W9-CCY-659

AMERICAN AUTOBIOGRAPHY

American
Autobiography
THE PROPHETIC MODE

G. Thomas Couser

University of Massachusetts Press   *Amherst, 1979*

Grateful acknowledgment is made to the following for permission to reprint copyrighted material:

The Estate of Gertrude Stein, for material from Gertrude Stein, *Brewsie and Willie*. Used by permission of The Estate of Gertrude Stein.

Random House, Inc. for material from Gertrude Stein, *The Autobiography of Alice B. Toklas*, copyright © 1933 by Gertrude Stein; for material from Stein, *Everybody's Autobiography*, copyright © 1937 by Gertrude Stein; and for material from Stein, *Wars I Have Seen*, copyright © 1945 by Gertrude Stein.

The Frank Lloyd Wright Foundation, for material from Frank Lloyd Wright, *An Autobiography* (1932) and (1943). Copyright © The Frank Lloyd Wright Foundation 1932, 1943, 1977. All previous copyrights renewed. All rights reserved; and for material from Wright, *Genius and the Mobocracy*. Copyright © The Frank Lloyd Wright Foundation 1949, renewed 1977.

Houghton Mifflin Co., for material from *The Education of Henry Adams*, edited by Ernest Samuels. Copyright © 1946 by Charles F. Adams. Reprinted by permission of the publisher.

The University of Texas Press, for material from G. Thomas Couser, "Of Time and Identity: Walt Whitman and Gertrude Stein as Autobiographers," in *Texas Studies in Literature and Language* 17, no. 4 (Winter 1976), pp. 787-804.

Bantam Books, for material from Robert M. Pirsig, *Zen and the Art of Motorcycle Maintenance: An Inquiry into Values*.

Rendezvous, for material from G. Thomas Couser, "*Zen and the Art of Motorcycle Maintenance* as Prophetic Autobiography," in *Rendezvous* 12, no. 2 (Fall 1977), pp. 31–38.

Dover Publications, for material from Louis Sullivan, *Autobiography of an Idea.*

G. P. Putnam's Sons, for material from Norman Mailer, *Advertisements for Myself.* Copyright © 1959 by Norman Mailer.

Princeton University Press, for material from *Walden: The Writings of Henry D. Thoreau*, edited by J. Lyndon Shanley, CEEA Edition. Copyright © 1971 by Princeton University Press. Reprinted by permission.

American Transcendental Quarterly, for material from G. Thomas Couser, "Thoreau's Cape Cod Pilgrimage," in *American Transcendental Quarterly*, no. 26, Supplement (Spring 1975), pp. 31–36.

University of Massachusetts Press, for material from Thomas Shepard, *God's Plot: The Paradoxes of Puritan Piety, Being the Autobiography and Journal of Thomas Shepard*, edited by Michael McGiffert. Copyright ©1972 by The University of Massachusetts Press.

Grove Press, for material from Malcolm X, *The Autobiography of Malcolm X*, with an epilogue by Alex Haley.

American Antiquarian Society, for material from "The Autobiography of Increase Mather," edited by M. G. Hall, in *Proceedings of the American Antiquarian Society* 71, pt. 2 (1961), pp. 271–360.

Oxford University Press, for material from John Woolman, *The Journal and Major Essays of John Woolman*, edited by Phillips P. Moulton.

Yale University Press, for material from *The Autobiography of Benjamin Franklin*, edited by Leonard W. Labaree, Ralph L. Ketcham, Helen C. Boatfield, and Helen Fineman. Copyright © 1974 by Yale University. Reprinted by permission of Yale University Press.

The New American Library, Inc., for material from *Armies of the Night* by Norman Mailer. Copyright © 1968 by Norman Mailer. Reprinted by arrangement with The New American Library, Inc., New York, N. Y., and by permission of the author and the author's agents, Scott Meredith Literary Agency, Inc., 845 Third Avenue, New York, New York 10022.

To my wife and the memory of my parents

ACKNOWLEDGMENTS

Although scholarship can be a lonely endeavor, it is never performed in isolation. My notes and bibliography document my debt to other scholars. But this apparatus does not indicate my debts to others whose contributions have been of another kind. Among my teachers, James M. Cox stands out as a model of intelligence and energy; his teaching and writing have inspired this book in more ways than he can know. As teachers and as friends, James A. Epperson and Alan T. Gaylord have encouraged me at times when professional prospects seemed dim indeed. Hyatt H. Waggoner, David H. Hirsch, and John L. Thomas read the manuscript in an earlier version and offered helpful suggestions. Alberta Colopoulos and Nancy Stebbins assisted me ably in the painstaking task of typing; a grant from Connecticut College helped defray the expenses of this process. Carol Schoen offered tactful editorial help with the final preparation of the manuscript. Without such inspiration, encouragement, guidance, and assistance, this book would not have come to be.

CONTENTS

AMERICAN AUTOBIOGRAPHY

ONE

Introduction

Prophetic Autobiography in America

The following chapters examine the development of an important mode of autobiographical writing in America, define and perhaps account for its distinctive characteristics, and demonstrate its variety and vitality. A coherent tradition—perhaps the mainstream of American autobiography from the Puritans to the present—is traced through autobiographical works by Thomas Shepard, Increase Mather, Jonathan Edwards, John Woolman, Benjamin Franklin, Frederick Douglass, Henry Thoreau, Walt Whitman, Henry Adams, Louis Sullivan, Frank Lloyd Wright, Gertrude Stein, Malcolm X, Norman Mailer, and Robert Pirsig. Generally, these autobiographies are characterized by the conflation of personal and communal history,[1] the conscious creation of exemplary patterns of behavior, and their didactic, even hortatory, impulses. These characteristics derive in turn from the writers' tendency to assume the role of prophet in writing autobiography. While prophetic autobiography is not exclusively American, it is characteristically American, and our tradition of prophetic autobiography seems to be a distinctive achievement of American letters.

My inquiry has been stimulated by the work of many scholars. Among them are the pioneers in the field of American autobiogra-

phy. In *The Examined Self*, Robert F. Sayre analyzed th∋ autobiographies of Franklin, Adams, and James in aesthetic terms and
encouraged further study of the larger tradition. James M. Cox's
essay, "Autobiography and America," traced developments from
Franklin to Stein with emphasis on the political significance and
formal innovations of his texts. In "Autobiography and the American Myth," William C. Spengeman and L. R. Lundquist explored
the way in which a wide range of American autobiographies communicate versions of a single myth central to American culture.
In *Spiritual Autobiography in Early America,* Daniel B. Shea, Jr.,
demonstrated decisively that the American tradition began before
Franklin, and argued that the stances and strategies of nineteenth-
century autobiographers are related to those of their Puritan and
Quaker predecessors. Scholars outside the field have also stimulated my thinking about the place of autobiography in American
literary history. Perry Miller's analysis of the New England mind,
and especially his revelation of the connection between Edwards
and Emerson, influenced my sense of the shape of our tradition,
and Sacvan Bercovitch's *The Puritan Origins of the American Self*
confirmed it by documenting the persistence of Puritan ideas
about the self and the nation (and the relationship between them)
long after Calvinism ceased to be a compelling theology. Finally,
Hyatt H. Waggoner's *American Poets* and Richard Chase's *The
American Novel and Its Tradition* have been important stimuli,
for both seek to identify the characteristic features of other kinds
of American writing. As I hope to show, prophetic autobiography
shares some of the characteristics cited by Waggoner as peculiar to
American poetry and by Chase as typical of American fiction.[2] Indeed, the prophetic mode of autobiography may be to American
autobiography what the romance is to American fiction—a literary
form which survives its initial, specialized uses because it is uniquely suited to expressing the complexity and contradictions of American experience.

The Old Testament prophets have been characterized as follows:
"The prophet was not a professional man nor was he concerned
with predicting the future for a fee or without it: a prophet was a
person filled with the divine spirit who, in such moments of inspiration, might utter the word of God; he was a preacher rather than

a fortuneteller, a forthteller rather than a foreteller!"[3] Without necessarily claiming divine inspiration, the prophetic autobiographer, like the Old Testament prophet, interprets the history of his community in the light of God's will; he speaks, then, for God to his community. But by virtue of this fact, he also functions as a representative of his community—as a reformer of its ethos, articulator of its highest ideals, interpreter of its history, and activist in the service of its best interests. Typically, his stance is one of opposition to the status quo or the apparent flow of history, but he is a critic rather than a schismatic; his ultimate loyalty is to a divine principle, but his immediate concern is with the community's destiny.

Prophetic autobiography flourishes in times of crisis—when change threatens communal values or when historical developments demand new modes of interpretation. It requires of the autobiographer a sense of his implication in the crisis and a theology or metaphysics capable of comprehending it. His presumption that he possesses a vision justifying his prophetic stance is matched by his sense of the community's need for it and perhaps balanced by his recognition that the vision is theirs as much as it is his.

Our tradition of prophetic autobiography has its roots in Puritan literature, for the Puritan minister identified closely with Old Testament models and functioned, in his writing, as an "interpreter, personification, guide, and forecaster of the corporate future."[4] Thus, the source for the distinctive concerns and literary strategies of the prophetic autobiographers can be located in their Puritan attitudes toward themselves and their history. Since the Puritan errand was, in Sacvan Bercovitch's words, an attempt to "actualize the metaphors of visible sainthood (for the individual) and national election (for the community),"[5] the Puritan mind tended to blur the distinctions between secular and ecclesiastical history, between political and spiritual exhortation, between private and public welfare, and between history and allegory. By virtue of a set of interlocking covenants joining them with God, the individual, the Church, and the colony were assumed to share a special role in the scheme of redemption. They became available as metaphors for each other. The Puritan imagination tended and intended to create a "colony in the image of a saint" and vice versa; it stressed the universal rather than the unique aspects of the individual's experience and focused on the corporate rather than the private dimension of the self. Thus, the tendencies to perceive the nation as unique and the individual as typical were related; the conflation of individual and communal history derived from the persistent notion that American history had redemptive meaning.[6]

The persistence of the prophetic mode of autobiography depends, to some extent, on the power of the Puritan legacy—a power deriving from the dominance of orthodox Puritanism in seventeenth-century New England. In England, where each of many sects developed its own autobiographical forms and functions, there was a broad range of possibilities for autobiographical expression—from the sober to the enthusiastic and from the naive to the sophisticated. In New England, where Puritanism suppressed its rivals, Puritan spiritual autobiography established the conventions for self-examination. Thus, although American Puritans had a theory of meditational literature, with the exception of the poetry of Edward Taylor, American literature boasts no achievement in a contemplative mode of self-examination comparable to that in England. That the primary mode of personal literature in seventeenth-century America was narrative rather than meditational, utilitarian rather than aesthetic, and allegorical rather than metaphysical proved to be important for the American tradition of autobiography.

Other aspects of our history and culture are equally significant. Certainly American culture has been conducive to autobiography as a means of expression, especially to autobiography with a religious dimension. If American society has been relatively fluid, putting little emphasis on class and manners as indices of worth and character, and if our cultural environment has been, as our novelists have complained, antipoetic, then American writers have been thrown back on themselves as the ultimate literary resource, and on individual experience as the ultimate test of significance and value.[7] If spiritual autobiography is "primarily concerned with the question of grace,"[8] most of the books discussed in the following chapters cannot, properly speaking, be considered such. Yet insofar as they tend to invest the idea of nationality or community with spiritual or sacred significance, they must be read as religious literature. Thus, Hyatt Waggoner's description of the distinctive qualities of American poetry applies nearly as well to American autobiography: "Characteristically, it has tested the validity of society and culture by the standards of the eternal. Even when most strongly in rebellion against their religious heritage . . . our poets have tended to take a 'supramundane' point of view."[9]

If the tendency to take a supramundane viewpoint derives from the high idealism with which the settlement of the continent was undertaken, the *necessity* of doing so results from the failure of American history to realize those ideals. While our national mythology endows our community with unique moral status and our history with redemptive significance, the historical record reveals the cost of our presumption. Prophetic autobiography does not tell us that we have fulfilled our destiny, but rather that it is still waiting to be fulfilled; it is at once a record of the opportunities and the burdens of being American. Often a way of measuring individual achievement against cultural standards, autobiography becomes, in the prophet's hands, a medium for measuring communal achievement against individually intuited standards. In this endeavor, the Puritan myth of a corporate identity has been a useful means of establishing stable correspondences between the individual and the community, the self and history, and of establishing coherent images of both the self and the community *through* history. Confronted with the contradiction between what America is and what it could be, our autobiographers have yielded again and again to the prophetic impulse: they have sought analogies between their own experience and that of the community; they have tested cultural myths in the crucible of their own experience; and they have distilled from that experience new visions and values to urge on their audiences. Confronted with a sense of declension or of uncontrollable change, they have insisted on their power not only to order their own lives but to influence the course of history.

I have not attempted to solve the complicated problem of the genre which preoccupies some students of autobiography, for my concern is not with a general theory of autobiography but with the development and persistence of a special way of writing it. I have kept in mind as a working definition of autobiography the following: "A retrospective account of a [person's] whole life (or a significant part of a life) written as avowed truth for a specific purpose by the [person] who lived the life."[10] In cases such as that of Transcendental autobiography, where my texts appear to lie beyond the bounds of such a definition, I have made my argument in the appropriate chapter. I have chosen to call prophetic autobiography a mode rather than a subgenre because it seems to me a way of writing autobiography that can adapt various conventional forms such as confession, memoir, and apology—and even other genres such as travel writing and journalism—to its own requirements and purposes. Indeed, inasmuch as the exemplary nature of prophetic autobiography makes it something of an anachronism after the eighteenth century, it owes its continuing vitality in part to its ability to exploit new forms and strategies.

Because autobiography, uniquely among genres, demands a certain content rather than formal characteristics, a student of autobiography will encounter a diversity of forms, intentions, and approaches.[11] Even so, many of the works discussed below challenge the general expectations a reader may bring to autobiography: that the individual will possess a unique identity; that time should be the most important dynamic of the development of the self, and chronology the most obvious structural principle of the narrative; and that the narrative will be a factual, retrospective account of the writer's life. To cite the most extreme example, Whitman tends to write collective autobiography in the present tense, raising the self above time, circumstance, and isolation from others. Generally, it might fairly be said that these books subordinate certain qualities we associate with nonfiction—objectivity and accurate historical documentation—to qualities we associate with fiction—symbolic density, experimentation with form and point of view, and careful selection and arrangement of material for thematic unity. Thus, these narratives seem to move from their roots in history toward the realm of fiction, poetry, and myth.

The imaginative freedom and power of some of these books have led some critics to suggest that they are really a form of fiction. But to argue that these books become, by virtue of their aesthetic success, something other than autobiography is to re-

fuse to take the genre seriously. It makes more sense to say that
books like *Walden* and *The Education of Henry Adams* become
not forms of fiction but simply classics of autobiography by making it a self-conscious art form. For although it may be true that
no definitional distinction between autobiography and fiction is
foolproof, criticism must distinguish between them. The careful
arrangement of incidents from one's life into a narrative may result in a work of fiction or of autobiography. The difference lies
neither in the content nor in the literary techniques employed but
rather in the signals the author sends about the nature of his narrative. The meaning of a literary work is, to some extent, genre-
bound, and the writer's signals rightly determine the way a reader
will take the text, the force it has for him. As Francis Hart has put
it, "in understanding fiction one seeks an imaginative grasp of another's meaning; in understanding personal history one seeks an
imaginative comprehension of another's historic identity. 'Meaning' and 'identity' are not the same kind of reality and do not
make the same demands. One has no obligation to fantasy."[12]

The matter of obligation is especially relevant to the works discussed here, for the prophetic autobiographer wishes to be understood as inhabiting the same world as his reader; he endeavors to
convert him to a vision of history or to commit him to certain values with an urgency uncharacteristic of fiction. Perhaps all skillful
autobiographers tend to subordinate historical documentation to
aesthetic values. What distinguishes the prophetic autobiographer
is the impulse behind his departure from historicity: he sacrifices
what he considers a superficial relationship between his narrative
and the *facts* of history in order to achieve a more profound correspondence between his narrative and the *truth* of history. In some
cases, of course, departures from biographical fact may seem to
manifest a prophetic pose rather than a truly prophetic impulse;
the autobiographer's manipulation of fact, his portrayal of himself as a prophet, may seem self-serving. But as it is probably fruitless to attempt to disentangle completely the related motives behind an autobiography, generally I have given the benefit of the
doubt to the autobiographer, stressing the way in which he gives
his experience a mythic shape which makes it more accessible to
and significant for the community.

The choice of texts has been determined by several criteria. First, and obviously, I have chosen autobiographical works that seem to me prophetic in impulse. Franklin and Stein, two exceptional figures who seem only quasiprophetic, are included because they are important autobiographers who had the opportunity and the desire, but not the equipment, to be prophetic; as a result, they help to illustrate more clearly what prophetic autobiography *is*. With a prophetic *tradition* in mind, I have chosen works from most periods of American history. Three autobiographies from different generations appeared the best way to represent the Puritan achievement, which varied with the temperament and circumstances of the individual in spite of strong pressures toward conventionality. Similarly, three autobiographies from the contemporary period suggest the persistence of the prophetic impulse despite the apparent fragmentation of cultural consensus.

Finally, in selecting texts I have considered literary quality. With the exception of some of the traditional spiritual autobiographers, these writers have had to generate both the form and the content of their prophecy in the absence of established conventions, and the dialectic between intuited vision and created form has been a focus for my inquiry. In large part, these autobiographers have been among our most innovative because their prophetic mission demanded a reexamination of the meaning of autobiography itself. Thus, while Gertrude Stein may have been no more prophetic an autobiographer than Lincoln Steffens or Emma Goldman—in conventional terms, she may have been less so —she was selected because her autobiographies challenge the notions of selfhood and history on which the autobiographical act is based.

The texts selected, then, are books that speak to us not only of the self but of *themselves*—of the nature of autobiography as an act. Furthermore, they are books that speak to each other; my choices were determined, in part, by my desire to understand the way in which—even when "influence" is not an issue—each book may be said to extend, revise, or answer certain of its predecessors. For the most part, models outside the American tradition seem to have helped it develop its own potential rather than to have deflected it from its course. Thus, I have emphasized the relationships among the works in the tradition to demonstrate its profound continuity. For the tradition is not a matter of a few similar, but isolated, masterpieces; it is an ongoing and almost obsessive inquiry into what it means to be an American.

TWO

Piety and Prophecy in

Puritan Spiritual Autobiography

Introduction

American autobiography surely derives many of its distinctive qualities from the way our earliest autobiographies were shaped by the Puritan culture, which both strongly encouraged personal literature in theory and limited the freedom of the autobiographer in practice. Required to serve community goals, all Puritan literature tended to be theological in content, didactic in purpose, plain in style, and allegorical in technique. The theological content was a result of the conscious function of literature—to define and articulate cultural values and to urge them upon the community. The didacticism and the plain style derived from the wish to communicate without distraction the urgency of the Puritan mission in America. The allegorical method resulted from the tendency to see their history as part of a divinely ordained plan and to associate it with biblical precedents; for the Puritans, allegory could be an objective mode of narration because, in their eyes, history was literally, not figuratively, ordered by God.

The Protestant elimination of institutional intermediaries between the individual and God, coupled with the Calvinist emphasis on justification by faith and the predestination of the elect, was a strong stimulus to scrupulous self-examination; hence the diary was a fundamental Puritan literary form. But the diary was essentially a devotional or confessional form. It differed from other Puritan literary forms in its intense introspection, its concentration on self-doubt, dullness, and depression, its presentation of the self in isolation from the community, and its meditational, or at least nonnarrative method. The Puritan self and community were publicly defined and evaluated only in narrative forms, which took account of interaction with God over a period of time.[1] Wholly public forms of writing, biography and history tended to present the life of the saint as unambiguously exemplary. Both subordinated the individualistic to the typical, and both associated personal and community history by suggesting parallels between the inward progression of grace and the outward progress of the Puritan experiment.[2]

Puritan autobiography was located at the nexus between the private, autodidactic diary and the public, explicitly didactic biography. Autobiography might be didactic in its examination of the overall pattern of the author's experience and devotional in its recording of his cumulative debt to God. But because the autobiography was not intended exclusively for the self, it shared more with the carefully composed forms of biography and history than with the diary. Puritan culture demanded that autobiography focus on the experience of grace, and Puritan autobiographies can be roughly classified according to whether the writer concentrates soley on his experience of saving grace or whether he examines a broader range of experience for signs of God's influence.

Conversion was the definitive religious experience, of course. But since the conversion narratives, or "spiritual relations," required of candidates for church membership, were designed to convince their audience of the genuineness of the author's conversion, they tended to conform to established patterns of conversion. Impersonal and conventional, they suggest the limitations within which the Puritan autobiographer worked and, with few exceptions, hardly deserve to be considered as autobiography.[3] A broader form was the full-life narrative, which concerned itself with the significance of the author's experience of common grace throughout his life. The full-life narrative clearly reveals the influence of

Puritan tribalism—the tendency of American Puritans to domesticate their God and to become an exclusive rather than an evangelical sect.[4] Addressed to the writer's immediate posterity, the full-life narrative was, in a sense, merely a supplement to education, domestic instruction, and parental example in the attempt to perpetuate Puritan values. By articulating the providential pattern of its own experience, one generation sought to encourage allegiance to God in the next generation, thus ensuring the continuing unfolding of the divine plan.[5]

The full-life narrative, then, was primarily didactic and hortatory rather than autodidactic and devotional. Hence, it tended to illuminate a different facet of the Puritan self from the diary: the autobiographer usually portrayed himself as an integrated rather than a tormented personality in a social context rather than in isolation. He was relatively certain of the significance of his experience, and he intended to foster Puritan piety in his audience. The relationship between writer and audience, intimate to begin with, was rhetorically heightened by the demanding mutual responsibility; in Paul Delany's words, "the reader's own life may be at stake, and as he reads he becomes, potentially, at least, a member of the community of saints."[6]

Implicit in the qualities of Puritan autobiography discussed above is its prophetic character. Insofar as the family is representative of the community, the Puritan autobiographer functions not only as a father but as a patriarch and prophet who interprets the community's history, discerns God's will working through it, and urges the community to fulfill its mission by conforming to certain patterns of behavior and piety. Identification with Old Testament prophets was natural and common for the Puritan clergy, and the prophetic stance was not limited to autobiography; indeed, it was more evident in forms like the jeremiad. But the prophetic mode of American autobiography appears to have its origins in Puritan culture, which believed strongly in the validity and necessity of prophecy. The autobiographies of Thomas Shepard, Increase Mather, and Jonathan Edwards demonstrate the consistency of the Puritans' prophetic impulse and the diversity of its manifestation.

Thomas Shepard's "My Birth and Life"

"My Birth and Life," the autobiography of Thomas Shepard (1605-1649), may be the first Puritan autobiography written in America, and it illustrates most of the general characteristics of the form.[7] A full-life narrative, Shepard's autobiography contains much biographical and historical information, revealing his firm commitment as a leader of the founding generation to outward experience in a public world. Its general theological argument or organizing principle is inherent in all Puritan autobiography: assembling evidence of divine favoritism toward the author. As Daniel Shea has shown, Shepard's experience, like that of other Puritans, at times resisted reduction to creedal assumptions.[8] Equally interesting are the ways in which Shepard shaped his experience through emphasis, organization, and analogy; in exploring the significance of his own life, he tended to fashion it into a myth representing and interpreting the experience of his whole generation.

As the narrative's dedication to his son suggests, Shepard's narrower and more explicit purpose was to leave a personal legacy and guidebook for his offspring; writing his autobiography was a way of ensuring his immortality at least as a parent. Thus, in a short narrative preceding the autobiography proper, Shepard described for his son five incidents in which the Lord had delivered Thomas Shepard, Jr., from death or disease in early life (twice while he was still in the womb). Clearly these incidents were selected to convince the son of his dependence on God and of God's interest in him. The whole prefatory narrative was calculated to inform him of his privileges under the covenant of grace and of the obligations implied by such privileges and deliverances. In spite of the Calvinist framework of predestination, God's sovereignty, and man's passivity, the clear implication was that young Shepard had a certain responsibility to continue his life in the pattern already established without his cooperation or even his consciousness.

The longer narrative which followed included these incidents within the context of a model of experience to be emulated—the father's life story. Having generated a son in England, the father attempted to generate a saint in America, using exemplary autobiography as one of the means. More than the father's behavior had to be emulated, of course. The son had to aspire to his father's vision and attitude—his piety. Thus, although the father could not, without divine assistance, accomplish the son's conversion, Shepard seized upon his son's deliverance from blindness to urge him to dedicate his healed eyes to God, to use them to discern and interpret God's influence on his life. Furthermore, in the short narrative, Shepard in effect presented his son with the first installment of his own autobiography. There he made available and interpreted for his son experience beyond his son's memory. Thus did one saint attempt to generate another, one autobiography attempt to inspire another.

By implication, Shepard's stance toward his son represents his stance toward the next generation. Like other Puritan genres, autobiography was a means by which one generation could shape the experience of the next in its own image. A distinctive feature of Shepard's autobiography demonstrates the way in which its scope broadened naturally and inevitably from the family to the community. This feature is the use of emigration as the structural and thematic center of the narrative in place of the conventional turning point, conversion. This shift from the usual pattern owes less to Shepard's paternal role than to his prophetic one; that is, it reveals his impulse to treat his own family's emigration as typical of that of the whole generation.

Occupying the center of the narrative, the account of the emigration divides it into two sections in which Shepard tends to perceive or portray himself very differently. The English section is dominated by a sense of personal tribulation. Shepard portrays himself as isolated and persecuted; he struggles for union with God and for efficacy as one of His agents, but is opposed by both Church and state. Images of disorder and dislocation begin with his childhood and culminate with his persecution as a Nonconformist, which leads him to consider emigration to New England as both a holy duty and a solution to his troubles.[9] Shepard's English experience, then, is characterized as a solitary pilgrimage in a hostile and profane world.

In contrast, the American section of the narrative reads like a chronicle rather than an autobiography; three of the four major incidents recounted are events of communal significance. This absorption of the individual self into the community serves three purposes. First, it solves the problem of suppressing the autobiographical ego for the second half of the narrative; broadening his autobiography to a kind of communal history allowed Shepard to report his own significant accomplishments impersonally, in the first person plural, as it were. Second, the new viewpoint expresses the Puritan sense that in America the social units of family, church, and state could become truly concentric circles by means of a series of interlocking convenants;[10] in place of the isolated, tormented self of the English section, Shepard portrays himself, in the American section, as a man engaged with his society in a communal submission to God's will.

Finally, the emphasis on communal rather than personal experience enabled Shepard to emerge as a prophet, interpreting recent history in such a way as to make it instructive for the next generation. For example, Shepard presents the founding of Harvard as a response to the simultaneous afflictions of the Pequots and the antinomians and as an attempt to perpetuate the values and vision of the founding generation: "Thus the Lord having delivered the country from war with Indians and Familists (who arose and fell together), he was pleased to direct the hearts of the magistrates . . . to think of erecting a school or college, and that speedily, to be a nursery of knowledge in these deserts and supply for posterity."[11] That the function of the autobiography is similar to that of the college underlines a theme implicit in Puritan autobiography in general: that of experience as education. The founding of Harvard was to do for future generations what Shepard tried to do for his son with his autobiography.

The process of emigration received close analysis in the narrative because it was the crucial act that made fulfillment of the Puritan mission possible. In addition to the discomforts and anxieties of life as a Nonconformist in England, Shepard cited the following reasons for emigrating: "I saw no reason to spend my time privately when I might possibly exercise my talent publicly in New England; I did hope my going over might make [others] to follow me" (p. 56). Here Shepard exposed the Puritan consciousness in action, weighing selfish against altruistic motives and personal against divine purposes until the call was effectually felt: "Though my ends were mixed and I looked much to my own quiet, yet the Lord let me see the glory of those liberties in New England and made me purpose, if ever I should come over, to live among God's people as one come out from the dead, to his praise" (p. 56). Shepard's reasoning here justified not only his own emigration but that of an entire generation. According to Shepard, emigration enabled the Puritan saint to become a more efficient, because unopposed, agent of God. Emigration was itself an exemplary act, and it could be likened to a kind of resurrection.

The last point, which suggests a parallel between the personal crisis of conversion (often compared to resurrection) and the communal process of emigration, is developed throughout Shepard's treatment of the crossing. With its dangers, setbacks, and eventual success, the emigration was, of course, a model of distress and deliverance, and typology and metaphor were used to reinforce this theme. More striking, however, than Shepard's rather conventional scriptural interpretation of the ship's salvation from threatening rocks on the first attempt to sail is his elaboration of the analogy between emigration and conversion. Though the ship was preserved, the passengers had to forego their attempt to cross, and Shepard's first son Thomas died from illness contracted during the rescue. Shepard interpreted this personal affliction as necessary to prepare him for life in the new world: "Here the Lord saw that these waters were not sufficient to wash away my filth and sinfulness, and therefore he cast me into the fire as soon as ever I was upon the sea in the boat, for there my first-born child . . . was smitten with sickness. . . . And I considered how unfit I was to go to such a good land with such an unmortified, hard, dark, formal, hypocritical heart, and therefore no wonder the Lord did thus cross me" (p. 61).

Shepard's special affliction set him off from the other passengers but also bound him to them, for he interpeted his son's illness as a result of his own failure to assimilate the lesson the storm was meant to convey to the whole group. The crossing, given special poignance by the loss of this first son, was given special significance by the birth, survival, and New England baptism of the second, also named Thomas. Shepard's consciousness of the replacement of one namesake by another and his construction of the entire narrative around the events of the emigration suggest that he perceived the process as a kind of second regeneration of himself—from an Old World Thomas to a New World Thomas. At the same time that he used an outward event to suggest an inward one, Shepard implied that his own experience had general significance, that he was typical of his entire generation. The effect of his narrative as a whole is to characterize the shared experience of emigration as equivalent to a second conversion—the regeneration of the first generation—and to render that lesson unforgettable to the son whose deliverance was coincident with that emigration. In the autobiography, then, we have not only a father speaking to his son, but one generation speaking to the next, and a prophet speaking for God to his peers and to posterity. In treating emigration as equivalent to conversion, Shepard seems to have established a convention followed in the biographies of early saints.[12] But in stressing the corporate dimension of experience, in treating himself as a representative of the community, he seems to have helped set the pattern for a mode of writing autobiography that extended finally beyond the confines of his own Puritan culture.

Increase Mather's "Autobiography"

If the overriding task of Shepard's generation was to establish the Puritan colony, that of the generation of Increase Mather (1639-1723) was to protect its original values against threatening forces—the growth of scientific rationalism and religious toleration, a decline in piety, and the revocation of the original charter. Mather's ministerial career spanned a period of time that saw what Larzer Ziff has called "a clerical withdrawal from the political scene into a position of commentary on its eternal implications."[13] Mather, who pioneered a new kind of jeremiad that singled out specific groups of the population for criticism, did not hesitate to adopt the role of the prophet to realize his extravagant, if desperate, hopes for New England.[14] As the gap between the dream and the reality of New England Puritanism grew wider, Mather felt obliged personally to bridge the gap. The pressures of his predicament are evident in his autobiography, which portrays him as a self-conscious prophet who was at times out of step with his society. If Shepard's autobiography may be said to mythicize the engagement of English Puritans with the New England cause, Mather's dramatizes his alternation between engagement and disenchantment with New England as a redemptive force.[15]

Although the autobiography was never published by Mather and was not printed until the twentieth century, he expected his children to use it, both as a lesson in itself and as material for an exemplary biography. For the Mathers, personal literature was a family preoccupation, and Cotton followed his father's example by writing both an autobiography, "Paterna," and a biography of his father, *Parentator* (1726).[16] In this context, it is not surprising to find that the theme of generational continuity is one that Mather's autobiography shares with Shepard's. For the most part, Mather's dedication simply reiterates Shepard's themes. Again, the writer professes to offer an objective interpretation of God's influence on his life. Again, the autobiography is intended to ensure not the writer's immortality—except in his role as parent—but that of his audience. Again, the autobiographer seeks to educate his children as he had been educated by God.[17]

Generational continuity and Puritan tribalism are emphasized throughout the narrative: in Mather's recording of his "particular faiths" for his children; in passages expressing concern that Cotton's speech impediment would prevent his taking up the ministry, "whereunto I had designed him" (p. 301); and in his decision in 1704 that no Puritan minister except his son Samuel, then in England, was worthy to succeed him (p. 353). But the tribalism differs from that in Shepard's narrative. Shepard's family was one of several concentric circles in an expanding enterprise; here, as Mather's confidence in the enterprise declined, his faith seems to have retreated to the narrowest circle. There are hints that, as a prophet, Mather conceived of himself as an adversary, rather than the guide, of the community.

While the second part of the narrative, largely an account of Mather's diplomatic missions to England, portrays primarily the public self, and the third part, which consists of journal entries, reveals the private self, the first part, a narrative which includes diary entries, presents the full spectrum of the Puritan experience. It offers abundant evidence of the conflict between Mather's desire for submission to an all-powerful God and his sense of pride in his personal achievements, between his pious intentions and the demands of the self. On the one hand is Mather's tendency to mystical ecstacies, suggested by many recorded meltings of the soul which occurred while he was preparing for or participating in communion. On the other hand is his attempt to harness such private encounters to his public endeavors; thus, he pleaded that he be given the "power of grace to be more than a conqueror over my special infirmities" (p. 292). However, in his pleading, he exploited the covenant promises in a revealing way: "I . . . begged of God, that Hee would give me leave to plead with him (and with Tears and meltings of heart I did plead with him,) that if hee should not answer me graciously, others after my decease, that should see the papers which I had written and kept as remembrances of my walking before God, would be discouraged" (p. 294). In effect, this passage shows Mather blackmailing God, threatening to leave behind autobiographical evidence of God's shabby treatment of a faithful servant. Confident of his favor in God's eyes, Mather apparently perceived Him not as an awful tyrant but as a ruler bound by covenant promises and obliged to favor Mather because of his prominence as a citizen and saint. This incident is but one example of Mather's tendency to "lobby" with God on the basis that to disappoint a Mather would be to alienate an important constituency.

As a parent, Mather attempted to mediate between God and his children; as a prophet, between God and New England. The two roles are connected, for the narrowness of his tribalism and his sense of God's obligation to his family affected his sense of his prophetic role. Whereas Shepard assumed the role of the prophet in his autobiography only to the extent of interpreting God's will as revealed in past history, Mather identified more completely with the Old Testament prophets and aspired to forecast the future as well. The autobiography furnishes the details of his assumption of this role in the 1670s: "Considering the sins of the Countrey, and the symptoms of divine displeasure, I could not rest in my spirit without giving Publick solemn warning of judgment near at hand" (p. 301). Subsequent events, including King

Philip's War and a smallpox epidemic, confirmed the truth of
Mather's prophecy: "And now the divine providence put into my
hands speciall advantages for service amongst his people. I had opportunities of preaching to the Generall Court, and thought it my
duty to stir them up to endeavor a Reformation of provoking
evils, by making Lawes for that end, and the Lord went along
with the word so farr as that several wholesome laws for the suppressing of sin were thereupon made and published" (p. 302).
Here Mather apprehended God's will in advance and helped a chastened New England enact it through legislation after their initial
failure to heed his prophecy.

Although the prophet is theoretically merely an agent of God
and a representative of the community, the role involves certain
pitfalls: his special role may lead him to glory in his elevated
status, or the indifference of the community may offend him.
Thus, the pastor who fully assumes the role of prophet may soon
become alienated from his society. Most of the time, Mather
found his congregation supportive, and he gratefully recorded the
beneficial effects of their prayers and fasts on his behalf. But the
following diary entry suggests that he did not completely escape
the prophet's occupational hazards: "If I be the Lord's servant,
when I am gone, the Lord will make some of my people sensible
of their neglects of me, though unworthy, in any respect, in myself considered" (p. 298). A similar note of self-righteousness and
self-pity is heard in Mather's reaction to his loss of the presidency
of Harvard: "But why should I think much of it, when Moses, yea,
our Lord Himselfe was ill rewarded by those whom He hath layd
under Infinite obligations of gratitude" (p. 351).

The difference between Shepard and Mather is both personal
and historical, of course. While Shepard functioned, in writing his
autobiography, as a prophet in the limited sense, he did not *portray* himself as a prophet and had no personal stake in the role.
Thus in the American section he was able to merge his own experience with that of the colony and to conform to the Puritan conventions of self-deprecation throughout the narrative. For Mather,
however, historical conditions demanded energetic and public
prophecy. The role of prophet seems to have become part of his
self-image as well as a public role; thus, in writing autobiography

Mather did not so much function as a prophet as he attempted to defend his career as a prophet and public servant. In the attempt to show himself as a true prophet, an efficient agent of God, and a devoted servant of New England, Mather isolated himself from the community instead of portraying his experience as representative of others'. At times, his self-portrayal does violence to the autobiographical conventions of human passivity and dependence on God.

As a public servant, Mather dutifully strove to remember that his ultimate loyalty was to God, but in his autobiography his sense of self-importance could taint even a pious declaration of his usefulness to the community: "Doubtless, there is not a government in the world that has been layd under greater obligation by a particular man than this government has bin by me. . . . Let not my children put too much confidence in men" (p. 352). Similarly, his great and sincere concern for the fate of New England led him to imply that he was personally responsible for its salvation through his intercession with God: "As I was praying that God would deliver New England I was much moved and melted before the Lord, not being able to speake for some time. . . . So I did rise from my knees with much comfort and assurance that God had heard me. . . . That very day King Charles dyed . . . and New England was that day delivered" (p. 313).

Mather's sense of personal responsibility for New England's fate is also suggested by the fact that his private pleadings with God in this example differ little from his later lobbying on behalf of New England before James II and William of Orange. Mather modestly gave credit to God: "My labors for the good of New England were not (through the grace of God which was with me) altogether without fruit" (p. 338). However, anxious to defend himself against criticism of the charter he obtained (and to be reimbursed for his expenses), Mather was careful to portray himself as a conscientious and indispensable champion of New England. The parallelism of his relationships with his natural and supernatural sovereigns was reinforced by his alternating between diary accounts of his prayers for New England and records of his appearances at court.

In the third and final section of the autobiography, Mather in-

creasingly expressed a mood of resignation, concern for his eventual sanctification, and a desire for death in preference to a period
of uselessness to God and society. Finally, after his wish to undertake another mission to England had been thwarted, Mather concluded with these words: "My times are in God's hands; and it is
good for me to be where he would have me be" (p. 360). Thus,
the narrative ends on a wholly conventional note, the theological
argument reasserting itself. But it is not only through Mather's
inclusion of his political and benevolent activities that his autobiography anticipates that of the deist, Franklin. For Mather's autobiography departs from the pattern set by Shepard to the extent
that he embraced more completely and self-consciously the role
of the prophet. Shepard functioned as a prophet in a modest way
in writing his autobiography; the role did not lead him beyond the
confines of Puritan conventions concerning the self. Mather's autobiography dramatized the career of a self-proclaimed prophet, and
his chosen role did lead him into conflict with the Calvinist assumptions about personal initiative. Writing in a less inhibiting
context, Franklin was able to take credit for his own achievements, but his adaptation of Puritan concepts to a secular and
nationalistic ethos resulted, finally, in a kind of false prophecy.

Jonathan Edwards's *Personal Narrative*

The *Personal Narrative* of Jonathan Edwards (1703–1757) is probably the classic expression in the personal literature of the American Puritans of what Perry Miller has called the Augustinian strain
of piety.[18] But it is by no means a typical Puritan autobiography.
Its striking differences from those of Shepard and Mather can be
attributed to a combination of historical and personal factors. If
the emigration of Shepard's generation crucially shaped his autobiography, and the declension of Mather's generation conditioned
his, the Great Awakening was the most significant historical influence on Edwards's narrative. Thus, the narratives of Shepard,
Mather, and Edwards are oriented respectively to the establishment, preservation, and revival of the Puritan mission in America.
In the Great Awakening, Puritanism attempted to recover its evangelical impulse by reemphasizing Calvinist theology and its focus

on the private relationship between God and man. Because Edwards was not only a prime mover of the Awakening but also its foremost interpreter and defender, his complex attitude toward the Great Awakening is relevant to the *Personal Narrative*. But the crucial influence on the narrative was finally Edwards's intense, mystical experience of grace.

Unlike Shepard and Mather, Edwards did not address his autobiography to his children, nor did he include a dedication revealing his conscious purposes.[19] To complicate matters, the narrative resists easy classification under the simple dichotomy between conversion narratives and full-life narratives: its temporal scope is equal to that of the full-life narrative, but it focuses almost exclusively on Edwards's experience of saving rather than of common grace.[20] For all its anomalies, it is clearly a didactic conversion narrative, but one in which conversion and instruction (and finally prophecy) have been radically redefined to express Edwards's personal version of Calvinism.

The circumstances of its composition help to establish its purpose. Although the date of its composition can only be narrowed down to the period between 1739 and 1746, Edwards was preoccupied throughout that period with the significance of the Great Awakening. Thus, implicit in the narrative is a concept that was increasingly important to Edwards as the Awakening reached its enthusiastic climax—the idea that saints could be distinguished with reasonable certainty from the unregenerate and that it was the duty of the congregation to make such distinctions. Like Edwards's *Treatise Concerning Religious Affections* (1746), the narrative was intended to serve as a guide to self-examination and the examination of others in this process. Indeed, the structure of the narrative roughly parallels that of the *Treatise*, for Edwards's early experience often displays "no certain signs" of truly gracious affections while his later experience clearly reveals the "distinguishing signs." In both works, Edwards employed a distinction between true and false religious affections in such a way as to validate the spiritual nature of the Awakening as a whole while criticizing certain of its embarrassing excesses.

Clearly, Edwards's developing attitude toward the Great Awakening strongly influenced the kind of spiritual autobiography he wrote and the kind of didactic purpose it served. The type of autobiography written by nineteenth-century evangelists Charles Grandison Finney and Lyman Beecher would not have served Edwards's purposes. Memoirs justifying their careers as evangelists, their narratives are not really spiritual autobiographies at all. They are self-serving rather than exemplary or prophetic. Instead of recounting spiritual experience or exploring the nature of grace, they monitor the outward progress of revivals. Nor would Edwards's purposes have been served by the kind of full-life narratives written by Shepard and Mather. Their narratives were not only exemplary but hortatory. To different degrees, both men urged certain values, attitudes, and actions on posterity. They offered models of experience not only worthy to be, but intended to be, imitated.

In sharp contrast, Edwards's *Personal Narrative* is less hortatory than instructive. For while Edwards was eager to distinguish between true and false religious affections, he was critical of the notion that conversion tended to take the form of a particular sequence of stages. He strove to avoid creating a model of the conversion experience, dwelling instead on certain signs that the process had truly taken place. As a result, his autobiography does not make urgent demands on its readers; it simply makes Edwards's useful experience available. It subordinates exemplary action to exemplary attitude by presenting the narrator as a recipient rather than a conduit of grace. Shepard and Mather all but promised grace to their intended audience; Edwards offers his experience of grace rather than grace itself to his readers. The pattern of that experience is exemplary through no achievement of Edwards's; it is exemplary because it is truly gracious. It is archetypal but not strictly imitable. With its unspecified audience and its soliloquizing manner, the *Personal Narrative* is both more private and more universal than the autobiographies of Shepard and Mather.

To make his narrative a guide to the experience of grace rather than a model or facilitator of it, Edwards strove to analyze as well as communicate his experience of grace. In accordance with this strategy, he deliberately underemphasized the actual moment of conversion because he himself understood it only in retrospect. Like Edwards, the reader may have to retrace his steps to pinpoint the moment at which the most profound change in human experience occurred. It is an elusive instant because it is a God-centered, not a self-centered moment, and because for Edwards conversion was like conception—the beginning of a new existence which might only be apparent later.

Conversion marked the initiation of a growth in grace that carried the saint progressively closer to God. Such a conversion caused profound changes in the individual's relationship to nature and to society and in his concept of himself. The infusion of grace changed the convert's perceptive faculties; he lived in a new relationship to the Creation: "After this my sense of divine things gradually increased, and became more and more lively, and had more of that inward sweetness. The appearance of every thing was altered; there seemed to be, as it were, a calm, sweet cast, or appearance of divine glory, in almost every thing."[21] The sense of the harmony of the soul with nature increased until, in moments of ecstatic vision or contemplation, the self seemed to merge with the universe.

A related effect of conversion was "a calm, sweet abstraction of soul from all the concerns of this world" (p. 60). Even as his narrative asserts this explicitly, it expresses it implicitly through its tendency to veer repeatedly from a specific time and place to a moment of contemplation removed from the social world. The narrative does reveal a progressive transcendence of the self through union with the divine, but it is an inward rather than an outward progression. Whereas Shepard and Mather rooted their narratives firmly in history and portrayed themselves as active and able servants of God, Edwards depicts himself being drawn passively from the world to God, from temporal to eternal concerns. In doing so, he gives unique autobiographical expression to the Calvinist version of the relationship between God and man.

The convert's "new sense" was primarily a feeling about God and not himself; insofar as conversion did involve a new sense of self it was a paradoxical one which made for an unstable emotional life. For even if the self could be completed and perfected in God, it was still in itself corrupt and worthless. The wish to be "Swallowed up in God" and increasingly "conformed to the image of Christ" invoked the obverse side of Calvinist self-conscious-

ness—the need to be "emptied and annihilated." Paradoxically,
self-transcendence required self-abasement, and self-fulfillment
meant self-annihilation. Growth in grace involved a progressive
loss of the sense of one's self as an individual personality bound
by human institutions; contemplating the divine glory alternated
with contemplating the worthless self one could not wholly transcend. Edwards consciously dramatized the strain of being pulled
by opposing emotional forces, but he understood his condition
to be paradoxical rather than contradictory. By organizing his narrative as a gradual progression toward complete sanctification, he
pointed to the eventual resolution of the paradoxes, one which
could occur only after death and hence lay beyond the scope of
autobiography.

Like any autobiography, the *Personal Narrative* is retrospective
in viewpoint, but thematically, at least, it is prospective in using
past experience to hint at an experience that can only be anticipated. The progressive and open form, the abstracted mood, and the
abrupt ending are all expressive of Puritan piety. In both form
and content, the narrative illustrates the way in which Puritan
autobiography, like Puritan experience, was to be oriented toward
goals unattainable on earth. The modern reader may wish that the
narrative offered an inside view of the Great Awakening or of the
workings of the theologian's mind, but Edwards chose to construct a narrative drained of individuality and history. His most
valued experience had been intensely personal and transcendently
impersonal, at once unique and universal. Thus, his autobiography
focused exclusively on the marrow of his life; even as it exposes
the limitations of Puritan autobiography, it fully develops its potential to reveal the inner dynamics of Puritan faith.

Looking backward, it is evident that the striking differences between Edwards's autobiography and those of Shepard and Mather
are the results of a shift in emphasis. Mystical tendencies, which
can be found in Shepard's *Journal* but not in his autobigoraphy
and which entered Mather's autobiography only in diary quota-
tions, became the dominant and organizing element in Edwards's
narrative. In an increasingly secular and rationalistic society, he
strove, as revivalist and autobiographer, to stress the original meaning of Puritan piety. His motives also determined the nature of the

prophetic dimension of his autobiography. Shepard and Mather
had portrayed themselves as community leaders and spokesmen
gifted with insight into God's will as revealed in history or in their
own predictions, as patriarchs and prophets engaged in the making
of history and urging the community to enact God's plan for it. In
his career as a minister, Edwards functioned in all these ways; indeed, he played a central role in an Awakening he hoped would
prove to be the beginning of the millenium.[22] But his interest was
not confined to his own time and place, nor to his own role in history, though he knew them to be significant. His tribalism was
expansive, not exclusive; his tribe was a community of the faithful
chosen by God, not created by human agreement. Hence in his
autobiography he ignored his role as a revivalist and eschewed literal prophecy for a more subtle, more universal kind.

If conversion was the crucial event in any saint's life, it was also,
on a different scale, the means by which awakenings and millenia
were effected. It was the ultimate dynamic of history. Thus, in the
Personal Narrative, Edwards only seems to retreat from history
and prophecy. In reenacting and analyzing his own conversion, he
was at once reenacting a significant personal and historical event
and prophesying a universal one. His narrative did not offer grace
to the reader, but it prophesied his conversion, and by foreshad-
owing the resolution of the paradoxes of his piety, Edwards prophesied the state of holiness that would characterize the millenium.
Like Shepard and Mather, but in a more universal way, he offered
his own experience as representative of that of the community.

THREE

John Woolman

A Prophet among Prophets

Quaker literature modifies the general characteristics of Puritan literature—its theological content, didactic aim, communal purpose, plain style, and its incorporation of Christian metaphors and myths—for the distinctive characteristics of Quaker culture conditioned Quaker personal literature in special ways. The characteristics of Puritanism most influential for Puritan personal literature—a preoccupation with conversion and with the purity of the congregation—took different forms in Quaker life and literature. Conversion remained significant, since man, though not totally corrupt, was born with a latent tendency toward sin. But in general the Quakers stressed the positive side of Reformation theology.

The center of Quaker theology was the doctrine of the Inner Light, which suggested that each man contained the divine spark, the seed of his own salvation, if he would submit to it. In describing his first attempts to speak in meeting, John Woolman (1720-1772) concisely enunciated his sense of this doctrine: "My under-standing became more strengthened to distinguish the language of the pure Spirit which inwardly moves upon the heart and taught [me] to wait in silence sometimes many weeks together, until I felt that rise which prepares the creature to stand like a trumpet

through which the Lord speaks to his flock."[1] This doctrine furnished the Quakers at once with a theory of God, a rule of life, a
concept of the ministry, and a theory of autobiography. The notion of the self as the passive vehicle of divine truth—of a revelation that supplemented Scripture—made each Quaker a potential
prophet in the original, Old Testament sense. Quaker theology
thus subverted the authority of Scripture and of an ordained, educated clergy as its interpreter. In their attempt to create a purer,
more primitive church than even the Puritans, the Quakers endorsed a less authoritarian and less dogmatic set of beliefs, all
of which influenced the conventions of the Quaker journal.

To counterbalance the enthusiastic and antinomian tendencies
of early Quakerism, the sect developed a strong sense of community. The individual Quaker retained access to the Inner Light, but
since divine truth was believed to be consistent, the individual's
revelations were expected to conform to the truth as interpreted
by the meeting. In effect, Quakers substituted the notion of consensus and the practice of censorship by the meeting for the Puritan reliance on clerical and scriptural authority as checks on
fanaticism. The hierarchy of meetings and the work of the traveling ministry also ensured consistency within the Quaker movement even as they broadened the religious community.[2] Another
significant check on enthusiasm was the development of a "practical mysticism"; Quaker mysticism "was tested by its outcome in
everyday life, notably by whether it gave a clear condemnation
of evil and brought men together in peace and fellowship."[3] The
dynamic tension between the mystical inwardness and the pragmatic benevolence of the Quakers, between the individualistic
implications of the doctrine of the Inner Light and the strong
communal emphasis of the Society of Friends, can be considered
the Quaker variations on the paradoxes of Puritan piety. This
dichotomy emerges as a central theme in Woolman's *Journal.*

The standard contents of Quaker journals include conversion
to Quaker beliefs and practices, the first motion to speak in meeting, the call to the public ministry, missionary journeys and suffer-
ings, and the progress of Quakerism.[4] Reflecting the Quaker
history of persecution in the seventeenth century, the early, influential Quaker journals were more concerned with the enactment

of divine truth in a hostile world than with isolated mystical experiences. They recorded not the inward progress of grace but the
establishment and growth of the Society of Friends. Like the
travels of the ministers, their journals, when published posthu-
mously with the approval of the meeting, were intended to bind
the faithful together.[5] However, the circumstances of American
Quakers during the eighteenth century were very different from
those of the seventeenth-century Quakers who had established
the conventions of the journal: "Eased conditions . . . prevailed
. . . in America, especially in Pennsylvania, where more than half
the colonies' 40,000 Quakers lived, where freedom of belief and
practice were guaranteed by William Penn's Quakerism, and where
the hands of the Friends wielded political control." Not surprisingly, the trials of American Quakers derived precisely from these
favorable conditions of prosperity and dominance, for to exercise political power and enjoy affluence was inevitably to compromise Quaker testimonies of peace, simplicity, equality, and
community.[6]

Significantly, the classic journal of American Quakerism emerged
from the attempt of American Friends to rediscover their heritage
during and after the collapse of Penn's Holy Experiment in the
crisis of 1755. Although the Quakers' utopian experiment was less
authoritarian than that of the Puritans, it was central to the Quaker mission in America. Thus the crucial dilemma for American
Friends in the eighteenth century was the fate of their faith after
the end of the Holy Experiment. The question was whether they
would retreat into an exclusive tribalism, like the Puritans, lapse
into quietism, like the English Quakers, or maintain a vital relationship between the world of the spirit and the world of power.

There were several causes of the crisis of 1755: the collapse of
the Quaker Indian policy; the need for defense during the French
and Indian War; criticism of Quaker pacifism from outside the
Society of Friends and criticism of the compromises of Quaker
assemblymen from within it; and the growing consciousness of the
Quakers' minority status.[7] The Quaker abdication of power was a
victory for purists like Woolman, but it was by no means a solution to the Quakers' dilemma. The subsequent internal response of
Quakerism consisted of a thrust toward asceticism, tribalism, and

group consciousness as evidenced in tighter organization and stricter discipline of members' behavior.[8] However, there was also an external response which provided a vital counterthrust to this exclusivism—an expansion of the Quaker notion of benevolence from a concept of charity among Friends to an inclusive concern which embraced even the Indian and Negro slave.

An unobtrusive but influential leader in the Quaker adjustment to the crisis of 1755, John Woolman adopted a stance that combined the two aspects of the Quaker response outlined above: he sought to foster group consciousness based on the essence of Quaker piety rather than on outward manifestations of it in dress and speech; and he desired that Quakers be useful to the larger society, not only through dedication to public projects but also as radical exemplars of a peaceful way of life. His close involvement in the Quaker dilemma is evident in two developments in his own life that coincided with the communal crisis. At about the time of the Quaker retreat from politics, he severely curtailed his business activities. Then, he used his increased "leisure" to do the journeying and writing that make the *Journal* such an effective dramatization of the dilemma of American Quakerism in the eighteenth century.

Woolman's opening sentence, though conventional, aptly introduces his *Journal* and suggests its essential Quaker qualities: "I have often felt a motion of love to leave some hints in writing of the goodness of God, and now, in the thirty-sixth year of my life, I begin this work" (p. 23). There is no suggestion here of the historical context nor any announcement of individual purposes; rather, Quaker piety is announced as both the motive and the theme of the journal. The reference to a repeated motion that finally issues in action suggests the pattern typical of Quaker experience, from the simple act of speaking in meeting to the process of agonizing, perhaps for weeks, over a decision on a course of action. This pattern and the Quaker notion of revelation it reflects account for an important distinction between Puritan and Quaker personal literature.

For the Puritan, revelation was essentially complete, and one's election, predestined. As a result, the Puritan autobiographer was less concerned with the nature of truth than with the way an ac-

cepted set of ideas applied to him—the way he fit into a preor-
dained scheme. For the Quaker, revelation was an ongoing process
through which the truth was progressively revealed to the faithful.
Moreover, the truth could be known only through a cycle of waiting, acting, and contemplating one's action; the repetition of this
cycle not only advanced the enlightenment of the individual, it
might change the communal notion of the truth. While the distinction is one of emphasis, the Puritan spiritual autobiographer generally recorded his concern for the correspondence between his past
experience and the will of a personal God, while the Quaker recorded his concern for the relationship between his future action
and God's will as expressed in moral principles. Thus, Puritan
autobiography tends to be deductive and retrospective, while
Quaker journals are more inductive and prospective.

Woolman's account of his conversion also illustrates the distinctive character of Quaker piety. Like a Puritan conversion, Woolman's was experienced in solitude; but it culminated in the
adoption of a universalistic interpretation of divine benevolence,
in contrast to the Puritan's relieved sense of his own election. Furthermore, a Quaker's conversion could be considered complete
only if it enabled him to return to the world with his virtue intact
and in a spirit of true friendship solicitous of the best interests of
even his unregenerate companions. For the Quaker, conversion
was less the crucial and all-consuming crisis of life than it was the
process that made possible the progressive education of his conscience and his submission to the motions of that conscience.
Woolman's first chapter ends with two incidents that make this
clear. First, he adopts the role of public conscience, reproaching
a Mount Holly innkeeper for the Christmas revelry at his inn. Second, he records his private anguish over his writing a bill of sale for
a Negro slave owned by his employer; out of that guilt grew a lifetime of devotion to the extension of the Quaker testimony of
equality.

For Woolman, of course, conversion led inevitably to the call to
the ministry. Just as inevitably, the narrative becomes an exploration of the complexities and paradoxes of the role of a public
Friend—a prophet among prophets. It achieves thematic unity by
weaving together the threads of the four Quaker testimonies it

progressively elaborates: those of simplicity, equality, peace, and community. Because of convention and because a Quaker could apprehend the truth only by enacting it, the journal focuses on Woolman's actions as a lay minister, especially his journeys to other meetings. Although Woolman averaged less than one month per year away from home, his journal expresses the essence of his life as a Quaker, for his journeys were both the expression and the test of his piety. Officially, he traveled as representative of his own meeting, but ultimately, of course, he served as an agent of God and a conveyor of divine benevolence. Proper submission to God, however, depended on his sensitivity to his environment; thus, he functioned in part as a kind of barometer measuring the moral atmosphere around him. A report of his own state of mind was often merely a reflection of the state of religion where he was traveling: "The sense I had of the state of the churches brought a weight of distress upon me" (p. 64). The result of this self-effacement is not impersonality; instead, as Paul Rosenblatt has said, "the paradox is that the self does not become incapacitated or dehumanized, but rather more discriminating, more imaginatively moral, more touching and humanizing."[9]

Already evident, then, is another underlying principle that distinguishes Woolman's *Journal* from its Puritan predecessors—the strong centrifugal impulse that derives from the traveling minister's function as the channel of communication between widely separated meetings. Though Woolman rarely used the term, his *Journal* becomes a true pilgrimage by virtue of the amount and purpose of his traveling. He used his journeys to suggest that physical travel was especially conducive to moral growth; his progressively more widely ranging travels to New England, the South, and finally England, were not only analogous to but necessary for his gradual elaboration of the Quaker social testimonies. Thus, although his travels performed the tribal function of binding the far-flung meetings more closely together, the essence of his journeying was antitribal. Woolman saw the whole Creation as organically unified, and in his travels he encouraged Friends to trace the moral consequences of their actions beyond the confines of the tribe, as he did.

As a prophet, Woolman was less concerned—in his journal as in his life—with literal prediction than with elaboration of the truth as expressed in the Quaker testimonies. Of these, perhaps the testimony of simplicity was the most fundamental: for the Quakers in general, because their interpretation of simplicity in terms of distinctive dress and habits gave them a communal self-image; for Woolman, because submission to an ascetic impulse opened his mind to the other testimonies. In the crisis of 1755, distinctive Quaker customs were reemphasized in an attempt to heighten group consciousness, but Woolman saw only too clearly that the superficial definition of solidarity would lead to an exclusive tribalism. In 1756, acting on his profound sense of this testimony, Woolman drastically cut back his thriving business enterprise and diverted his energies from the business of shopkeeping to the humbler craft of tailoring. Typically, his concern was not only to free himself from excessive involvement in wordly affairs, but also to set an example discouraging trading in superfluities. His thrust, then, was toward a radical personal witness to the essence of simplicity rather than toward rigid conformity to tribal customs. If the Quakers were to reemphasize simplicity in a time of crisis, Woolman, as a prophet, would help them to define it properly.

Woolman never departed from this fundamental testimony; rather, he elaborated it throughout his life and *Journal*. This concern is especially evident in his Thoreauvian theory of economy: "I believe [God] hath provided that so much labour shall be necessary for men's support in this world as would, being rightly divided, be a suitable employment of their time, and that we cannot go into superfluities, or grasp after wealth, in a way contrary to his wisdom, without having connection with some degree of oppression and with that which leads to self-exaltation and strife" (p. 120). Utopian as such a theory may seem, Woolman's concern for economic conditions also manifested itself in some very sharp and specific social observation, another feature distinguishing Woolman's *Journal* from Puritan spiritual autobiographies, in which providential views of history and tribal concerns precluded any interest in utopian economics or radical social criticism.

The testimony of simplicity was inextricably linked to those of equality, peace, and community; violation of the principle of simplicity led to oppression, war, and the disruption of human broth-

erhood. Woolman's testimony against slavery, which dominates
the *Journal*, probably is the most historically significant of any of
his social concerns. Typically, the concern for slavery grew from
the circumstances of his personal life to universal scope. Early in
his career he found that drawing up wills in which slaves were be-
queathed implicated him in the slaveholding of the Friends in his
community. His first antislavery gesture, then, was his refusal to
write a will which, in his eyes, violated God's wish that all men be
free. Soon, his concern drew him to the South where he could ob-
serve the treatment of slaves under harsher circumstances. There
he expressed his opposition to slavery by paying slaveholding
Friends for their hospitality and by journeying on foot, "that by
so travelling I might have a more lively feeling of the condition of
the oppressed slave, set an example of lowliness before the eyes of
their masters, and be more out of the way of temptation to un-
profitable familiarities" (p. 145). Woolman's multiple intentions
illustrate the economy of his ethics: with one gesture, he delivered
himself from evil, conveyed a moral lesson to his hosts, and broadened his sympathy. While acting in a calculatedly exemplary fashion, he still left room for learning; the action was not only didactic
but autodidactic. Furthermore, his concern was antitribal, for he
stressed Quaker responsibility to the "Gentiles, who do not profess Christianity" (p. 129).

Woolman's growing concern for slavery moved him to deliver
prophetic warnings to gatherings of influential Friends. Included
in the *Journal* is a speech before the Yearly Meeting of 1758 which
ended: "Should we now be sensible of what [God] requires of us,
and neglect to do our duty in firmness and constancy, still waiting
for some extraordinary means to bring about their deliverance, it
may be that by terrible things in righteousness God may answer us
in this matter" (p. 93). Such prophecies share much with Puritan
jeremiads, but there is a crucial difference. Woolman demanded
not a reversion to neglected tribal values but an advance toward a
utopian or millenial interpretation of the testimony of equality.

Woolman's dealings with the Indians followed a similar pattern,
but they were as much concerned with the testimony of peace as
that of equality. Furthermore, they were closely conditioned by
the communal crisis faced by his generation of Friends. In this

crisis, he held firmly to the pacifist position against pressuring
Quakers to participate in the war effort—as Assemblymen, in raising a militia and paying for arms; as citizens, in paying war taxes;
and as soldiers, in the defense against Indian raids. Woolman's pure
pacifism involved the risk of great suffering, and to guide his people, Woolman placed their troubles in the context of the Providential theory of history characteristic of the Old Testament and
Puritan prophets. Woolman especially stressed the crucial role
of his generation in defining their values for the next: "By our
constant uniform regard to inward piety and virtue, let them see
that we really value it" (p. 101).

The tribalistic theme was part of the Quakers' internal response
to their communal crisis. However, for Woolman, peace was not
simply a distinguishing trait to be passed down to later generations, but part of the core of values which could make Quakers
truly useful to the larger society: "We trust [that] as there is a
faithful continuance to depend wholly upon the Almighty arm
from one generation to another, the peaceable kingdom will gradually be extended 'from sea to sea and from the river to the ends
of the earth,' to the completion of those prophecies already begun, that 'nation shall not lift up sword against nation nor learn
war any more' " (p. 49). Thus, Woolman's missions to the Indians were at once part of a practical (but unsuccessful) attempt to
achieve a nonpolitical diplomatic settlement and an expression of
a desire to spread the peaceable kingdom.

A sense of Quaker declension which had haunted Woolman
since childhood furnished both a motive and a motif for the *Journal*. But his complex attitude toward the ultimate fate of the
Quaker community was perhaps best expressed not in his occasional prophecies of catastrophe, but in this passage: "Though our
Society in these parts appeared to me in a declining condition, yet
I believe the Lord hath a people amongst them, who labour to
serve him uprightly, but have many difficulties to encounter"
(p. 43). He clearly recognized the responsibility of this pious minority and especially of the individual prophet to reawaken the
Society. But his own drawings led him to such radical extremes
that he was in danger of falling into an adversary relationship with
his people, as Increase Mather had. The consequences of his role

first came home to him with regard to his antislavery stance: "I saw at the time that if I was honest to declare that which Truth opened in me, I could not please all men, and I laboured to be content in the way of my duty, however disagreeable to my own inclination" (p. 52). His resolve was firm, but as a Quaker, he could not welcome the role of eccentric, as Thoreau later did. The Quaker prophet, though not as tightly bound to Scripture as his Puritan counterpart, was held more closely to the community's version of the truth. Consensus was a Quaker ideal; a too-radical individual challenged that value and risked drawing attention to himself rather than to his message. The challenge for the prophet was to change the consensus without violating the process by which it was reached. Thus, the Quaker practice, expertly executed by Woolman, was to address evil not by denouncing the evil-doer, but by appealing to the seed of God in him.

This predicament was typical of the Quaker's existence; it pertained in meeting, in prophecy, and in autobiography. Woolman's most severe crisis involving his departure from group customs came in 1761 when he decided to give up wearing dyed clothes. His objections to the use of dye were several: it was unnecessary, hurtful to the cloth, and conducive to uncleanliness, since it hid dirt; but his strongest concern was for the role of dye in the West Indies slave trade. Yet in spite of the depth of his concern, his fear of appearing publicly different from his fellow Quakers caused him to delay the decisive change. He worried that his gesture would be misinterpreted as issuing from vanity, fashion-consciousness, or sheer eccentricity. Significantly, his fear focused on the prospect of appearing "singular" among a strongly group-oriented people. Only after a psychosomatic crisis did he fully resign himself to this new form of witness to the testimonies of simplicity and equality. More than his original conversion, in fact, this process involved a sense of death and rebirth as a new man: his new clothing became not only an expression of a social concern but an external manifestation of the profound inner change that enabled him to make such a public gesture.

This episode vividly illustrates the predicament of the Quaker prophet and the central tension in Quakerism between the individualistic doctrine of the Inner Light and the emphasis on consensus.

Woolman found it necessary to address this dilemma directly. For example, speaking in the debate on slavery at the yearly Meeting of 1759, he tried to "show how deep answers to deep in the hearts of the sincere and upright, though in their different growths they may not all have attained to the same clearness in some points relating to our testimony" (p. 97). The object of perception was the same for all, but different powers of perception caused different Friends to perceive the same object differently. Woolman later gave a historical dimension to this concept. Contemplating the progress of the Reformation, he described the historical role of the prophet: "The uprightness of the first reformers to the Light and understanding given them opened the way for sincere-hearted people to proceed further afterward, and thus each one truly fearing God and labouring in those works of righteousness appointed for them in their day findeth acceptance with them" (p. 147). Woolman recognized that the Society's notions of truth and hence of good and evil were conditioned by historical circumstances. The radical and the conservative were merely at different points on the route to the same destination. The role of the prophet was not to outdistance the others but to hasten their progress by humble leadership.

Significantly, these passages balance Woolman's sense of declension with a sense of the progress possible if conscientious prophecy is heeded. He recognized the central role of the prophet in the progressive enlightenment of the community; similarly, he recognized that the prophet's significance depended as much on his relationship with the Society of Friends as on his special relationship with God. Woolman's radical concerns for peace, simplicity, and equality were derived from an equally radical interpretation of the testimony of community. But as a Quaker he found that his responsibilities to the whole human brotherhood had to be tested and made meaningful within the context of the smaller community first. His ethical concerns clearly transcended tribal considerations, but his role was to extend rather than to ignore or denounce the concerns of the tribe.

In autobiography as in life, Woolman needed to merge with the community as well as to subordinate his will to God's. The conventional formal expression of submission to God's will was, in

Quaker as well as in Puritan spiritual autobiography, the use of the passive voice. But Woolman added to this the frequent substitution of the first-person plural for the first-person singular in phrases such as, "Our hearts were sometimes enlarged in the love of our Heavenly Father amongst these peoples" (p. 36). The inclusion of collective documents—sometimes in fact written by Woolman but presented as products of the committees that approved them—was also a formal expression of the Quaker ideal of consensus, as was Woolman's presentation of his emotions as a reflection of the moral atmosphere around him.

These characteristics point to a distinction between the mysticism of Woolman and that of Edwards which was symptomatic of the differences between Quaker and Puritan piety in general. Both men were true mystics and both autobiographies focused on growth in grace through mystical experiences. Moreover, their autobiographies are the classic expressions of Puritan and Quaker piety because they explored the implications of the two faiths at times when they were undergoing redefinition in response to crisis. But Edwards defined growth in grace as a progressive annihilation and fulfillment of the self in an exclusive intimacy with God, whereas Woolman's submission to God was achieved by means of the extension of his human sympathies. This growth in grace was evident in his progress from childhood sin through a solitary conversion to an expansive concern with all mankind. It was also evident in a vision Woolman had, late in life, during a severe attack of pleurisy. This vision brings the *Journal* toward a conclusion: "I was brought so near the gates of death that I forgot my name. Being then desirous to know who I was, I saw a mass of matter of a gloomy colour between the South and the East, and was informed that this mass was human beings in as great misery as they could be and live, and that I was mixed in with them and henceforth might not consider myself as a distinct or separate being. I then heard a soft, melodious voice, . . . and I believed it was the voice of an angel who spake to other angels. The words were, 'John Woolman is dead' " (p. 185).

Only the following morning, when Woolman realized it "meant no more than the death of my own will" (p. 185), was it clear that the vision confirmed his complete submission to God's will and

prophesied his own death. But unlike Edwards, who perceived his
resignation to God's will and his death in terms of a mystical merging with God, Woolman saw his loss of individual identity in terms
of a merging with all of mankind as well as with God. Edwards's
mysticism reflects the tendency of Puritan piety to conceive of the
individual ultimately in terms of an exclusive relationship with
God, while Woolman's mysticism reflects Quakerism's universal-
ism. Like Edwards's *Personal Narrative*, Woolman's *Journal* suggests the nature of the eventual resolution of the paradoxes of
piety, while recognizing that the actual resolution lies beyond
death and hence beyond autobiography. Yet for Woolman, one
of the paradoxes concerned the relationship of the individual to
the community. His resolution of that paradox is closer to the
spirit of Whitman's "Song of Myself" than to that of Edwards's
Personal Narrative.

Such a vision would have made a fitting conclusion to the book.
Nevertheless, the *Journal* does not actually conclude with that passage. Depending on the editorial decision, it ends in one of several
other ways, each fitting in its fashion. The most authoritative edition ends with a passage in which Woolman returned to two issues
that continued to preoccupy him in England—slavery and the
wearing of dyed cloth. The final passage consists of an account of
a Friend's death, and includes his deathbed vision of the corruption and violence of slavery. After describing that vision, Woolman
wrote: "He appeared calm . . . , death in about one hour appeared
evidently upon him, and I believe about five hours from my going
in he quietly breathed his last; and as I believe he left no more
memorandum in writing of that dream or vision of the night, at
this time I believe it seasonable for me to do it" (p. 192). This
conclusion is perhaps the most fitting. Having prophesied his own
death, Woolman might have made any conclusion seem anticli-
matic, but by recording a vision of slavery similar to his own, he
offered evidence of his own influence without claiming it. Furthermore, by substituting his friend's death for his own as conclusion
to his *Journal*, he carried on the self-effacement he had struggled
for throughout his life—and achieved a final selfless autobiographical act.

FOUR

Deism and Prophecy

Benjamin Franklin's *Autobiography*

In spite of disagreement over its
greatness and its place in our literary history, Benjamin Franklin's
Autobiography has established itself as a classic to be reckoned
with in any account of American autobiography. The crucial question here is whether it belongs to the tradition of prophetic autobiography. For those who read it as a smug, self-congratulatory
success story, the answer is easy. But although the book is a success story—the classic, if not the original American success story—
it is not fair to blame Franklin for what that form became in others' hands. Franklin's ideal of success was enlightened and humane.
It included moral and intellectual as well as economic advance-
ment, and it was not entirely individualistic; for Franklin, true
success manifested itself in benevolent and altruistic action. Because Franklin sensed a responsibility to the community, and act-
ed on it, his autobiography goes beyond self-advertisement to assume some of the characteristics of prophetic autobiography. It is
not only an exemplary narrative but one that urges certain values
on the entire community to help it achieve its historical destiny.
In reading it, we witness and, to some extent, participate in the
transformation of personal history into a narrative which has the
shape and resonance of a myth. Still, Franklin's view of the self

and its relationship to God and the community was such that he could be at best a kind of prophet manqué. His autobiography effected important innovations, but it is not truly prophetic in conception.

Although Franklin was acutely aware of, and respectful of, the Puritan and Quaker heritages, he tended to transform their values in the direction of a secular and utilitarian ethos. His debt to his Puritan background was neither incidental nor wholly superifical; his emphasis on diligence in one's calling, his preoccupation with ethics, and his sense of responsiblity to an ordered community all derived from that source.[1] But as a descendant of the Puritans in an enlightened age, he approached their tradition with detachment and selectivity; while he maintained a certain tenuous continuity with them, his modifications of their conventions often amounted to radical innovations. Although he perpetuated the Puritan ethic by further secularizing it, his autobiography is devoid of any expression or understanding of Puritan piety. Hence the strong contrast between Franklin's autobiography and that of Edwards, his contemporary. Edwards focused on the nature of God and on his own mystical participation in that divine being; Franklin stressed his activities in the world of men. Edwards weaned himself from the world; Franklin realized himself within it, devoting his career to achieving concrete results with men and things.

If Franklin's career moved him a considerable distance in time and space from the influence of New England Puritanism, Philadelpia Quakerism was a force he had to contend with throughout his adult life. In general, he was favorably disposed toward the Quakers, whom he regarded as less dogmatic and tribalistic than the Puritans. Insofar as Quaker merchants exemplified a variation of the Puritan ethic, he had a natural affinity with them, and his civic projects often depended on close cooperation with benevolent and pragmatic Quakers.[2] With its emphasis on travel and public service and its tendency to expand its intellectual, moral, and geographical dimensions simultaneously, Franklin's autobiography shares more with Woolman's *Journal* than with Edwards's *Personal Narrative*. Furthermore, in his letter urging Franklin to complete his autobiography, Abel James implied that the narrative might serve didactic purposes similar to those of the Quaker journal.

Like the Puritans, the Quakers represented a culture Franklin both admired and criticized; his own autobiography was forged, in part, out of his ambivalence toward their examples.

The text of the autobiography bears out one's sense that Franklin's temperament and values differed in important ways from those of the Quakers. Except for his acknowledgment of Thomas Denham as a sponsor of his business career, Franklin gives Quaker influence no credit in his personal development. Instead, he humorously recalls that the first house in the Quaker city in which he slept was a meetinghouse, a recollection that succinctly characterizes his relationship with Quakerism. This anecdote at once portrays him the way pious Quakers must have perceived him—as insensitive to spiritual experience—and portrays the Quakers as he must have regarded them—as tolerant (he was not awakened until the end of the meeting) but a little dull (the meeting was not sufficiently engaging to keep him awake). Franklin's admission that he added a thirteenth virtue, humility, to his own list at the suggestion of a Quaker acquaintance may appear at first to be a concession to Quaker piety. But his subsequent argument for the usefulness of the *pose* of humility in persuasion illustrates his significant transformation of the Quaker concept.

Just as it exposes Franklin's subtle but decisive transformations of Puritan and Quaker values, his autobiography reveals that deism furnished a radically different context for autobiography from those supplied by Puritanism and Quakerism. Those two religions encouraged introspection and autobiography by imposing on the individual an overriding concern with grace and salvation. Furthermore, their communal emphasis established the conventions in terms of which the saint would perceive and portray himself. Deism did none of this. The deist was able to consider his fate as self-determined and his life as a process of self-education rather than one of instruction by a paternal God. Deism shifted the index of an individual's worth from his beliefs to his behavior, from faith to works. Because deism tended to lodge initiative, will, and responsibility with man rather than God, it liberated the autobiographer from the providential framework and tribalism of traditional spiritual autobiography, broadened the scope of his autobiography, and gave him new latitude in the interpretation of his exper-

ience. At the same time, it eroded some of the preconceptions
conducive to the writing of prophetic autobiography: the sense
that one's vision derived its authority from its transcendent source;
the idea that both the individual and the community were bound
to God by special covenants; and the belief that the history of the
community was characterized by urgent crises with profound moral implications. Thus, as Franklin moved away from the other-
worldliness of Puritan piety and the radical moral testimony of
Quaker piety, he gave up some of the distinguishing characteristics
of the prophetic autobiographer: his supramundane viewpoint;
his sense of history as divinely ordained; and his complex, sometimes antagonistic relationship with his audience. As we shall see,
Franklin's autobiography reveals that his concepts of self, God,
and history were fundamentally different from those of the prophetic autobiographers we have considered.

Franklin's conception of his autobiography as a revised edition
of his life clearly distinguishes his vision of autobiography from
that of a Puritan or Quaker. Long before he began writing the autobiography, he had composed an epitaph for himself using a similar
metaphor: "The Body of B. Franklin, Printer; Like the Cover of
an old Book, Its contents torn out, And Stript of its Lettering and
Gilding, Lies here, Food for Worms, But the Work shall not be
wholly Lost: For it will, as he believ'd appear once more, In a
new and more perfect Edition, Corrected and amended by the
Author."[3] Except for his confidence in his own sanctification,
there is nothing here to alarm an orthodox Puritan, and much of
the wit would have pleased a Puritan elegist. However, the ruling
metaphor in the opening passage of the autobiography has radically different implications from those of the epitaph. For in play-
fully begging the advantage, in writing his autobiography, that
"Authors have in a second edition to correct some Faults of the
First" (p. 43), Franklin has assumed the role previously assigned
to God, and the book takes the place of the immortal soul as the
revised edition of the man's life. For the Puritan, God was ultimately the Author of the autobiography even as he was the Creator of the saint; here, Franklin boldly claims full responsibility for
his autobiography and, by implication, for his life and his afterlife.
His intent is no less didactic than the Puritan autobiographer's;

however, the process is not one of passing on lessons taught by God but one of creating a model of self-education. The deity may still make the rules and occasionally intervene in the game, but for the most part, the initiative has passed to Franklin, who plays the game shrewdly and aggressively. Franklin's vision of his act as autobiographer clearly reflects his deistic view of the human predicament and of human possibilities.

Franklin's deism both permitted and required a new degree of self-consciousness in writing autobiography; lacking the conventional, though sincerely felt, formulas of the Puritan or Quaker saint, Franklin had literally to invent himself as a character. Responding to his challenge with wit and intelligence, he gives the impression of having experienced much of life as play, entering into a succession of roles easily and always with a certain detachment.[4] It is partly this sense of delight in his experience, of his value and consequence as an individual, that sets his autobiography apart from the spiritual autobiographies preceding it. Much of the pleasure of reading the book derives from the satisfying correspondence between narrative and character. Personality is revealed in incidents which in turn shape it; the result is a coherence, whether discovered or contrived, between the character observed and the observing persona. For autobiography as a self-conscious art form, there is clearly an advance here over traditional spiritual autobiography.

Franklin's deism and his sense of responsibility for himself also contributed to the feature of the autobiography most distasteful to modern readers—the self-advertisement he engages in both as a businessman and as an autobiographer. If he could conceive of his self as his own creation, he could also treat it, at times, as a commodity. Thus, he candidly recommends self-advertisement as a means to success, stopping just short of sanctioning hypocrisy: "In order to secure my Credit and Character as a Tradesman, I took care not only to be in *Reality* Industrious and Frugal, but to avoid all *Appearances* to the contrary" (p. 125). On the one hand, Franklin tried to minimize the offense to the reader by practicing the art openly and skillfully. On the other hand, conscious of the Puritan strictures on the autobiographical ego, Franklin strove to make the vanity of the secular autobiographer a virtue in disguise. After all, he argues in his opening paragraph, vanity is "often productive of Good to the Possessor and to others that are within his Sphere of Action" (p. 44). Still, the notion of autobiography as self-advertisement is at odds with the notion of autobiography as prophecy, which demands some kind of subordination of the individual ego to the needs of the community. When simple self-congratulation takes over as the dominant impulse, as it does in the individual success story, the autobiography belongs to a tradition essentially opposed to the prophetic one. This tradition has a kind of precedent in Franklin's *Autobiography*, but actually represents a debasement of his example.

Part One concludes with an account of Franklin's first public project—the organization of a subscription library. Thus far, the narrative has been largely a story of success and self-improvement, an account of Franklin's achievement of personal independence and prosperity. But at this point, he begins to transcend strictly private enterprise to engage in philanthropic endeavors, and the narrative seems to move toward the prophetic mode. From here on the theme of success is subordinated to that of benevolent public service (a pattern followed in the autobiographies of Booker T. Washington and Andrew Carnegie). Thus, the overall pattern of Franklin's experience is more accurately characterized as a gradual but dramatic extension of the scope of his interest, knowledge, and influence than as a vertical rise through social ranks. (The pattern of Woolman's experience was similarly expansive, but his desire was to expand the scope of his social conscience whereas Franklin sought to extend his personal power.) The library project is a good introduction to this new aspect of the narrative because here Franklin portrays himself as the originator of a project which in turn generates others. The library is seen as an agent of progress and enlightenment contributing to the pride and self-consciousness of the American colonists. The actions of the individual at this point begin to influence and even to become the history of the community. This hint of Franklin's later activities as an American propagandist and revolutionary is the first suggestion of his identification with the nation. The conclusion of the first part, with its reference to the colonial resistance to English tyranny, foreshadows the conflict that completed his self-realization and induced him to adopt a quasiprophetic role as he continued his autobiography.

In the short second part of the autobiography, written in France in 1784, Franklin consciously enlarged his conception of the book as a result of two letters urging him to finish it. Of the two, Benjamin Vaughan's rather effusive letter more specifically indicates the broadened significance of the autobiography, for Vaughan explicity links it to the international image of the newly independent nation. Reminding Franklin that "all that has happened to [him] is also connected with the detail of manners and situation of a *rising people*," Vaughan requested a model of self-education which would serve as an "efficacious advertisement" for America, inviting to it "settlers of virtuous and manly minds" (pp. 135–36). In particular, he desired a narrative whose characterization of a virtuous revolutionary would both justify American independence and inspire worldwide progress. Finally, he envisioned the *Autobiography* as encouraging "more writings of the same kind . . . and [inducing] more men to spend lives fit to be written"; Franklin's narrative was to inspire other lives worthy of autobiography and other autobiographies worthy of imitation. It was, like his projects, to shape the American nation in his image.

It is impossible to determine to what extent these expectations provided a new stimulus and to what degree they simply made Franklin aware of the possibilities of the narrative already begun. However, it is certain that in Part Two he deviated from his outline of 1771 to dwell on his religious beliefs and his project for attaining moral perfection.[5] The passage concerning his religious principles stresses his substitution of universal principles for the "unintelligible dogmas" of his Puritan upbringing. But while Franklin's elaboration of a creed appropriate for an enlightened, progressive nation is a prophetic *gesture*, his system of beliefs, as has been suggested, jettisoned precisely those elements of religion conducive to true prophecy. Deism encouraged faith in reason rather than in inspired utterance.

The project for achieving moral perfection has a similar thrust—the isolation and pursuit of personal values which are then implicitly recommended as appropriate to the new nation. Admitting

his own failure (or only partial success), Franklin nevertheless recommended his thirteen virtues and his method as valid means of
self-improvement.[6] Here Franklin sought a practical modern alternative to Puritan and Quaker self-examination. His scheme was
not intended to provoke anguished introspection, a radical extension of the social conscience, or a closer personal relationship with
God; rather, it was to produce objective self-knowledge and de-
monstrable improvement in moral conduct. Unlike a Puritan or
Quaker prophet, who might invoke impossible ideals or exhort his
audience to virtue without showing them the way, Franklin felt
responsible for inventing a method (one wants to say a technology) capable of producing the desired result. However, in spite of
the fact that he had been a revolutionary, his ethic, like his creed,
was far from radical; it drew heavily on common sense and middle-
class values. While Franklin's sense of the need for new values
moved him to a gesture that seemed prophetic, his values themselves reduced the need for, and respect for, prophecy in the original sense. Franklin spoke, finally, only as a founding father to his
proliferating progeny.

In Part One, Franklin's pursuit of success and independence involved a process of self-liberation from restrictive institutions and
involuntary associations. In Part Two, his pursuit of perfection demanded rigorous self-discipline. The result was a structure that
demonstrated sequentially the two complementary aspects of
Franklin's highest ideal and his unifying theme—self-government.
Self-liberation and self-control, individual freedom and social order, were the values Franklin attempted to reconcile implicitly in
his autobiography. In a way, the implication of the entire *Autobiography* is that the personal self-government of men like Franklin
had made the Revolution possible and that the continued well-
being of the Republic depended on the universal emulation of
their example.

In Part Two, then, the Revolution emerges as the decisive historical context of the autobiography. Here Franklin lets the reader
witness his discovery of the analogy between his experience and
that of the nation. Just as America was creating itself as a nation,
Franklin was revealing, in his autobiography, how he had created
himself as an American and how much he had contributed to the

creation of the nation.[7] Thus, without even mentioning his participation in the event, he created an autobiographical analogue of the
Revolution—"the life of a self-made, self-governing man, written
by the man himself."[8] By virtue of its being consciously fashioned
to represent communal history, the narrative, in a sense, "prophesies" the Revolution just as Edwards's narrative prophesies the
millenium; it isolates the values and attitudes conducive to the imagined change and suggests the dynamics by which the transformation would occur.

But Franklin's autobiography is, even at this point, prophetic
only in a very limited sense. After all, by the time Franklin began
Part Two, the Revolution had occurred, whereas Edwards's millenium had not. Franklin's narrative corresponds in a way to the Revolution; it justifies and validates it. But as the narrative continues,
Franklin reveals a sense of history inconsistent with a truly prophetic autobiography. In Part Three he portrays himself primarily
as a projector,[9] the shaper of the new nation on many levels—from
his visionary but unsuccessful Albany Plan to his proposals for
street cleaning and street lighting. No detail was too small for his
flexible mind as it expanded its scope of comprehension and control. Underlying his social service was a view of history very different from the Puritan's providential one: "Human felicity is
produced not so much by great pieces of Good Fortune that seldom
happen as by little Advantages that occur every Day" (p. 207).
This philosophy of history gave man control of his destiny, but it
lacked the urgency and drama of the providential view and it offered no basis for prophetic utterance. For the Puritans' sense of
crisis, Franklin substituted a sense of gradual but inevitable progress. Thus, Franklin functioned less as a critical interpreter of the
community's history than as its enactor and embodiment. His
autobiography is exemplary and representative but not prophetic
because he achieved self-definition by sacrificing the supramundane
viewpoint of the prophet. Franklin's authority as an autobiographer was not derived from his vision but from his accomplishments—the institutions he created to embody his limited vision of
America. Furthermore, he perceived no fundamental moral gap
between himself and his audience or between the community's
history and its proper destiny. For him, the differences between

the real and the ideal America were matters of detail rather than of conception.

Indeed, as the autobiography continues, the suggestion of the ideal is progressively subordinated to the narrative of the enactment of the historical reality. Moreover, as the power of the autobiographical *character* increases and his personal influence is extended over greater spheres of action, the power of the *narrator* wanes and the narrative becomes increasingly dull and drained of individuality. The effect is as though Franklin sacrificed the personal dimension of his life when he assumed a place on the public stage. As his interests and those of the community became increasingly identical, his autobiography became history and there was no need for him to continue the narrative. Although the ending seems inconclusive, it is, in a sense, appropriately final. His ultimate role in the autobiography was that of the representative of several American colonies before their English oppressors. Thus, at the point when he had become literally the representative of the community, his self was, after a fashion, annihilated. Whereas Edwards and Woolman had, in their separate ways, foreshadowed their deaths and prophesied their union with God, Franklin simply "died" into history as the servant of his community.

As Benjamin Vaughan saw it, Franklin's narrative was to determine the shape of American history and American autobiography. Coming at the time of the birth of the Republic and the emergence of autobiography as a self-conscious genre,[10] Franklin's autobiography achieved important innovations and broadened the possibilities for American autobiography. Yet, as Daniel Shea has observed, for nineteenth-century American writers, the patterns of spiritual autobiography were more appealing and influential.[11] Certainly, autobiographers inclined toward a prophetic stance often found those patterns a useful resource in their attempt to restore a spiritual dimension to American autobiography and culture. Still, while they might have to resist Franklin's invitation to advertise themselves instead of communicating their visions, they could also learn from Franklin's self-conscious artistry and his freedom as an autobiographer.

FIVE

Frederick Douglass

Abolitionism and Prophecy

The *Narrative of the Life of
Frederick Douglass* (1845) reveals the impact on the slave narrative of most of the acknowledged literary influences—the Bible,
Pilgrim's Progress, abolitionist oratory, and sermon rhetoric.[1] But
more significant than these literary influences were several experiential ones—Douglass's experience of slavery, of the antislavery
movement, and of religious conversion. The relevance of the first
two is obvious enough. Indeed, they combine to give the narrative
a polemical purpose which may compromise its validity as autobiography for some readers. Those readers may find more comprehensive and balanced accounts of Douglass's life in *My Bondage
and My Freedom* (1855) or *The Life and Times of Frederick
Douglass* (1881). But in spite of the changing perceptions and
viewpoints of the later versions, Douglass's lifelong involvement
in the reworking of his autobiography underlines the importance
of slavery to his self-understanding. Instead of writing sequels to
his first volume, and thus escaping from the experience of slavery
in his successive autobiographies, Douglass chose to revise and expand his narrative periodically; this involved returning to slavery
and liberating himself from it over and over. Thus, the large
chunks of exposition which seem to interrupt and impede the

flow of the narrative are a necessary part of it. Reenacting his own experience led Douglass inevitably toward an analysis of slavery; and analyzing the institution that attempted to define and confine him contributed in turn to his understanding of himself.[2] As a result of the narrative's pattern, the reader, like Douglass, finds "slavery" obstructing his progress; Douglass used this pattern to teach the reader, through form as well as content, that one must understand slavery before reaching freedom.

How Douglass's conversion is relevant to the *Narrative* is less obvious, for it is never mentioned in the text. Nevertheless, it plays an important role, for Douglass employs the structure of the conversion narrative to organize and focus his autobiography. He might well have been familiar with John Woolman's *Journal*, which combined an account of spiritual growth with antislavery testimony, but Douglass's piety and his antislavery sentiment are essentially different from Woolman's. If he had literary sources for his conversion model, they remain obscure. More likely, his sense of the shape and significance of conversion derived from his own conversion experience (which was, of course, shaped by Southern Methodism), his later churchgoing, and his experience as a preacher once he reached the North.

According to *My Bondage and My Freedom*, his religious mentors were both black and white, and his conversion occurred in three stages: first, a sense of being in need of salvation, but without the means; next, a period of humiliation and doubt; and finally, after a "change of heart," a sense of faith in God and love for all mankind. Douglass observes that his awakening to religion (that is, to his spiritual condition) occurred before his awakening to the antislavery movement (that is, to a full awareness of his political condition). And he admits that the preaching of the white minister left him somewhat confused: "He thought that all men, great and small, bond and free, were sinners in the sight of God; that they were, by nature, rebels against his government, and that they must repent their sins, and be reconciled to God through Christ."[3] At that point in his life, Douglass's sense of himself as a man did not correspond to his sense of himself as a slave or as a Christian. Thus, although his conversion gave him a new and needed sense of status and of his special destiny, it was treated some-

what perfunctorily and did not serve as a decisive turning point in
the narrative.

My Bondage and My Freedom, a longer narrative which gives
separate treatment to the several dimensions—political, religious,
and personal—of Douglass's self-understanding, may be truer to
the literal facts of Douglass's experience; but the early, telescoped
narrative fuses these elements in an efficient and powerful way.
Whatever the nature of his models of conversion, the significant
point is that he was familiar with the experience and the terminology of conversion and, more important, that he forcefully adapted
those models to his own purposes, making central to his narrative
an analogy between the process of conversion and that of liberation.

According to this analogy, slavery is equivalent to a state of sin
or existence in Hell, freedom to grace or Heaven, and escape or liberation to salvation or conversion. While the analogy itself may
not have been original with Douglass,[4] the consistency of its application in the narrative suggests that it was a conscious narrative
and rhetorical strategy. It is the development of this analogy, I
think, that structures and controls the narrative, giving it a classic
shape unique among slave narratives. Like other American autobiographers in the nineteenth century, then, Douglass exploits the
patterns of spiritual autobiography for prophetic purposes; for
throughout the book, he writes not merely as an autobiographer
concerned with his own experience but also as a prophet commenting upon American history from a supramundane viewpoint.
However, Douglass's strategy is a double-edged sword, for he manages at once to use Christian values to condemn the institution of
slavery and to use his knowledge of slavery to criticize some of the
preaching and practice of nominal Christians. As a prophet, he
calls not only for the abolition of slavery but also for the purification of American Christianity.

The implications of Douglass's conversion analogy provide an
ironic commentary at every point on the doctrines of Southern
Methodism, as reported in *My Bondage and My Freedom*. For example, Douglass portrays himself as having been born innocent
into a sinful condition; instead of revealing man to be innately
sinful, Douglass exposes slavery as inherently evil. When he calls
the experience of witnessing the whipping of his aunt "the blood-

stained gate, the entrance to the hell of slavery, through which I was about to pass,"[5] he makes explicit part of his analogy. But the implications the metaphor holds for the slave differ from those it holds for the master. The sin of slavery is most obviously the master's, as is evident from his cruelty. But just as it is evil to be a master, it is also a sin to be a slave, if the slave accepts his condition as proper and accepts fallen Christians as his true superiors. The common denominator between the sin of being a master and that of being a slave is that both betray the democratic values of equality, self-sufficiency, and self-government. The slave's sin of ignorant or unwilling self-sacrifice is far more forgivable than the master's, which is committed consciously and willfully, out of self-interest. But the slave's spiritual predicament is perhaps the more complex.

Douglass's penetrating perception of the slave's moral dilemma is expressed in his discussion of a garden kept by his first owner, Colonel Lloyd. Abounding in fruit, the garden is described as a kind of worldly paradise from which slaves are excluded. In one sense, it serves as a metaphor for the plantation system; it stands for all the goods, comforts, and pleasures denied to the slaves. Naturally, and justifiably, they seek access to it. The colonel's response is to tar the fence around it and to interpret tar on a slave's clothing as evidence of sin. According to Douglass, the plan succeeded because the slaves realized "the impossibility of touching *tar* without being defiled" (p. 33). The implication here is that the slaves are morally superior to their masters, who feel that they can participate without guilt in a sinful social system. By the very fact of its exclusiveness, the garden becomes a place of corruption rather than of Edenic innocence. But the sin inherent in its existence is complicated by the temptation the system offers the disadvantaged slaves. There is little danger of their committing the sin of the master—the exploitation of others; rather, the temptation is to submit to mastery by another. Colonel Lloyd is a powerful but not an omnipotent master; rather, he is a false god—irrational, unjust, vengeful, and dishonest. To maintain his integrity—to be saved—the slave must look beyond his master's authority and resist the lure of white values. It may appear to the slave that he has been expelled from a white paradise, but he must remember that his master is the true denizen of the hell of slavery.

Douglass's condition was somewhat mitigated by his belief in his eventual deliverance from slavery: "From my earliest recollections, I date the entertainment of a deep conviction that slavery would not always be able to hold me within its foul embrace; and in the darkest hour of my career in slavery, this living word of faith and spirit of home . . . remained like ministering angels to cheer me through the gloom" (p. 47). The first confirmation of his sense of election, and hence the first use in the narrative of the providential framework, comes with his transfer from the plantation to Baltimore. There is, however, a certain irony in his sense of divine favoritism, for the real benefits of his selection become evident only as the apparent advantages are revealed to be illusory. Only after his expectations of benevolent treatment are dashed do the truly redemptive features of life in Baltimore emerge. It is not the relative leniency of slavery there but its transparency that proves helpful. It is, ironically, through the revocation of certain privileges that Douglass comes to understand the means of his enslavement. Thus, in being denied instruction in literacy, he learns a more signficant lesson about "the white man's power to enslave the black" (p. 49). The idea that slavery depends on the ignorance of the enslaved is "a new and special revelation, explaining dark and mysterious things" (p. 49).

The essence of his new insight is that his proper goals for himself are inevitably the opposite of his master's: "What he most dreaded, that I most desired. What he most loved, that I most hated. That which to him was a great evil, to be carefully shunned, was to me a great good, to be diligently sought" (p. 50). Similarly, his valuation of himself must differ from his master's. Since his sinful condition is his master's creation, Douglass's salvation lies in committing what are sins in his master's eyes. Hence he undertakes a course of self-improvement, bribing poor white boys to teach him to read. Newly aware of his master's vision, values, purposes, and methods, Douglass begins to equip himself to subvert them. Implicity and instrumental in the quest for self-mastery is a sense of loyalty to a higher master; Douglass must betray his white master to be faithful to himself and to God.

Once he has been exposed to the gospel of freedom—the arguments against slavery—as set forth in "The Columbian Orator," Douglass's condition is analogous to that of the convert in the stage of conviction. He is aware of his sin, but helpless to avoid it, aware of grace but unable to possess it. Thus, he says of his reading: "It had given me a view of my wretched condition without the remedy. It opened my eyes to the horrible pit, but to no ladder upon which to get out" (p. 55).

Douglass's spiritual progress enters its climactic phase when, after his transfer to rural St. Michael's, he is put out to be broken as a field hand by a man named Covey. The narrative veers toward allegory here, for Covey, a notorious slave-breaker, is characterized in fairly explicit terms as a satanic figure: "He had the faculty of making us feel that he was ever-present with us. . . . He always aimed at taking us by surprise. Such was his cunning that we used to call him, among ourselves, 'the snake' " (p. 73). Covey's role is to tempt (actually, to threaten) Douglass into slavish behavior and attitudes that betray not only his humanity but his divine potential. Just as the convert's heart is broken before it is made new, Douglass's spirit is broken before it is regenerated. The nadir of the narrative comes when, during his first six months with Covey, he goes through a stage analogous to the stage of humiliation: "I was broken in body, soul, and spirit. . . . The dark night of slavery closed in upon me; and behold a man transformed into a brute!" (p. 75).

Not Douglass's flight from the South but a fight between him and Covey completes the conversion analogy. Having suffered an especially savage and unjustified beating at Covey's hands, Douglass appealed to his owner for relief. Finding no protection there, he sought it next in a magic root given to him by a fellow slave. Finally, however, it is only the spontaneous impulse to resist Covey's next attack that saves Douglass. Retrospectively, he portrays this battle, in which he gave more punishment than he received, as a crisis conversion: "This battle . . . was the turning-point in my career as a slave. . . . It was a glorious resurrection from the tomb of slavery, to the heaven of freedom. My long-crushed spirit rose, cowardice departed, bold defiance took its place; and I now resolved that, however long I might remain a slave in form, the day had passed when I could be a slave in fact" (p. 83).

The source of freedom, then, is not dependence on one's legal master or faith in superstition but reliance on one's self. The slave must not only invert his master's values, he must finally act out his resistance to his master's intentions. In this instance, Douglass's behavior won him a certain grudging respect and better treatment from Covey. But the real reward was his salvation from the psycholgical and spritual oppression of slavery. He had finally and decisively resisted the temptation to act slavishly and willed his own freedom. Thus, although his admission that his impulse surprised him leaves room for divine inspiration, and although he portrays this struggle as the culmination of a long process of preparation for conversion, Douglass emphasizes his own initiative. His implicit "theology," then, rejects not only superstition and slaveholding but also the otherworldly Christianity of slaves who would wait passively for the Lord to deliver them.

Throughout the narrative, Douglass's prophetic motive impels him to generalize from his own experience and to shift back and forth between the narrative of events and the analysis of a social system. He not only participates in the communal "rites" inherent in the slave and fugitive experience, he often gives explicit interpretations of such rituals.[6] At this point in the narrative, as if to explain why his crisis experience was not more common, Douglass explains the ulterior purpose of granting holidays to the slaves at Christmas time. According to Douglass, these holidays function as "safety-valves" which carry off the "spirit of insurrection" (p. 84). Released from work and encouraged to use their leisure for dissipation, slaves understandably become disgusted with what they take to be freedom. However, Douglass points out that those who mistake license for liberty are, in effect, obstructing their own liberation and participating in a kind of idolatrous rite.

Douglass's treatment of his escape represents a striking and significant deviation from the conventional pattern of the slave narrative. Often, the story of the escape provides the climax of the fugitive narrative. Furthermore, typically the geographical movement from South to North serves as "a conscious metaphor for the fugitive's personal and social movement from anonymity to identity, from self-contempt to self-respect, from ignorance to enlightenment, and from sin to salvation."[7] However, Douglass

entirely omits this anticipated episode from his book. He makes
the strategic reasons for this omission explicit. He does not wish,
by divulging details of his escape, to endanger those who have
helped him, nor does he want, by alerting slaveholders to his
method, to hinder future attempts at flight. Thus, Douglass's
annotated omission reminds the reader that flight from slavery,
which provides the readers of most slave narratives with easy
wish-fulfillment, is still a matter of life and death for fugitives.
Furthermore, his assertion that he is not "at liberty" to tell all of
his tale suggests that the full realization of his freedom depends on
the emancipation of all slaves. Finally, the omission of the conventional climax emphasizes his use of the conversion analogy. The
fight with Covey—the crisis of liberation-as-conversion—remains
the structural and symbolic center of the book; the achievement
of freedom in mind and soul replaces bodily flight to Northern
soil as the crucial event of his life.

Sidonie Smith has observed that there is a double pattern inherent in the slave narrative—that of the fugitive's break *away* from
an oppressive community and that of his entry *into* a community
which would permit his self-realization.[8] The conclusion of Douglass's narrative shows that the pattern remained, for him, existentially and historically incomplete. Two episodes in particular
qualify the affirmation of the ending. According to the logic of his
analogy, the North, the land of freedom, ought to be described as
a kind of paradise. But the fugitive slave can no more find absolute
security than the convert can, and, on his arrival, Douglass finds
New York a forbidding and anxiety-producing place. So long as
the sin of slavery exists, the fugitive is threatened with capture,
and his freedom remains tentative.

A similar lesson is suggested by Douglass's account of his induc-
tion into the abolitionist movement with which the narrative concludes. His career as a professional abolitionist commenced when
he rose to speak of his bondage at an antislavery convention on
Nantucket in 1841: "It was a severe cross, and I took it up reluc-
tantly. The truth was, I felt myself a slave, and the idea of speaking to white people weighed me down. I spoke but a few moments,
when I felt a degree of freedom, and said what I desired with considerable ease. From that time until now, I have been pleading the

cause of my brethren . . . " (p. 119). Again, Douglass recognized the incompleteness of his transition from slavery to freedom, but he accepted responsibility for completing the process, in two ways. First, while his reluctance to express himself before a white audience betrayed a vestige of the slave mentality, his decision to do so reenacted and reinforced his liberation from the community that fostered that sense of his inferiority. Unlike Franklin, who merely created an analogue of revolution in his autobiography, Douglass actually committed a risky and rebellious act in writing his.[9] And whereas Franklin confidently attested to his ability to govern himself, Douglass candidly admitted the difficulty of mastering himself. Second, having failed to *discover* a free community into which he and his brothers could enter in a new relationship, Douglass here began the task of *creating* one.

The signficance of the conclusion, then, refers us back to the importance of the conversion analogy. For if, as John L. Thomas has said, "the American abolitionists constituted a religion,"[10] then Douglass's narrative records not only his conversion to the faith but also his ordination as a minister. When he wrote the book, he was one of Garrison's most prominent and precious converts, and Garrison's "Preface" reinforces one's sense that the use of the conversion analogy was deliberate. In it, he used the terms borrowed from revival preaching to describe the response desired in the reader: "He who can peruse [this book] without a tearful eye, a heaving breast, an afflicted spirit, —without being filled with an unutterable abhorrence of slavery and all its abettors . . . without trembling for the fate of this country in the hands of a righteous God . . . must have a flinty heart and be qualified to act the part of a trafficker in slaves and the souls of men" (p. x). Garrison suggested, then, that the narrative was calculated to awaken the reader from his spiritual lethargy, to alert him to his implication in the sin of slavery, to melt his heart, and to convert him to the abolitionist cause.

Douglass's remarks in the appendix further characterize the impulse behind the narrative. Having emphasized at every opportunity the cruelty of his churchgoing masters, Douglass felt impelled to point out that he was not an opponent of Christianity: "What I have said respecting and against religion I mean strictly to apply to the slaveholding religion of this land, and with no possible reference to Christianity proper; for, between the Christianity of this land and the Christianity of Christ, I recognize the widest possible difference—so wide that to receive the one as good, pure, and holy is of necessity to reject the other as bad, corrupt, and wicked" (p. 120). Douglass did not identify slaveholding religion with Southern Christianity, however. Far from intending to reassure his Northern readers, he wished to show that their Christianity was nominal, and hence hypocritical, if it did not include the belief that slavery was a sin. If the reader found himself included in the indictment of slaveholding religion, Douglass invited him to come out of his corrupt institution into the abolitionist church—out of a slave community into a free one. Thus, like most conversion narratives, Douglass's *Narrative* was written not only to record the author's conversion but to precipitate or confirm that of the reader. It was the abolitionist movement that provided Douglass with the nearest thing to a free community, and he joined it in the hopes that that select group would succeed in abolishing not only slavery but prejudice in the larger community.

The benefits of modeling his slave narrative on the conversion narrative were many. Although Douglass's "theology" might have offended some conservative Christians, the religious language and providential apparatus of the narrative encouraged them to read it as an enactment of God's plot for Douglass. Moreover, the radical implications of Douglass's theology would have been acceptable to the religious groups most influential in the antislavery crusade—Quakers and evangelical Arminians. These Christians would have been comfortable with Douglass's belief in the divine potential of the individual, with his implication that the individual could, with divine inspiration and assistance, achieve his own regeneration, and with his sense that conversion needed to be followed by reform activity. Indeed, like the theology of Charles G. Finney, Douglass's had perfectionist implications, for following his original "conversion," he experienced greater and greater degrees of freedom, as he explored its existential and political implications.

Douglass's analogy had the further advantage (for his rhetorical purposes) that it presented something with which his audience was not directly familiar—the experience of slavery—in terms of something with which they were presumably familiar. Without violating the integrity of his experience as a black slave, Douglass managed to cast it in a form accessible to his predominantly Northern white audience. His adaptation of a well-known narrative formula to his materials encouraged the reader to expand his sphere of moral concern to include the issue of slavery. As a strategy for organizing a slave narrative, the use of the conversion analogy had a certain elegance, for it employed one of the premises of radical abolition-ism—that slavery was a sin—as the foundation of the structural framework of the book. By means of this gesture, the narrative achieved in its form the convergence between religion and reform it tried to bring about in life; Douglass created a historical as well as a literary model.

Finally, for Douglass, the conversion-liberation analogy must have seemed an appropriate way of giving his experience coher-ence and shape. While it sacrificed some factual detail and com-plexity, it was an apt metaphor for his life. It offered him, then, a way of expressing the significance of his experience in a conven-ient, symbolic shorthand which gave his life the resonance of a myth and the power of prophecy.

SIX

Henry David Thoreau

Retreat and Pilgrimage

In any account of American literary history, the period of the American Renaissance is crucial. This holds especially true for the development of the native tradition of autobiography because it was Thoreau and Whitman, acting out the theories of Emerson, who first raised American autobiography to the level of an art form. Since Transcendental literature brought together as its main tendencies "the impulse to prophesy, to create nature anew for oneself, and to speak in the first person singular,"[1] it may seem inevitable, in retrospect, that Emerson's followers should have enriched the prophetic tradition of American autobiography. But in fact, the predicament of the Emersonian autobiographer was ambiguous, for while Transcendentalism in many respects recovered the essential piety of earlier American Protestantism, it rejected the dogmas and conventions which had channeled the expression of that piety into specific autobiographical forms. Furthermore, the writing of autobiographical narratives was inhibited by certain aspects of Transcendentalism. For example, the tribal functions of traditional spiritual autobiography did not pertain for Transcendental writers. And in the absence of a morphology of spiritual development, let alone a belief in the necessity of conversion, there was no model for spiritual autobiography. Indeed, the theme of the growth of one's mind was itself foreign to Transcendentalism, which preferred to stress the present moment as the only reality and one that contained all of life's possibilities.[2] Finally, Emerson's ideas about the self tended to challenge, if not deny, the assumptions underlying conventional autobiography—that the self exists trapped in time and in an individual identity. Thus, even as Transcendentalism encouraged introspection as both a spiritual endeavor and a literary strategy, it fostered a concept of the self which tended to dissolve under scrutiny, and it supplied little in the way of useful models, guidelines, or limits for the autobiographer. Hence the paradox that while Transcendental literary theory was favorable to autobiography, the literature of the movement included few clearcut examples of autobiography as it was conventionally understood.[3]

Thoreau and Whitman followed separate but similar paths to autobiography. Their intuitive sense of the analogues in their own experience for the history of the nation and for traditional patterns of autobiographical writing places them firmly in the tradition we have been tracing, while their genius for discovering forms that expressed the Emersonian concept of the self made them innovative and highly sophisticated autobiographers. Finally, because they viewed nature as a divine language, all experience as symbolic, all history as potential mythology, revelation as ongoing and accessible, and the American nation as having a special destiny, they assumed the roles and functions of the prophet in their writing.

It was in *Walden* that Thoreau first successfully fused his life and his art by totally embracing autobiography—by living self-consciously in order to write his life. However, in a discussion of Thoreau's place in the tradition of American autobiography, it must be admitted that *Walden* is not autobiography in any conventional sense. Its highly selective use of material, its pervasive symbolism, and its idealized persona make it seem more fictive than factual. Yet Thoreau's comments on truth, reality, and myth throughout his writings provide an explanation for the kind of autobiography he wrote. For example, a theory of autobiography is implicit in this passage in *A Week on the Concord and Merrimack Rivers*: "The poet is he who can write some pure myths today without the aid of posterity. . . . We moderns . . . collect only the raw materials of biography and history, memoirs to serve for a history, which is itself but materials to serve for a mythology."[4] Throughout his life, Thoreau strove to reduce facts of the imagination to facts of the understanding and to realize the sacred dimensions of his daily activities.

Thus, the fictive quality of Thoreauvian autobiography is largely a result of the attempt to telescope the process of converting history into myth, and the features that seem to have no place in autobiography can all be understood as part of Thoreau's unique response to the predicament of the Transcendental autobiographer. For example, his pervasive allusions, in *Walden* and *Cape Cod*, to mythic or biblical parallels for his experience and his "extravagant" writing were not intended to create fiction but truth as he understood it. Seen in the light of Emerson's view of nature, Thoreau's nature description indicates a method of assimilating the highest values, and suggests, without calling attention to personal achievement, the autobiographer's success in reaching his goal of harmony with nature. Similarly, the overall pattern of the book stresses the natural cycle rather than the linear progression of history because Thoreau was attempting to exemplify man's ability to transcend historical circumstances. He chose to compress two years into one because the seasonal cycle included all the possibilities of life and elevated his narrative to the level of universal myth. Thus, the tendency to endow autobiography with mythic significance took a quantum leap in the American Renaissance not because Thoreau and Whitman preferred fiction to fact or because they wished to falsify their biographies, but because they embraced an idealistic metaphysics and a prophetic mission and because they assigned a noetic function to the imagination.

This new approach to autobiography is illustrated by the difference between Franklin, who began to create his own myth retrospectively in old age, and Thoreau, who attempted to live his life as myth. There is a kind of double artistry to Transcendental autobiography because events were enacted with conscious artistic and prophetic intent instead of being shaped retrospectively for a certain effect. It was no coincidence that the Transcendentalists first raised autobiography to the level of an art; they had already raised life itself to that level. Furthermore, just as Emerson's view of man encouraged him to shape his life in conformity with an ideal, his aesthetic theory gave autobiographical confession a role in the attainment of the ideal. Thus autobiography could be not merely a record of self-transcendence but a tool in the process of self-creation. Autobiography itself became prospective rather than retrospective—prophetic in the predictive sense.

The comparison with Franklin is worth pursuing, because there are hints in "Economy" that *Walden* was conceived as a criticism of Franklin's values and vision, if not as an answer to the *Autobiography* itself. Thoreau's life story was not called for, as Franklin's had been, by a nation seeking to bolster its confidence and international image. But Thoreau did take advantage of his neighbors' curiosity to portray his narrative as an answer to public inquiries rather than an expression of egotism—a witty variation of Franklin's strategy in Part Two. If Thoreau used Franklin's strategy, he did so with the intent of undermining his values, for *Walden* reads, in part, like a declaration of personal independence from Franklin's America. Throughout the book, Franklin's prudential values are revealed to be shallow, materialistic, and selfish. Against Franklin's endorsement of competition and cooperation in an urban setting in a technological society, Thoreau set his own experience of self-realization through contemplation in a pastoral retreat. In place of discipline and industry, Thoreau urged the value of idleness and meditation; against the profession of doing good, the vocation of being good; instead of the role of public projector, that of holy prophet. Perhaps Thoreau's most telling revision of Franklin is in his redefinition of independence and economy: in the first chapter, Thoreau uses scrupulous accounting and arithmetical calculation to set forth a theory of economy which asserts values that defy understanding in terms of dollars and cents.

Thoreau's frequent use of proverbs also recalls Franklin only to undercut him. Whereas Franklin, both as proverbwriter and public conscience, used his influence to reinforce the practical and conservative wisdom prevalent in his society, Thoreau, as a prophet, directly challenged conventional wisdom with radical alternatives.[5] Another telling criticism of Franklin's vision is implicit in Thoreau's brief parody of the success story in "Economy." In explaining his move to Walden Pond, he portrays himself, like Franklin moving to Philadelphia, as a frustrated writer and public servant seeking to launch his business career in a more favorable location. Having failed to gain the appreciation and support of his towns-people for his service as "inspector of snowstorms" and "surveyor . . . of forest paths," Thoreau determines "to go into business at once," and selects Walden as a "good port" due to the advantages of the ice trade and the railroad. The facts of his predicament, of course, made any such rationale patently absurd; his true purpose, punningly revealed, was evangelical rather than entrepreneurial— to get his faithfully kept accounts audited at last.[6] In addition to reversing Franklin's progression from private to public life, Thoreau demolished the kind of opportunistic reasoning on which Franklin's career had been built.

Thoreau rejected religious institutions, forms, and rituals not— like Franklin—in quest of a useful religion, but in an attempt to recover the original piety and the sense of the miraculous which those forms were meant to communicate. Like Emerson, Thoreau retreated from the Unitarian church not to reject Christianity but to fulfill its promise. Perhaps because of his orthodox family back-ground, his version of Transcendentalism retained more aspects of Puritan piety than either Emerson's or Whitman's; the most obvi-ous are his extreme conscientiousness, his ascetic self-discipline, and his sense of man's habitual alienation from God and nature. But he also inherited, probably from Emerson, elements of the Quaker faith. He shared the Quakers' sense of the immanence of God in man and nature; their insistence on the priority of the in-dividual conscience over biblical, clerical, and political authority; their tendency to experience grace through intuition rather than through more obvious and outward means; and their tendency to define the faithful by their vision rather than by their doctrines.

It was perhaps inevitable, then, that Thoreau should reject Franklin's secular model of autobiography, the success story, to revive and perpetuate some of the distinctive qualities of both Quaker and Puritan autobiography—a task neglected by such prominent theologians and religious leaders of his day as Charles Grandison Finney and Lyman Beecher. Daniel Shea has linked *Walden* with the Quaker or "illuminist-antinomian" mode of auto-

biography because it establishes, like Woolman's *Journal*, an exemplary way of seeing rather than a pattern of action, a fresh vision rather than a doctrinal system.[7] Thus, although the chapter
"Sounds" develops certain lessons about the impact of the railroad
on American civilization, those specific ideas are no more significant than the vision of nature that underlies them.

Although *Walden* shares much with Woolman's *Journal*, it also
displays many of the characteristics of the conversion narrative.
Certainly it records moments of transfiguration, suggests that a
profound conversion has taken place, and attempts to induce a
similar conversion in the reader. Indeed, there are striking parallels
between *Walden* and Edwards's *Personal Narrative*. Like Edwards,
Thoreau sought to create a narrative that communicated his own
sense of grace and prophesied his reader's conversion without establishing a rigid or imitable model of conversion. And both narratives are organized around the metaphor of "seasons of awakening."
Furthermore, Thoreau's nature mysticism links him closely to
Edwards. Thoreau's "innocent" enjoyment of storms echoes Edwards's, and Edwards's recurrent use of the term "sweet" to
describe his new sense of the goodness of God is recalled by Thoreau's sense of the benevolence of nature: "I was suddenly sensible
of such sweet and beneficent society in Nature, . . . an infinite and
unaccountable friendliness all at once like an atmosphere sustaining me, as made the fancied advantages of human neighborhood
insignificant" (p. 132). Finally, Edwards's metaphor of the soul
of a true Christian as "a little white flower as we see in the spring
of the year . . . opening its bosom to receive the pleasant beams
of the sun's glory"[8] anticipates Thoreau's more pervasive use of
the natural images to suggest the workings of God in the soul.

Perhaps *Walden* comes closest to the Puritan vision of life in the
chapter, "Higher Laws," where Thoreau's sense of life as an arduous spiritual struggle is most clearly set forth. Even here, to be
sure, Thoreau expresses confidence that "spirit can for the time
pervade and control every member and function of the body, and
transmute what in form is the grossest sensuality into purity and
devotion" (p. 219). But his insistence on the necessity of a constant sublimation of man's natural impulses is closer in attitude to
Puritan theology than to Franklin's Art of Virtue. Unlike momen-

tary mystical ecstacy, Thoreau finds that lasting transcendence and moral progress—for the race as well as for the individual—depend on perpetual struggle, for "there is never a moment's truce between virtue and vice" (p. 218).

Although *Walden* offers no chronological record of spiritual transformation, it does contain analogues or loose parallels to various stages of Puritan conversion. Thus, when Thoreau admits, "I never knew, and never shall know, a worse man than myself" (p. 78), he adopts temporarily the traditional role of the Puritan convert in the period of conviction—the chief of sinners. The stage of humiliation, in which the Puritan is convinced of his inability to earn saving grace by his own efforts, is paralleled by Thoreau's fruitless pursuit of a diving loon, which culminates in the loon's derisive laughter at Thoreau's futile attempts to anticipate his movements. And Thoreau records a sense of divine favor closely analogous to a Puritan's feeling of unmerited grace: "Sometimes when I compare myself to other men, it seems as if I were more favored by the gods than they, beyond any deserts that I am conscious of; as if I had a warrant and surety at their hands which my fellows have not, and were especially guided and guarded" (p. 131).

However, Thoreau stresses the result rather than the process of conversion and lets the passing of the seasons mark the change from doubt and introspection to exuberance and ecstasy. The narrative is designed not so much to document Thoreau's spiritual growth as to accomplish a change in the reader, to prepare *his* heart for conversion. Having begun by accusing the reader of living a corrupt life in a fallen world, Thoreau removes him to a prelapsarian site, coaches him in meditation and symbolic vision, and invites him, at the end, to share in the universal possibilities of redemption. Thus, Thoreau's report, in "Solitude," of his private and exclusive sense of grace gives way, in "Spring," to the universal and natural process of absolution: "In a pleasant spring morning all men's sins are forgiven" (p. 314). If the reader has exercised himself as suggested in "Reading," he may mark a new era from the reading of this book, which may, in that sense, become his autobiography as well as Thoreau's

In discussing *Walden* as spiritual autobiography, the emphasis up to this point has been on its didactic and exemplary qualities. Implicit in these features, however, is its prophetic nature, for Thoreau desired to perform the traditional prophet's role of isolating and perpetuating the spiritual values of the community, and by doing so, facilitate the unfolding of God's plan in their history. His night in jail and "Civil Disobedience" provide the first clear example of the double pattern of his prophetic action: first, the considered symbolic act; then the commentary interpreting and justifying the act.[9] Significantly, the night in jail came during the Walden years, and his notion of prophecy shaped his account of that period; for Thoreau aspired to be the inspired interpreter of American civilization in the middle of the nineteenth century and the personification and forecaster of its future possibilities.

In performing this role, he was closer to Woolman than to Edwards or any of his other predecessors because he called not for a reversion to old values but for a radical revision of the prevailing ethos. In some respects his predicament was unique, accounting, in part, for the nature of *Walden* as prophetic autobiography. To put it simply, he lacked the obvious qualifications and advantages of those before him. Unlike Franklin, he was not a public figure with established authority. Unlike the Puritan and Quaker autobiographers, he lacked clerical status and a preexisting audience of saints. Emerson's axiom that a poet was by definition a prophet encouraged him to play the role but did not guarantee him listeners.

Justification of his prophetic status would thus depend on his acting like a prophet—giving his prophecy autobiographical validity—and on his writing like a prophet—giving his prophecy force by a convincing literary performance. For Thoreau as for Woolman, prophecy was to take the form of criticizing society from a transcendent viewpoint. Hence he made a direct assault on the values of his audience: "The greater part of what my neighbors call good I believe in my soul to be bad, and if I repent of anything, it is very likely to be my good behavior" (p. 10). Unlike a Puritan, Thoreau could not simply base his testimony upon scriptural authority, and unlike Woolman he could not present his prophecy as a refinement of the community's already radical social testimony. Thus, he had the double burden of creating a scripture on which to base his testimony[10] and of creating the visible saints he wished to bind in covenant with God. "Economy" bore the burden of testament-making; in it, Thoreau forged the transcendent system of values that justified his social criticism. But like Woolman, Thoreau developed the testimonies of peace, equality, simplicity, and community throughout his autobiography. In addition to spiritual values, Thoreau had to instill saintly vision in his readers. He also initiated this process in "Economy," using familiar words and concepts in unfamiliar ways and recasting old proverbs to express new insights.[11] In this way, *Walden* became a rhetorically sophisticated and intensely hortatory autobiography.

Eventually, of course, Thoreau hoped to win over, rather than alienate, his audience. Woolman had accomplished this by combining prophetic action and personal visiting. Thoreau excelled at the unilateral symbolic gesture, whether it involved spending a night in jail or two years at Walden, but he was not very successful at personal visiting. It is thus to his credit that, in "Baker Farm," he revealed his failure to convert an Irish immigrant to his way of life and thought. John Fields had to bear the initial responsibility for trying to live "by some derivative old country mode in this primitive new country" (p. 208), but Thoreau had to admit his failure as a prophet with at least this one neighbor in need.

In writing *Walden*, Thoreau found a kind of substitute for Woolman's reliance on the community. Whereas Woolman could lower his prophetic profile by submerging his ego in the meeting, relying on the committee letter or group visitation to alter the consensus, Thoreau invoked nature as mediator between him and his audience. After giving his readers, in the first few chapters, a heavy dose of philosophy, a lesson in reading, and instruction in listening and seeing, Thoreau relied on immersion in nature to accomplish their conversion. Having shared his vision of nature with them, he was able to conclude by encouraging them to make his unique autobiography their own and thus make it truly universal.

The validity of *Walden* as prophecy depended on its having roots in history as well as in biography, in communal as well as personal experience. At times Thoreau alluded to specific current events, as when he satirized the Mexican War in "Brute Neighbors."

But generally, he sought to establish a more profound relationship between autobiography and history by invoking historical events or conditions with broader scope. By setting his awakening in a kind of wilderness, Thoreau associated his experience with the mythology surrounding Indian captivity and the hunt—and with literary genres that sprang out of the unique conditions of American history.[12] Similarly, by the simple act of moving to the wilder environs of Walden, he invoked as historical context both the contemporary westward movement and the original settlement of Massachusetts. In "Former Inhabitants," he reminds us that migration has always been the means of creating America and that it has always failed, or at least fallen short of the ideal. The geographically short but spiritually long remove from Concord village to Walden would determine what migration could still accomplish: "Again, perhaps Nature will try, with me for a first settler, and my house raised last spring to be the oldest house in the hamlet" (p. 264).

Thoreau's reference, in *A Week*, to Franklin as a demigod who "aided Americans to gain their independence, instructed mankind in economy, and drew down lightning from the clouds,"[13] is more flattering than the implicit criticism of him in "Economy." But to some extent Thoreau must have seen himself as superseding Franklin as the educator of Americans in the areas of independence, economy, and nature. Thus, in moving to Walden on July 4, Thoreau also invoked the American Revolution as context for his experience. For Thoreau, the Revolution had been, at best, incomplete because it had not brought about true freedom.

Finally, in moving to Walden, Thoreau prophesied another war for freedom—one that had not yet happened. But in enacting a personal secession from a slaveholding Union, Thoreau predicted more than the Civil War; he predicted its failure to abolish slavery in America.[14] For in "Economy" Thoreau exploited both the antebellum crisis and his readers' consciousness of the bondage of blacks in the South to broaden the concept of slavery until it transcended regional and race lines and political considerations. Like Douglass, Thoreau saw slavery as ultimately a spiritual rather than a legal condition; he, too, sought not only a personal escape from that condition but the creation of a community into which the individual could be freely reintegrated. Without minimizing the dire predicament of the black slaves, Thoreau urged his audience to see that the peculiar institution imaged forth an American as well as a Southern problem, a white as well as a black condition, and that all previously attempted, even imagined, solutions would fail to touch its roots.

Ultimately, then, Thoreau managed to allude in some way to nearly all of the communal experiences behind the autobiographies we have discussed—the Great Migration, the subsequent declension and Awakening, the Holy Experiment, the Revolution, and the development of slavery—and to nearly all the indigenous genres—narratives of discovery and exploration, of hunting and Indian captivity, of conversion and success, and of slavery and escape from it.[15] Like Henry Adams, Thoreau read American history and American literature as failure. He envied his predecessors their opportunity, but he deplored their achievement.

Yet he remained optimistic: the individual and the community could enact, through spiritual regeneration, what no war or migration could accomplish unaccompanied by inner change. If prophecy is heeded, if the creation of new myths to embody and new language to express a radically new vision can make the nation faithful to its highest ideals, "Who knows what beautiful and winged life . . . may unexpectedly come forth from amidst society's most trivial and handselled furniture to enjoy its perfect summer life at last!" (p. 333).

The link between *Walden* and *Cape Cod* is textual, biographical, and thematic. In "Spring," Thoreau's recognition of the need to be "refreshed by the sight of inexhaustible vigor, vast and Titanic features, the seacoast with its wrecks" (p. 318), emphasized the close and complementary relationship between the two books. The pattern of life at Walden, however satisfying, threatened to become static, and Thoreau was impelled to pursue a restless quest for a renewal of faith and vision. Thus, even as *Walden* was taking shape through successive revisions, Thoreau traveled repeatedly to the Cape to explore a landscape which partly reflected, partly stimulated, his sense of growing alienation from nature and of the lapse of mystical ecstasy. In the transition from the green and pastoral surroundings of the inland pond to the barren seashore and boundless ocean of Cape Cod, Thoreau found a severe challenge to his Transcendental faith—a kind of temptation in the wilderness. It required another life to explore this other landscape and this other aspect of nature; *Cape Cod* became the spiritual autobiography of that life, compressing three trips taken over a period of six years into one symbolic excursion to the Cape.

The baffling reality of the environment, which is conducive to mirages, helps to account for the book's peculiar empirical method and its spare prose style: the faith of this pilgrim, at once Darwinian scientist and Transcendental prophet, had to depend on accurate observation rather than comfortable preconception. Hence Thoreau's constant measuring and classifying and hence the long historical digressions that clutter the book. Confronted with Cape Cod, Thoreau felt it necessary to supplement even his perceptive eye with all the corrective lenses at his disposal—guidebooks, historical sources, local lore, and his skills as naturalist and surveyor. Not every detail is necessary, of course, but the book's unfinished quality is expressive of the fact that Cape Cod offered no simple realities or easy affirmations; perspective and proportion became paramount because an indigenous faith rested not on stable correspondences but on a vital balance between dynamic opposing forces.

If *Walden* took the form of a Transcendental rendering of the conversion narrative, *Cape Cod* shows Thoreau expelling himself from his Edenic garden to undertake a pilgrimage through a potentially hostile environment. Yet it shares with *Walden* the basic pattern of the hero's withdrawal from society into nature and his eventual return to society in a state of regeneration, and it has affinities with both Puritan and Quaker spiritual autobiography. More than *Walden*, *Cape Cod* dramatizes the Puritan view of life as ceaseless struggle between opposing forces, and the structure of the hero's pilgrimage is reinforced by analogues of the stages of Puritan conversion. The dynamics of the narrative are perhaps closer to those of Woolman's travels than to those of any Puritan narrative, for Thoreau's success as a pilgrim depends not on allegiance to established doctrine and scriptural authority but on sensitivity to his surroundings. If he is to achieve growth and insight, his state of mind, like Woolman's, must at times reflect his environment. Thus, his description of his surroundings indicates, indirectly, the progress of his pilgrimage.

The ultimately optimistic conclusion of *Cape Cod* depends in part on the fact that Thoreau found there "a people who were, almost out of necessity, specimens of life as it should be when lived in closest contact with Nature."[16] In a sense, he sought to emulate their adaptation to the Cape and thus recapitulate the whole process of the Cape's exploration and settlement. But the process had to be one of personal initiation rather than simple imitation; turning his back on the towns, Thoreau performed his private experiment with no certainty of reaching the same conclusions as the natives. In quest of a new vision, Thoreau found he had to risk his old faith and experience setbacks. But the narrative does culminate in a kind of fulfillment and at least a tentative resolution. At its conclusion, Thoreau is, in his own terms, saved.

Although Thoreau does not even reach Cape Cod in "The Shipwreck," he uses this opening chapter to offer his reader a preview of it and to introduce the book's concerns, by quickly addressing the fundamental challenge of Cape Cod and exploring several possible responses to it.[17] He is drawn by news of a shipwreck to Cohasset Rocks where his attention focuses on "the livid, swollen, and mangled body of a drowned girl, . . . the coiled up wreck of a human hulk."[18] In this stark scene, he confronts the essence of the ocean's challenge—its power to destroy humans and their constructs, whether physical, like the brig, or mental, like the Transcendental concept of a benign nature. Although he portrays himself as a detached observer, he is aware that he too is in danger of being wrecked, like the brig, the bodies, and the seaweed washed up by the storm. Having faced this fact early, he spends the rest of the narrative attempting to investigate, understand, and respond to it.

Thoreau's explicit response to the wreck has two aspects: a naturalistic one, which involves identification with the forces of nature, rather than with their human victims; and a Transcendental one, which sees order and supernatural compensation—a heavenly reward for the drowned—behind apparent chaos and loss. Yet such a response fails to convince at this point because it represents a retreat to a long view of the event; such a leap from the natural fact to its supernatural significance is uncharacteristic of the book, whose value is in its proximate vision and empirical method. Here Thoreau seems to revert to a strained application of his Concord faith rather than to test his faith in the circumstances of Cape Cod, to assume rather than to discover the morality of nature.

A more satisfactory solution is suggested implicitly in the chapter's conclusion, which records his visit to the same cove a year later. Thoreau still perceives the perpetual challenge of the ocean behind the placid appearance of Pleasant Cove: "As I looked out over the water, I saw the isles rapidly wasting away, the sea nibbling voraciously at the continent, the springing arch of a hill suddenly interrupted . . . showing by its curve against the sky, how much space it must have occupied where now was water only" (p. 15). Here, however, the challenge of the elements is resolved without recourse to a supernatural frame of reference. Thoreau has been reminded that the natural order maintains its own dynamic equilibrium: "On the other hand, these wrecks of isles were being faithfully arranged into new shores, as at Hog Island, inside of Hull, where everything seemed to be gently lapsing into futurity" (p. 15). The perspective of time and the flexibility of his mind allow him to see that the ocean's destructive power is inextricably linked to its creative force.

The chapter ends with a kind of existential resolution of the problem—his immersion in the ocean. Although the water is threateningly chilly, it is also pure and transparent, and he finds the sea-bathing "perfect." The ability to adapt his inlander's skills, acquired in ponds and rivers, to this alien element, is especially significant because one of his crucial and saving discoveries on Cape Cod was of the possibilities of human accommodation to this bleak landscape. His immersion in the sea on his return trip suggests both the completion of his initiation and the refreshment that his pilgrimage brought him. Thus the conclusion of this preliminary survey suggests the wholeness and coherence that his Cape experience eventually assumed.

Thoreau hints at the spiritual and prophetic dimensions of the narrative in the conclusion to "The Plains of Nauset." In an apparent digression, he probes the ecclesiastical history of the local towns for its relevance to the natives and to himself. This passage is merely one manifestation of his continuing search for a native faith. While he rejects the doctrines, the theocratic government, and the suppression of heterodox ideas characteristic of the Puritans, he identifies with them as pilgrims and even envies them their assurance: "If I could but hear the 'glad tidings' of which they tell, and which, perchance, they heard, I might write in a worthier strain than this" (pp. 55–56).

Once Thoreau is on the Cape itself and has had some of his preconceptions removed, he can further explore the implications of the seashore for his faith both in nature and in human nature. On the one hand, he finds comforting the fact that where there are wrecks there are wreckers—ingenious and resourceful men who salvage usefulness from misfortune and profit from loss. On the other hand, he perceives the shore unflinchingly as a chaotic neutral ground: "Before the land rose out of the sea, and became *dry* land, chaos reigned; and between high and low water mark . . . a sort of chaos reigns still" (p. 71). The challenge such a place poses to human faculties is a serious one, and the chapter ends with a grim vision of the insufficiency of human mercy in this environment. Peering, through a knothole, into the dark interior of a Charity-House constructed to shelter the shipwrecked, he finds the poorly provided shelter "but a stage to the grave" (p. 74), "not a *humane* house at all, but a seaside box, not shut up, belonging to some family of Night or Chaos" (p. 78). Significantly, in this passage Thoreau weaves together allusions to the Sermon on the Mount (Matthew 7:7–12) to reveal the gap between the Christian ideal and institutional charity. This gloomy vision of the inadequacy of human mercy is the nadir of the narrative—a kind of dark night of the soul for Thoreau.

The narrative proceeds toward its climax in a dialectical fashion. The central insight of "Across the Cape" is that the land can be as threatening as the sea. Circular valleys, sometimes containing whole villages, as if they were sinking or the "sands had run out," hint to Thoreau of the apocalypse. Still, in the next chapter, the Highland Light becomes a landmark in Thoreau's quest for a steady faith in an unstable world. The lighthouse provides an affirmative counterpart to the dark Charity-House and a wry analogue of the divine and supernatural light which illuminates the

Puritan saint. Although the steadiness of the beacon is threatened by the fallibility of institutional mercy, Thoreau is deeply impressed by the patience, integrity, and devotion of the lighthouse keeper. Whereas the Wellfleet oysterman encountered earlier was an example of Calvinistic fatalism, this man, who struggles "to keep his light shining before men" (p. 170), is a model of a positive, but not naive, indigenous faith. Biblical allusions and Thoreau's assertion that, on the night he spent at the lighthouse, he found himself in "no danger of being wrecked" (p. 175) make it evident that the lighthouse is a symbol of salvation. Moreover, Thoreau's identification with the beacon, at the foot of which he sleeps, suggests that he conceives of himself as a prophet or the bearer of a redeeming message: "I thought as I lay there . . . how many sleepless eyes . . . were directed toward my couch" (p. 172).

In the climactic chapter, "The Sea and the Desert," Thoreau's quest reaches fulfillment in a process consisting of several stages. A preliminary stage involves a full recognition of the threatening nature of the land itself. Again the sand is likened to the ocean: "On the edge of the shrubby woods the sand had the appearance of an inundation which was overwhelming them. . . . It is here a tide of sand impelled by the waves and wind, slowly moving from the sea toward the town" (pp. 204-5). This apocalyptic image of the landscape's destructive force is balanced by a consideration of the resourceful strategies which allow the natives to survive there. The epitome of their ingenious adaptation is their use of beach grass to anchor firm sand hills which hold back the sandy tide and prevent the Cape from becoming an uninhabitable wasteland.

The next step in Thoreau's pilgrimage is his confession of faith in this communal project, which clearly embodies many of his implicit values in its ingenuity and its combination of natural and human resources: "Thus, Cape Cod is anchored to the heavens, as it were, by a myriad of little cables of beach grass, and, if they should fail, would become a total wreck, and erelong go to the bottom" (p. 207). The central significance of this passage may be inferred from the way it integrates various images used separately earlier in the book—the leitmotif of the wreck, the image of the Cape as a ship, the recurrent image of the tenacious beach grass, and the anchor as the emblem of faith. Though the anchor cables are fragile, they have held, and Thoreau chooses to believe in their future security. Faith has found a focus that relates nature to human nature.

Perhaps it is this assurance that allows Thoreau to push his quest to its culmination in his final exposure to the unbridled Atlantic. At that moment, he finally professes his conviction of the essential difference between the ocean and a pond: "As we stood looking on this scene we were gradually convinced that fishing here and in a pond were not, in all respects, the same" (p. 211). This terse understatement contrasts sharply with the triumphant conclusion of *Walden* and hardly seems like an affirmative climax. However, the real force of this deceptively simple assertion lies in the succession of observations, insights, and analogies which prepared for it and which elaborated its experiential implications; its impact lies in our recognition that Thoreau has actually been fishing in the ocean all along.

Thoreau's pilgrimage carried him, both in time and in space, to the edge of America. On Cape Cod, he consciously sought an eternal frontier, as the western one receded from him. The knowledge gained in this neutral zone might be challenging to one's preconceptions, for "it is a wild, rank place, and there is no flattery in it" (p. 186). Yet this is only one aspect of the shore; Thoreau also recognized that the ocean was "the origin of all things" and "the laboratory of continents" (pp. 127–28). In the evolutionary process, at least, the shore is the site of creation, and it is still giving life. It is this aspect of the Cape to which Thoreau alludes in his concluding sentence. For if "a man may stand there and put all America behind him" (p. 273), he may also, simply by reversing his perspective, put America before him. Thus, traveling to the shores where American history began is for Thoreau the equivalent of the busk he called for and enacted in *Walden*. Undoing American history, Thoreau discovered the original ingredients of the American experience and affirmed the possibilities of the endless rediscovery and recreation of America by the reawakened pilgrim.

Ultimately, *Cape Cod* functions, like *Walden*, as a prophetic spiritual autobiography in which the narrator becomes a divine interpreter of communal history and the embodiment of its possible future; but, in keeping with its darker view of nature, *Cape Cod*'s prophecy is less flamboyantly uttered than that of *Walden*. In *Walden*, Thoreau undertook to create a synthetic Scripture employing Eastern religions as well as Christian sources; hence, the book took on a philosophical and meditative quality not found in *Cape Cod*. Here he focuses on personal testimony rather than testamentmaking; he is largely content to invoke the Bible as his authoritative Scripture. Of course, the parallels between Thoreau's experience and the stages of Puritan conversion are oblique and ambivalent, for Thoreau's experience was not one of internal transfiguration in a crisis conversion but of encouragement won from external circumstances. However, these analogues do link him with the region's past, and help to clarify the relationship between the outer excursion and the inner pilgrimage. Furthermore, although he criticizes the Pilgrims as timid explorers in his digression on the discovery of America, he admits that they "were pioneers, and the ancestors of pioneers, in a far grander enterprise" (p. 257). It is this same enterprise, the creation of a spiritual community in the New World, that impels Thoreau's adoption of the prophetic role, and his recurrent references to the Pilgrims reveal his grudging admiration for their faith. While certain of their doctrines remain repugnant to him, he finds their harsh view of life somehow appropriate to the Cape, and he reveals growing respect for their collective strength. Thus, while *Cape Cod* reflects a less optimistic view of nature, Thoreau finds himself encouraged by the possibilities of human cooperation, at least as historically practiced in this distinctive region. In short, whereas in *Walden* Thoreau drew on many religions and summoned virtually all of American history as the context for his radical prophecy, here he draws largely on Christianity and invokes only the historical context of migration, exploration, and settlement to fashion a personal but more subdued prophetic autobiography. Having trekked to the site of the original settlement of New England, Thoreau returns confident that America can still fulfill her unique destiny, and, inviting his reader to retrace his journey, he challenges America to recapitulate his personal pilgrimage on a communal scale, using *Cape Cod* as a spiritual guidebook.

SEVEN

Walt Whitman

Vision and Revision

           Although Whitman was not among the original group of Transcendentalists, he qualifies as one for our purposes by virtue of his discipleship to Emerson. As an autobiographer, he found himself in a predicament similar to Thoreau's, but his tendency to act out the role of the Emersonian poet more literally than Thoreau resulted in an even more innovative contribution to the tradition. Two autobiographical works which bracket his career—"Song of Myself" and *Specimen Days*—reveal his unique solutions to the problem of expressing the concept of Transcendental egoism; moreover, they portray Whitman as a prophet. Taken together, these complementary works form a kind of prophetic autobiography which reveals significant continuity with the tradition of American spiritual autobiography, especially with its Quaker component.

In addition to absorbing Quaker ideas through Emerson's influence, Whitman was exposed to them through more immediate channels. Though not herself a practicing Quaker, his mother came from Quaker stock, and Whitman's father was a friend and admirer of the radical Quaker, Elias Hicks, who made a strong impact on young Walter when he was brought to hear Hicks preach.[1] Unlike Emerson, then, Whitman did not have to rebel against a Puritan-

Unitarian tradition to accept the doctrine of the Inner Light; it formed the core of his religious thought from the beginning.[2] Late in his life, Whitman paid tribute to Hicks in a brief essay he included in *November Boughs* (1888); there, in commenting on Hick's belief in "the universal church, in the soul of man," he indirectly defined himself and his relationship to the Quaker tradition. Furthermore, his characterization of Hicks as one of the "most *democratic* of the religionists—the prophets" suggests that Whitman found inspiration in Hicks as well as Emerson for his role as the prophet of democracy.[3] Indeed, his explicit association of the two men acknowledges the similarity of their principles; Emerson's influence was important not only because it reinforced Whitman's Quaker heritage but also because it suggested to him how to translate it into poetic expression.

Of course, Whitman went beyond both Hicks and Emerson in some respects. Whitman tended to collapse the dualism between man and God, and between body and soul, maintained by the Quakers and even, to a lesser degree, by Emerson and Thoreau. He expanded the scope of man's divinity, asserting that since man was part of God, rather than vice versa, everything in man was sacred. For Whitman, the most dangerous sin was man's sense of guilt, which was derived from outmoded conventions and morals that obscured man's sense of his own divinity. His democratic religion depended on all men loving each other as they were.[4] Thus, although Transcendental literary theory supplied a general context for Whitman's poetry, his prophecy and his autobiography also had to express Whitman's unique religion, which went beyond the assumptions of Transcendentalism.

Although the essentials of Whitman's faith and hence the content of his eventual prophecy must have been established much earlier, there is no hint of prophecy or autobiography in his writing before the publication of the first edition of *Leaves of Grass* (1855). Whitman had available to him, of course, several Romantic examples of autobiography or prophecy—Goethe's *Poetry and Truth*, Wordsworth's *The Prelude*, and Carlyle's *Sartor Resartus*. However, none of these provided Whitman with a model because none of them combined prophecy and autobiography in the way Emerson seemed to encourage. For example, although Wordsworth flirted with the notion of prophecy, he neither portrayed himself as a prophet nor functioned as one in writing his poetic autobiography. *The Prelude* is essentially a retrospective account of a gradual growth to poetic and spiritual maturity, whereas "Song of Myself" is the announcement, rather than the record, of a poetic career; substituting vision for meditation and prophecy for retrospection, Whitman created himself as a poet with a radical act. His composition of the poem was an autobiographical and prophetic gesture for which *The Prelude* offered no precedent.

Sartor Resartus may have provided some inspiration for what Whitman attempted in "Song of Myself," and in *Specimen Days* Whitman conceded America's need for a scornful Hebraic prophet like Carlyle, but his remarks also reveal that indigenous models of prophecy were at least as important as Carlyle's example: "The word prophecy is much misused; it seems narrowed to prediction merely. That is not the main sense of the Hebrew word translated 'prophet'; it means one whose mind bubbles up and pours forth like a fountain, from inner divine spontaneities revealing God. Prediction is a very minor part of prophecy. The great matter is to reveal and outpour the Godlike suggestions pressing for birth in the soul. This is briefly the doctrine of the Quakers."[5] The allusion to Quaker doctrine at this point is by no means accidental, for Whitman goes on to point out that Carlyle's serious failing as a prophet was his lack of a quality essential to the "truest cosmical devotee or religioso and the profoundest philosopher." This quality, which is central to Quaker as well as Emersonian and Hegelian thought, Whitman defined as "a soul-sight of that divine clue and unseen thread which holds the whole congeries of things, all history and time, and all events, however trivial, however momentous, like a leashed dog in the hand of the hunter" (p. 106). Lacking a sense of the divine harmony of the whole, Carlyle was, in some respects, constitutionally unsuited to the prophet's role of interpreting communal history from a divine perspective; by implication, he was also an inappropriate model for Whitman.

Whitman's discussion of Carlyle suggests that in some ways, his acquaintance with examples of Romantic autobiography and prophecy merely served to drive him back on his Transcendental and Quaker tenets. Later we shall see how much "Song of Myself" and *Specimen Days* share with traditional spiritual autobiography. But first it may be helpful to consider in what sense "Song of Myself" can be called autobiography, since it seems to violate even the concept of autobiography developed by Thoreau. In *Walden* and *Cape Cod*, Thoreau subordinated the factual or literal truth to the ideal or symbolic truth of his experience in order to invest his autobiography with a mythic dimension. In "Song of Myself," however, there are few, if any, verifiable autobiographical facts; Whitman abolishes the distinction between literal and symbolic truth as he collapses so many other conventional dualisms. If *Walden* and *Cape Cod* move from autobiography toward prophecy and myth, "Song of Myself" moves from prophecy and myth toward pure vision. It is true that in a Quaker journal, the narrator might recount a vision in order to help establish his prophetic authority; Woolman, for example, did not always distinguish sharply between dream and waking, vision and reality.[6] But in "Song of Myself," Whitman's vision tends to take over the whole poem, displacing conventional narrative entirely. Vision is not tested against reality; it is assumed to *be* reality.

Even though Whitman's prophetic impulse seems to have overwhelmed his autobiographical impulse, one can still argue that "Song of Myself" is simply a more radical form of "mythic autobiography" than *Walden.*[7] Whitman thought of all of *Leaves of Grass* as a new kind of autobiography, for he described the book as "the outcropping of my own emotional and other personal nature—an attempt, from first to last, to put a Person, a human being (myself, in the latter half of the Nineteenth Century, in America), freely, fully, and truly on record. I could not find any similar personal record in current literature that satisfied me."[8] Elsewhere he referred to it as autobiography "in the high, the uncommon sense,"[9] perhaps meaning the Emersonian sense, according to which the *Divine Comedy* was Dante's autobiography written in colossal cipher. For, like *Walden*, "Song of Myself" should be understood as autobiography which reflects an Emersonian concept of the self; thus, it is intended to be a means as well as a record of self-transcendence.

There is no hard external evidence that Whitman had a mystical experience like that described in section 5, and the biographical

evidence suggests that Whitman was not, in 1855, the man he portrayed as himself in the poem. But the poem evidently issued out
of some genuinely transcendent sense of himself. The mystical
experience may stand for a crucial spiritual or psychological transformation Whitman was undergoing, but it may just as well refer
to Whitman's growing awareness, in the early 1850s, of his poetic
and prophetic faculties, his sense that Emerson's ideas about the
poet applied in some special way to him. Thus, in writing "Song
of Myself," he simultaneously enacted and recorded a crucial self-
transformation. As Hyatt Waggoner has put it, "Walter Whitman
first imagined a 'fictional' character, 'Walt Whitman,' then devoted
himself to becoming that character. . . . Whitman was to discover
that becoming Emerson's kind of poet enabled him finally to be
the kind of man he wanted to be. . . . Making art out of life, he
was able to make his life a work of art freely created."[10] Fully
aware of the discrepancies between his real and ideal selves, he
managed to gradually diminish the distance between them, not
by counterfeiting himself, but through arduous emotional and
spiritual growth. This lifelong process is amply documented in
Roger Asselineau's *The Evolution of Walt Whitman: The Creation
of a Personality*.

"Song of Myself" is profoundly involved with the tradition we
are tracing, for it is prophetic autobiography in at least the two
senses Whitman distinguishes in his discussion of Carlyle. First, it
is prophetic in the sense that it attempts spontaneously to communicate divinely inspired truths about Whitman's self. Second,
it is prophetic autobiography in the minor sense that it predicted,
because it shaped, Whitman's subsequent development as a person
and poet. Over the years, as Whitman lived to realize in fact his
Emersonian vision of himself, the poem became a kind of self-
fulfilling prophecy of self-fulfillment. In addition, it can be described as prophetic autobiography because in it Whitman's
prophetic persona, like a spiritual autobiographer, recalls a conversion experience and its consequences. Considering it in this
light will reveal its close relationship with the tradition.

Although Whitman was familiar with at least one example
of Quaker spiritual autobiography—Hicks's *Journal*—that one
work was probably no more influential than any of the other

models available to him, since Whitman was uncomfortable with some of its conventional qualities. Thus, the important links between Whitman and the Quaker journalist are not to be found in Whitman's occasional affectation of Quaker terminology, but in more subtle manifestations of similar religious beliefs and prophetic intent. As a whole, *Leaves of Grass* imitates the pattern of composition of the Quaker journal; a conversion narrative is supplemented periodically by installments probing the significance of subsequent experience in the light of a new vision. More specifically, there are intriguing similarities between "Song of Myself" and Woolman's *Journal.* [11] Both men wrote in the context of communal crisis; both turned from outward pursuits to inward experience in response to these crises; both cited a divine call which led them to adopt the role of minister or prophet; both referred to private visions to convey their prophetic message; both were led by a divine impulse into wide-ranging travel which brought them into empathetic contact with strangers; both attempted to forge a larger spiritual community by extending the tolerance and expanding the consciousnesses of individuals; both were advocates of a radical revision of community values; both encountered as the primary paradox of their piety the tension between their mystical inwardness and their desire for communal solidarity. Finally, as Daniel Shea has observed, their didacticism, like Thoreau's, is a matter of isolating the essential principles of their lives and recommending their vision, rather than their acts, as exemplary. [12]

Like a spiritual autobiographer, Whitman begins his song speaking as one full of grace, but unlike a traditional spiritual autobiographer, he openly celebrates his divinity and insists that his listeners are equally worthy of celebration. The contrast between Whitman and his predecessors can be illustrated by comparing his opening lines to those of a seventeenth-century Puritan poem, *Auto-Machia*, by George Goodwin:

> I sing my *Self:* my *Civil-Wars* within;
> The *Victories* I howrely lose and win;
> The dayly *Duel*, the continuall Strife,
> The Warr that ends not, till I end my life. [13]

All of the spiritual autobiographers we have discussed, including Thoreau, welcomed their readers to a world of constant strife between virtue and vice. In contrast, Whitman announces at the beginning of his poem the end of the civil war within, the victory of divine union, and universal amnesty.

In preparation for the vision of section 5, Whitman withdraws from the artificiality of society to intimacy with nature and his invited soul. His loafing, like Thoreau's passive contemplation, contrasts with Franklin's busy and efficient progress, and he promises a vision which will entirely supplant Franklinian values:

> Have you reckon'd a thousand acres much? have you reckon'd
>   the earth much?
> Have you practis'd so long to learn to read?
> Have you felt so proud to get at the meaning of poems?
> Stop this day and night with me, and you shall have the origin
>   of all poems,
> You shall possess the good of the earth and sun,
>   (there are millions of suns left,) . . . [14]

Whitman proposes to dispense with conventional methods of education—"Creeds and schools in abeyance, . . . I permit to speak at every hazard,/Nature without check with original energy" (ll. 10-13)—and to eschew the highly charged rhetoric and logic of conventional edification for reliance on empathy and the reader's divine intutition—"Only what proves itself to every man and woman is so,/Only what nobody denies is so" (ll. 655-56). Finally, before recalling the mystical experience, Whitman warns his reader that his will not be a conventional autobiography; disregarding the curiostiy of "trippers and askers" about superficial matters such as his early life, his friends and his surroundings, he will attempt to communicate the truth about his detached and transcendent "Me myself" (ll. 66-74). Whereas he once "sweated through fog with linguists and contenders," he now strikes a Quaker pose, witnessing and waiting (ll. 80-81).

His waiting is rewarded by the memory of the mystical union of his body and his soul, and the vision which accompanied that experience; this experience and this vision establish his prophetic author-

ity and provide him with the substance of his prophecy. From
here on, the song is like no other spiritual autobiography, partly
because Whitman is concerned with giving adequate formal expression to radical ideas. Take, for example, the Emersonian concept of the individual's relationship to time. In "Self-Reliance,"
Emerson had said, ". . . man postpones or remembers. . . . He cannot be happy and strong until he too lives with nature in the present."[15] *Walden* was, in part, Thoreau's record of his attempt to
accomplish this; carefully setting off his Walden experience from
his previous life, he framed it in a seasonal cycle rather than conventional chronology. In "Song of Myself," Whitman expressed his
sense of the self's transcendence of time by freely manipulating it
and entirely subverting chronology.

In section 5, he summons the memory of a recent past to ob-
literate his past life and to initiate his present timeless existence.
He replaces literal chronology with a loose symbolic chronology—
from the conception of the poet in the sexual imagery of the
mystical experience to his gestation, birth, death, and rebirth.
Even this symbolic progression is implied only to be disrupted by
Whitman's compression and expansion of normal time sequences.
Now he projects himself backward beyond birth to identify with
the entire process of evolution—"All forces have been steadily employ'd to complete and delight me" (l. 1168); now he propels himself forward beyond death with the promise to wait and welcome
the reader to eternity. Throughout the poem, the loose, fluid, associational structure and the constant flow of present participles
express Whitman's confidence in his transcendence of time and
mortality: "I have the best of time and space and was never measured and never will be measured" (l. 1201). The ultimate effect
is paradoxical—that of an autobiography written in the present
tense. That is, "Song of Myself" can be seen as an attempt to express not only the Emersonian ideal but the sensation of living
above time's inexorable passage to death.

Just as the mystical union of body and soul releases the integrated self from chronological time, so it fuses the self with the
cosmos and hence with others. At first, Whitman merely states
this aspect of his vision:

Swiftly arose and spread around me the peace and the knowledge
  that pass all the argument of the earth,
And I know that the hand of God is the promise of my own,
And I know that the spirit of God is the brother of my own,
And that all the men ever born are also my brothers, and the
  women my sisters and lovers,
And that a kelson of the creation is love. [ll. 91–95]

Even at this point it is clear that Whitman's mysticism is closer to
Woolman's than to that of Thoreau and Emerson, who cherished
a sense of their individual election and a somewhat private relationship with God. In contrast, both Woolman and Whitman experienced divinity through the brotherhood of man. But Whitman
went beyond both Woolman and Thoreau by portraying salvation
as a process not of restricting and purifying the natural self but of
recognizing and celebrating its inherent divinity.

Both Whitman's mysticism and his notion of salvation demanded to be enacted as well as stated, however, and part of the drama
of the poem concerns the elaboration of Whitman's radical prophecy. He was a prophet of a new consciousness—of innocence rather
than guilt, of transcendent souls rather than social roles, and of
union rather than division among men; and his democratic as well
as his sexual themes challenged the values of Victorian America.
Like Thoreau, he was concerned for the salvation of the nation
in its crisis over slavery. But for Thoreau, the proper response
to citizenship in a slaveholding Union was a personal secession
followed by exemplary self-reform; as a prophet he assumed an
adversary relationship with the American public, challenging them
to bring their behavior and their institutions into conformity with
divine ideals. In contrast, Whitman called upon Americans to recognize that they were actually free—from time and circumstance
as well as from restricting institutions—and actually bonded to each
other in a transcendent union that could not be dissolved by secession or civil war. Rather than requiring a withdrawal from society
and a radical conversion, he demanded allegiance to a democratic
Union divinely ordained. In Quaker terms, Thoreau gave priority to
the testimony of peace and equality, while Whitman gave priority
to the testimony of community. Because Whitman neither engaged

in acts of social protest nor set forth a probing critique of society
like Thoreau's, he may seem like a milder or more affirmative
prophet than Thoreau, but in some ways his vision was more radical.

Thoreau opened *Walden* with an attempt to convict his audience of their sins, and accomplished a rhetorical identification
with them only through the medium of nature. Whitman begins
"Song of Myself" by assuring his audience of their innocence,
and attempts to transform them simply by accepting them and
merging with them. He demands not self-reform but self-revelation
from them:

> Undrape! you are not guilty to me, nor stale nor discarded,
> I see through the broadcloth and gingham whether or no,
> And am around, tenacious, acquisitive, tireless, and cannot be
>   shaken away. [ll. 145–47]

Both Thoreau and Whitman encourage the reader to adopt the autobiographical habit, but Thoreau recommends self-exploration,
which suggests an activity carried on in private and over a period
of time, while Whitman requres only an Emersonian confession,
which brings immediate absolution.

Whitman's role as a prophet and especially the content of his
prophecy tend inevitably to make his autobiography a collective
one. Thus, while his mystical vision establishes his claim to special
spiritual status, he immediately tempers this claim with the assertion that he possesses no capabilities the reader lacks, only knowledge of capabilities they share: "I am the mate and companion of
people, all just as immortal and fathomless as myself,/(They do
not know how immortal, but I know)" (ll. 137–38). Furthermore,
he portrays the relationship between prophet and listener as one
of mutual need. Only by offering the reader his vision of the possibilities of self-transcendence does Whitman himself achieve
self-fulfillment. His message, he believes, is not original and is
meaningless unless shared: "These are really the thoughts of all
men in all ages and lands, they are not original with me,/If they
are not yours as much as they are mine they are nothing, or next
to nothing" (ll. 355–56).

To speak for the inarticulate is a function of the traditional
prophet. But Whitman goes further; he desires intimacy, even iden-

tification, with the reader. To achieve this, Whitman makes innovative use of common pronouns. Using the "I" of the poem to refer variously to his body, his soul, and the poem itself, he expands the bounds of the ego to universalize his autobiography. Similarly, he often addresses the reader directly, a strategy which closes the gap between the "I" and the "you" by dramatizing the speaker's presence before the reader. This technique also exploits the fact that in English the second-person singular and plural take the same form; addressing the reader as "you," Whitman can be at once intimately personal and universally inclusive.[16]

The catalogues in which he celebrates as many human types as possible are another means of making the poem everybody's autobiography. His empathy for scorned or outcast types is reminiscent of Woolman's:

> In me the caresser of life wherever moving, backward as well as
>   forward sluing,
> To niches aside and junior bending, not a person or object
>   missing,
> Absorbing all to myself and for this song. [ll. 232–34]

Whitman's mystical vision, like the one Woolman experienced near the end of his life, reveals that he has no existence separate from the mass of men. But Whitman takes his vision more literally than Woolman, and his complete identification with others brings dangers as well as rewards. On the positive side, there is the opportunity for self-transcendence, an escape from the narrow viewpoint of the isolated self, and an apparent victory over individual mortality. On the negative side, identification with the oppressed brings a burden of pain and suffering and, more ominously, the possible loss rather than transcendence of self. For Edwards and Woolman, complete sanctification lay beyond death and beyond autobiography. But Whitman, for whom sanctification involved merging with the entire cosmos, desired to achieve that state in this life and to express it in autobiography. As he absorbs others to himself in one of the major patterns of the poem, he dilutes his individuality and risks having it entirely drained from him. As the poem becomes everybody's autobiography, it threatens to become nobody's;

self-transcendence through mystical merging threatens to become a kind of death-in-life rather than a life-beyond-death.

When, at the end of section 37, Whitman's unrestrained identification with others has nearly obliterated his sense of himself, he resurrects himself by means of one further identification—with the crucified Christ. The intended meaning may be that, properly perceived, suffering can be redeeming and that, properly understood, identification with others need not result in loss of self. But the reversal is not entirely convincing. Here Whitman came up against both the dilemma of the Transcendental autobiographer, whose concept of self tended to dissolve into something universal, and the paradox of his mysticism, in which a personal vision removed the conventional boundaries between himself and others. Unlike Woolman, Whitman did not confront these problems directly, and he rescued himself from his predicament by a rather literal *deus ex machina.* Lawrence Buell has called "Song of Myself" the epitaph of literary Transcendentalism because in it, Whitman carried Emersonian ideas as far as they could go—perhaps to a kind of dead end: ". . . if one denies the assumption of a unifying essential soul, personality disintegrates into chaos."[17] Whitman never denied the assumption of the unifying soul, of course, but his tendency to sacrifice personality to it exposes the limits and limitations of Transcendental autobiography. In this sense, "Song of Myself" anticipates the predicament Henry Adams would face as an autobiographer.

Whitman strikes a better balance when he insists on his prophetic status and simultaneously offers to share his vision with the reader. His relationship with the reader is never aggressive or condescending because of the assumption of the equality and mutual needs of the speaker and listener. Climactic moments occur when Whitman poses not only as a prophet but as a savior or healer—as a conveyor of grace and vitality:

To any one dying, thither I speed and twist the knob of the door,
. . .
Let the physician and the priest go home.
. . .
O despairer, here is my neck,

> By God, you shall not go down! hang your whole weight
>   upon me.
> I dilate you with tremendous breath, I buoy you up.
> [ll. 1008-14]

But always there is the reciprocal gesture of acknowledgment of
the divinity of the ordinary: "Accepting the rough deific sketches
to fill out better in myself, bestowing them freely on each man
and woman I see" (l. 1036). Having asserted that his faith sums up
all "worship ancient and modern and all between ancient and
modern" (l. 1098), Whitman apparently emerges from his mystical trance to state his central insight again, as a simple proposi-
tion: "It is not chaos or death—it is form, union, plan—it is eternal
life—it is Happiness" (l. 1318).

The poem ends with a surprisingly conventional but more satisfying vision of Whitman's sanctification than that implied earlier
in the poem. First, Whitman envisions his final union with God, in
images that legitimize, by spiritualizing, his homoerotic impulses:

> My rendezvous is appointed, it is certain,
> The Lord will be there and wait till I come on perfect terms,
> The great Camerado, the true lover for whom I pine will be there.
> [ll. 1198-2000]

Then Whitman prophesies his eventual reunion with the reader
and, by implication, *his* sanctification: "I stop somewhere waiting
for you" (l. 1346). The song has not been a narrative of growth *in*
grace but of the growth *of* grace until, at the end of this communal spiritual autobiography, it embraces all in a divine union.

If "Song of Myself" created Whitman as a poet and prophet, he
subsequently undertook, in life and in letters, to give the poem a
factual basis, to incarnate his ideal. Parallel to his struggle to become the self he had imagined was a lifelong process of self-pro-
motion in which he attempted to associate his person with his
poetic persona. To this end, he not only reviewed his own poetry
anonymously, he participated in writing his own biography. Scholars have established that Whitman was largely responsible for writing John Burrough's *Walt Whitman As a Poet and Person* (1867).[18]
Later, Whitman revised the manuscript of R. M. Bucke's biography

of him before its publication. In part, *Specimen Days* is another expression of his impulse to establish a positive image of himself for future biographers. In fact the first section of *Specimen Days*, the reminiscences of the prewar years, was based on impressions gathered on a trip taken with Bucke to acquaint him with the scenes of his youth and was sent to Bucke to provide him with information for the biography.[19]

Despite the complexity of Whitman's motives, it is not fair to characterize *Specimen Days* as a self-advertisement. In advancing age and poor health, Whitman thought frequently of death, and one motive was simple self-preservation: "I suppose I publish and leave the whole gathering . . . from that eternal tendency to perpetuate and preserve which is behind all Nature, authors included" (p. 3). Ultimately, the book became a kind of spiritual autobiography or journal which verified in more conventional form the reality of the self prophesied in *Leaves of Grass* and especially in "Song of Myself."[20] Like the poem, it is a prophetic autobiography which offers the reader regenerative vision or strength. Furthermore, it is written largely in the present tense and it tends to become collective as autobiography.

But it is prophetic in a less dramatic way than "Song of Myself." In the poem, Whitman announced the creation of a poet-prophet, offering a mystical vision and his literary performance as evidence of his inspiration. *Specimen Days* is more modest in its claims; at times, Whitman seems to function as a prophetic autobiographer, but more often he merely portrays himself as a prophet, offering factual evidence of the trials and triumphs of his prophetic vocation. In mood and method, its relationship to "Song of Myself" is analogous to that of *Cape Cod* to *Walden*. In their later works, both Whitman and Thoreau attempted to recapture and reaffirm (albeit with qualifications) the mystical ecstasies of their early books. Thus, whereas Whitman's autobiographical poem had envisioned a timeless existence following from a mystical experience, *Specimen Days* attempts to substantiate the existence in fact—in time and in space—of the idealized persona of the poem. The narrative, grounding itself in historical and biographical fact, recapitulates crucial episodes in Whitman's life up to 1882—his actual physical intimacy with nature, his experiential knowledge of war and death, his actual performance as a healer, and his physical travels across the United States. *Specimen Days*, then, both summarizes his progress toward his ideal and memorializes his transcendent self in a prose narrative complementing his more visionary poem.

Inevitably, in writing autobiography, Whitman again confronted the problems of time and individual identity. As he tells it, the impulse to collect and publish his spontaneous jottings came to him as a moment's inspiration on July 2, 1882 (p. 3), and it is doubtful if the ensemble was carefully composed. Yet in *Specimen Days* he seems to have intuitively found a new autobiographical form which managed both to ground the self in time and space and to express the possibilities of transcendence of time and identity envisioned in "Song of Myself." Like the poem, the prose work is written largely in the present tense. Although the four sections are arranged chronologically—reminiscences of the early years (1819-1855), memoranda of the war years (1860-1865), nature notes (1876-1878), and travel diaries and literary essays (1878-1882)—only the first section is written in the past tense, and the overall effect is not to portray development in time but to re-create a series of present moments. Like the Quaker journalist, Whitman begins his autobiography with a retrospective narrative summarizing his life before he began to keep a journal; the successive "entries" are, or seem to be, spontaneous notes written in the present tense.

In most of the book, then, the past is preserved as a continuous present, an "eternal now," as Whitman presents the reader with a succession of immediate and concrete impressions of the war, of nature, and of the American landscape. The sense of the ongoing moment is conveyed by the use of seemingly endless sentences, sentences without verbs, and the frequent use of present participles. Typical of his immediacy and of his emphasis on his presence at the scene is the opening of a section called "A Cavalry Camp": "I am writing this, nearly sundown, watching a cavalry company, . . . just come in through a shower, making their night's camp" (p. 24). The impression gained is not of Whitman's growth in chronological time but of his ability to live deeply in the moment and to share it with others.

In the overall structure of the book, the Civil War is the turning point at which the summarized past gives way to the ongoing present and at which the history of the individual broadens to include others. Thus, in *Specimen Days*, an event in the community's history replaces the mystical experience of "Song of Myself" as the turning point and the analogue of the conversion experience in traditional spiritual autobiography. This shift of emphasis from inward to outward history, the substitution of an actual historical event for a private—perhaps imagined—experience, indicates more than Whitman's desire to "ennoble and advance his literary reputation by joining it to the drama of war and the 'majesty' of the Union cause."[21] Whitman may have exaggerated the war's significance for his literary development, but it undoubtedly confronted him with a challenge crucial to his personal development; it "intensely sharpened his sense of the appalling cost even of the partial realization of the democratic ideal, [and] summoned him to make his own faith stronger in that which endures beyond death."[22] He interpreted this threat to his ideals as requiring a personal purification or sacrifice to the cause;[23] conversely, he came to see that identification with the nation in a time of crisis could bring him self-realization. Thus, as a wound-dresser, he was able to sublimate some of his homoerotic urges, to divert emotion from solitary and sensual outlets into a spiritual communal cause. Similarly, the war, and especially the eventual victory of the Union, tended to vindicate him as the prophet of union. For him, the war years were both "the real parturition years (more than 1776–'83) of this henceforth homogeneous Union,"[24] and the years that provided him with "the greatest privilege and satisfaction . . . and, of course, the most profound lessons of my life" (p. 58). Thus, in this version of his autobiography he uses the Civil War, rather than a mystical experience or the publication of the first edition of *Leaves of Grass*, to date his emergence as a prophet.

In the Civil War section, then, we see Whitman assuming the prophet's function of interpreting communal history in relation to transcendent values. Not surprisingly, he views President Lincoln as another exemplar of "(a new virtue unknown to other lands, and hardly yet known here, but the foundation and tie of all, as the future will grandly develop), UNIONISM" (p. 41). As a communal historian, Whitman endeavors to record the "real war" with its "interior history." This means including its "hell-scenes" as well as its more inspirational moments, but always with the goal of "illustrating the latent personal character and eligibility of these states, in the two or three millions of American young and middle-aged men, North and South, embodied in those armies" (p. 60). To this end, Whitman included as many diverse specimen soldiers as possible, making his autobiography collective in a rather literal way. Under headings like "Typical Soldiers," "Spiritual Characters among The Soldiers," or "A Connecticut Case," he includes biographical sketches of soldiers he has met, extracts from their diaries, letters he has written for them, and lists of their names and regiments.

In "Song of Myself" he had declared, "I act as the tongue of you,/Tied in your mouth, in mine it begins to be loosen'd" (ll. 1248–49). Here he becomes the voice of the soldiers in a literal, yet still prophetic, way. His inclusion of specimen soldiers recalls the catalogues of "Song of Myself" in which he had identified successively with many types, but here the individuals are real people and the contact is more vividly felt. Here, too, Whitman is a distinct person, and in the unifying context of a historical event, he finds he can speak for others without losing his own sense of identity: "I can say that in my ministerings I comprehended all, whoever came in my way, North or South, and slighted none. . . . It has given me my most fervent views of the true *ensemble* and extent of the states" (p. 58). Their stories may temporarily displace his personal history, but his empathy for them reinforces, rather than weakens, his sense of himself. Again, the relationship is reciprocal. Whitman serves the wounded by emanating his vitality, serenity, and confidence; they in turn serve him by helping him to become his ideal self. In memorializing them, he is able to create a valid memorial image of himself.

In *Specimen Days*, as in "Song of Myself," Whitman sought to include the reader, as well as specimens, in his autobiography. Thus, in the war memoranda, he addresses the reader, not as in a letter, but as though he were physically present. For example, in describing a visit to an army hospital ward, he wrote: "In Ward H we approach the cot of a young lieutenant of one of the Wisconsin regiments. Tread the board lightly, here, for the pain and panting of death are in this cot" (p. 27). Denying the distinction between the experience and its record, he refused to record his experience in isolation from the reader. He sought to combine the "I" and the "you" in the "we" by including the reader in the scene or, alternately, by projecting his own experience into the reader's; his goal was for him and his reader to coexist in the presence and present of one another, as equals in a collective autobiography.

Although there is a gap of about ten years between the war memoranda and the nature notes, Whitman implies an autobiographical link between them. Although his stroke of 1873 was probably not related to his hospital service during the war, he attributed his physical decline to the stress of the years of national trauma, suggesting that although he was not wounded *in* the war he was wounded *by* it. Thus, he muses on his years of recuperation: "Dear, soothing, healthy, restorative hours—after three confining years of paralysis—after the long strain of the war and its wounds and death" (p. 61). The nugget of truth in Whitman's sense of having been a victim of the war resides in the fact that the war did more for his self-image as a prophet than for his career as a poet. The literary fruits of his war experience were by no means as impressive as those of the creative surge of the early 1850s, and by 1870, he had begun to doubt his ability to be the prophet of a new democratic literature.[25] *Specimen Days* reflects this chastened sense of his own capabilities, and the nature notes record the process of restoring himself to physical, emotional, and spiritual health after a long decline.

Timber Creek, where Whitman sought regeneration through harmony with nature, was in a sense his Walden Pond. But for Whitman, harmony with nature meant physical contact, as though sensuous immersion—whether by bathing naked in the sun and the mud, by wrestling with saplings, or by merely loafing in nature's ambiance—might induce a transformation like that of section 5 of "Song of Myself." The results were beneficial but gradual: "It seems as if peace and nutriment from heaven subtly filter into me, . . . as I sit here in solitude with Nature. . . . I merge myself with the scene, in the perfect day" (p. 71). Like Thoreau, Whitman found a kind of companionship in nature: "Here I realized the meaning of that old fellow who said he was seldom less alone than when alone" (p. 72). But Whitman's use of nature is more direct than was Thoreau's, who sought to read it like a language. Whitman sought a sense of identity with nature that brought both self-transcendence and reinforcement of private impulses: "Babble on, O brook, with that utterance of thine! I too will express what I have gathered in my days and progress, native, subterranean, past. . . . I will learn from thee, and dwell on thee—receive, copy, print from thee" (p. 61). Finally, on July 22, 1878, while contemplating the whole "stellar concave spreading overhead," he seems to have experienced a mystical communion with the cosmos reminiscent of "Song of Myself": "As if for the first time, indeed, creation noiselessly sank into and through me its placid and untellable lesson . . . the visible suggestion of God in space and time—now once definitely indicated, if never again" (p. 79).

But Whitman does not merely record this evidence of divine favor, in the manner of the Puritan spiritual autobiographer; rather, as in "Song of Myself," he achieves self-transcendence only to offer it to the reader. As he had drawn the reader into the interior history of the war in the previous section, here he attempts to make the "notes of that outdoor life . . . as glowing to you, reader dear, as the experience itself was to me!" (p. 61). As the "natural-medicinal, elemental-moral influences" of nature flow into him, he hopes to include the reader in the circuit of healing energy: "who knows . . . but the pages now ensuing may carry ray of sun, or smell of grass or corn . . . to serve as cooling breeze, or Nature's aroma, to some fevered mouth or latent pulse" (p. 61n).

The last section of the book is the most miscellaneous and the least prophetic; that is, Whitman, in closing out his autobiography, tends to remind us that he is a prophet, rather than act as one. The travel diaries, of course, correspond to and realize the visionary exploration of America in "Song of Myself," and Whitman finds, in both the American landscape and the American people, confirmation of his earlier prophecy. In the Rockies he found the law of his own poems (p. 91), and in the Mississippi River, vindication of the Union cause: "One almost thinks it *is* the Union—or soon will be" (p. 94). The mood of this section is confident about the nation's future, as though its health had been restored along with his own, and Whitman finds in his reimmersion in society "the directest proof yet of successful democracy, and of the solutions of that paradox, the eligibility of the free and fully developed individual with the paramount aggregate. . . . I find in this visit to New York, and daily contact and rapport with its myriad people, on the scale of the ocean and tides, the best, most effective medicine my soul has yet partaken" (p. 78). Always sympathetic toward the scorned or unfortunate, Whitman finds nothing in a visit to an insane asylum to destroy his faith in man: "Nothing at all markedly repulsive or hideous—strangely enough I did not see one such. Our common humanity, mine and yours, everywhere" (p. 99-100). Here, in a moving passage, Whitman justifies his earlier image of himself as the voice of the downtrodden.

Although Whitman's literary essays are not so integral a part of his autobiography as Thoreau's chapter on "Reading" is of *Walden*, they serve similar purposes. By isolating the essential qualities —potential and actual—of American literature, Whitman seeks to give his readers a lesson in reading. Thus, posing as a kind of benevolent patriarch of American letters, Whitman sifts through Emerson, Carlyle, Poe, Longfellow, and others for their essential ideas and their import for American letters. It is significant and appropriate that this discussion of crucial literary problems should include two concerns central to the tradition of American autobiography. We have already noted Whitman's definition of prophecy, his association of it with Quaker doctrine, and his implication that it is central to his own work. In addition, he identified as "the most profound theme that can occupy the mind of man" another preoccupation of American autobiographers, "the query: What is the fusing explanation and tie—what the relation between the (radical, democratic) Me, the human identity of understanding, emotions, spirit, etc., on the one side, of and with the (conservative) Not Me, the whole of the material objective universe and laws, with what is behind them in time and space, on the other side?" (p. 106). Stated thus, in philosophic terms, Whitman's concern clearly adumbrates Henry Adams's essential quandary, but it is equally a religious question, to which our earliest spiritual autobiographers had addressed themselves.

It is a long way from the poetry of "Song of Myself" to the

literary criticism of *Specimen Days*, but the shift is partly a result
of Whitman's attempt to create a more conventional autobiography
to complement and validate his earlier visionary autobiography.
Recognizing perhaps that his prophecy had carried him beyond
the limits of conventional autobiography in "Song of Myself," in
Specimen Days he created a more historical account of himself
which was still innovative and expressive of the Transcendental
vision of the self. Taken together, the two works frame Whitman's
career, and serve as his contribution to the tradition of prophetic
American autobiography.

EIGHT

Henry Adams

Heretic and Prophet

In the case of Henry Adams, there is no shared system of beliefs which can be said to have conditioned his autobiography. In fact, in writing it, he assumed the role of an iconoclast, demolishing conventional wisdom and undercutting the latest scientific advances. Still, in spite of his pessimistic temperament, in spite of his protestations of failure, ignorance, and impotence, his autobiography is guardedly optimistic, successful as art, and didactic in a complex and powerful way. In spite of his heresy and iconoclasm, he forged an intellectual synthesis audacious enough to support a prophetic impulse in *The Education of Henry Adams.*

During the Civil War, Adams may have been reluctant to act on his brother Charles's suggestion that he was "capable of teaching the people and becoming a light to the nations," but he never ceased to be intrigued by the notion.[1] Increasingly concerned throughout his lifetime about the nation's failure to realize its ideals, he attempted to bring about reform directly, through personal influence, and indirectly, through his writings, always sustaining a belief that a "saving remnant" could reform society. Thus, when his impulse toward leadership and public service in the family tradition was frustrated by his exclusion from public office, he moved naturally toward the role of a reformer. When his activities as a reform journalist failed to affect the corrupt machinations of the Grant administration, he became a university professor and historian. The succession of roles—reformer, professor, historian, autobiographer—gives the impression of a retreat from power. But ultimately it led toward a different kind of power—that of the prophet.

Adams assumed the role of prophet only late in life and even then with much ambivalence and detachment. But in retrospect, we can see that some of his earlier activities served as rehearsal for the final role. Thus, in writing his *History of the United States during the Administrations of Thomas Jefferson and James Madison* (1889–1891), he dissented from a naive, native faith in American democracy, measured the republic's history against its professed ideals, and outlined its probable development. In *Mont-Saint-Michel and Chartres* (1905), Adams celebrated a culture, a faith, and a world view in which "Church and State, Soul and Body, God and Man are all one."[2] This ideal, in declension, produced both New England theocracy and American democracy—evidence that history is degradation rather than progress. At the same time, however, Adams urged upon his readers a sense of how multiplicity could be confronted; and, unwittingly, in his assessment of Aquinas's synthesis of faith and rationalism, Adams prepared for his own attempt at an intellectual synthesis in the concluding chapters of the *Education*. With his analysis, in the *Chartres*, of the "useful fictions" medieval culture employed to organize society, Adams prepared his audience to accept the Dynamic Theory of History as a myth useful to twentieth-century American society.

In writing the *History*, Adams had been more historian than prophet; in the *Chartres*, he had moved toward prophecy, and treated poetry as history; subsequently, in the *Education*, he treated his life as history, and made that history both poetic and prophetic. In a sense, the *Education* followed from the *Chartres*, for it detailed the inevitable decline implied by the changes in medieval Christianity between the eleventh and the thirteenth centuries. In another sense, it followed from the *History*, for it extended the narrative of communal history into the twentieth century, answering, in the process, some of the questions raised in the earlier work. In a third sense, it followed from both, for in it Adams emerged as a prophet who combined the intuitive approach of one with the scientific objectivity of the other. He used history, which he thought had become predictive, to prophesy the future development of society along lines of force he perceived; and he used intuition to suggest new values and a new vision which, if adopted, might change the course of history. In the *History*, he scorned the notion that America had a unique destiny. In the *Education*, he suggested that American history had special, if not unique, significance because the future was to be enacted first in the New World; American history was literally prophetic because it tended to reveal the course of universal history.[3] Thus, in writing his autobiography, Adams functioned as a prophet in many different ways: as interpreter of communal history, as recorder of prophetic historical developments, as speculator about the future, and as creator of a vision he hoped might somehow alter history. In the end, in spite of its apparent impersonality, the *Education* is a more personal and authentic profession of faith than the *Chartres* and closer to the essence of spiritual autobiography.

A connoisseur of autobiography, Adams was, of course, familiar with a wealth of models, both American and European. There was ample precedent in the Adams family for writing diaries and autobiographies, and Adams may have found other hints in autobiographical works by Rousseau, Tocqueville, Mill, Darwin, Carlyle, and Newman, among others. But it is the complex relation of the *Education* to its American predecessors which demands consideration here. According to Adams's testimony in the *Education*, he envied the Transcendentalists their world view but found it, like the idealistic metaphysics of Carlyle and the nature mysticism of Saint Francis, inaccessible to him: "In spite of the long-continued efforts of a lifetime, he perpetually fell back into the heresy that if anything universal was unreal, it was himself and not the appearances; it was the poet and not the banker; it was his own thought, not the thing that moved it."[4] With their assumption of a unified soul in harmony with God and nature, the Transcendentalists seemed anachronisms to him; their faith, however attractive, was naive and untenable. Still, he shared certain characteristics with Thoreau and Whitman. With the Thoreau of *Cape*

Cod, he shared a sense of nature as potentially chaotic and of life as a dynamic struggle between opposing forces. With Whitman, he shared a sense of the multiplicity of the self and an impulse to identify himself with the historical process. Like both Thoreau and Whitman, but for very different reasons, Adams was driven finally to establish his own cosmology, and behind his self-depreciation lay a "transcendent and irrepressible egoism," as Ernest Samuels has shrewdly observed.[5]

Finding inspiration, perhaps, but no formal model in Transcendental autobiography, Adams went behind the Concord faith to Benjamin Franklin, whom he cited in his "Preface" as an example of self-education of a more traditional, empirical sort (p. xxix). However, his invocation of Franklin is laced with irony, for the *Autobiography* and the *Education*—which frame the nineteenth-century history of America between them—contrast sharply, as though Adams had created a conscious autobiographical answer to the earlier success story and a refutation of its optimistic expectations for America. Adams shared Franklin's preoccupation with politics and nature—with power in all its forms. Yet, like Thoreau, Adams found efficiency insufficient by itself, and he was alarmed by the effect of Franklin's Promethean gestures in the realms of science and democracy. Indeed, the thrust of his treatment of Franklin is to transform him from a Prometheus into an Epimetheus: confident of his ability to control power, Franklin had helped to release forces that threatened to overwhelm later generations. Although Franklin did offer a model of self-education, the form of his autobiography derived from the assumptions of scientific rationalism, which Adams questioned. Furthermore, his myth depended on his successful experiments with various careers and his role as a maker of history. As a self-proclaimed failure in many careers and, at best, a writer of history, Adams would have to look further for a formal model.

This he claimed to have found in St. Augustine's *Confessions*. Attempting both to recount a spiritual conversion and to refute the heresies of his youth, Augustine initiated a form of spiritual autobiography which took the form of an intellectual progress as well as a moral reformation. Adams, of course, was to invert the developmental aspect of his model, portraying himself as proceeding from youthful faith in democracy and progress to more and more heretical beliefs, his aim being to overthrow the "ersatz religions" of the nineteenth century like Social Darwinism.[6] Yet he, like Augustine, demanded the freedom to consider metaphysical questions in his autobiography. Thus Augustine's exemplary meditation on theology is matched by Adams's meditation on history. The crucial difference between the two autobiographers, as Adams realized, lay in his lack of divine inspiration and hence of absolute faith in his cosmology; the only conclusion he could reach was an intellectual synthesis comprehensive enough to embrace contradiction and vigorous enough to be worthy of a temporary commitment. Still, as Robert Sayre has observed, Adams cherished the hope that if, "like the Augustine of the *Confessions*, he could discover the meaning of his own life, then, like the Augustine of *De Civitate Dei*, he could also give order to the world."[7]

In turning to Augustine for a model, of course, Adams returned to the source of the piety expressed in Puritan spiritual autobiography, and his ambitions for his autobiography place him firmly in the tradition of prophetic autobiography which began with the Puritans. In fact, in "A Dynamic Theory of History," Adams associated Luther, Calvin, Bunyan, and the American Puritans with Augustine's quest to substitute the Civitate Dei for the Civitate Romae (p. 483). His reverence for Augustine and his own puritanical temperament help to account for the fact that his *Education* shares more with Puritan autobiography than with any of his other American predecessors. Adams was certainly not a Puritan in any historical sense, but, as J. C. Levenson has observed, in Adams "the Puritan character survived Puritan belief."[8] Aware of this, Adams associated his pessimism with his heritage from New England Puritanism.[9]

Like a Puritan spiritual autobiography, the *Education* portrays history as a constant combat between opposing forces: it portrays life both as a pilgrimage and as a process of being educated by forces beyond one's control; it professes determinism and prophesies inevitable apocalypse but implies that human initiative can play a role in salvation; it chooses posterity as its audience in the hope of maintaining continuity between the generations; and it assigns America special status as an exemplary nation. Like his

Puritan predecessors, Adams makes his personal experience representative by diminishing rather than expanding the concept of the individual's power and anticipates the prospect of the self's final annihilation. Of course, he differs from them in many respects. Most notably, whereas the Puritan possesses a fixed theology and attempts to ascertain whether he has the faith required for salvation, Adams portrays himself as possessing faith but lacking a theology able to sustain it. Thus, like the Transcendentalists, he undertakes a personal inquiry into the nature of things and invents a personal cosmology. In summary, in many ways and on many levels, Adams is intricately involved with the American tradition. In some ways he submits to it; in others, he rebels against it. The result of his complex and varied response to the attractive forces of his predecessors is a highly individualistic autobiography which carries the tradition into the twentieth century.

In one sense, the *Education* is an intellectual autobiography, for Adams is obviously intent upon testing the validity, or the educational value, of many influential Victorian ideas. But insofar as he pursues this activity as a quest for a world view which will endow his life with order and significance, the book becomes a metaphysical or even a spiritual autobiography. He attacks the ersatz religions of his time not because they have replaced traditional religion but because they are poor substitutes for it—because they are not worthy of faith. He objects to these "useful fictions" not because they are fictions but because they have ceased to be useful. Knowing his own "religion" to be, ultimately, illusory, he calls on his reader to accept it or fashion his own, suggesting that the more skeptical the reader is, the more useful and lasting his own myth will be. Because Adams accepts the nineteenth-century tendency to blur the distinction between theology and secular philosophical thought, we may consider the tensions of his thought to be the paradoxes of his piety.

Without exhausting them, we can identify the following as central polarities in his thought: optimism versus pessimism, moralism versus naturalism, free will versus determinism, intuitive faith versus scientific rationalism, effectual action versus passive contemplation, and self-assertion versus self-annihilation. Using the third person to emphasize the gap between the youthful character and the mature narrator, Adams generally characterizes his younger self in terms of the "positive" side of the polarities: he is optimistic and moralistic, a believer in free will and progress, and eager to assert himself by controlling power. Yet his experience tends to confound all of his expectations, and the narrator tends to impose a "negative" or corrective vision on his early life. Thus, in the first section (chapters 1–20), he portrays his experience as frustrated action resulting in accidental education; education befalls the youth, usually in the form of the shattering of his inherited ideas. The effect is to imply that the two poles are irreconcilable and that Adams's experience led him irreversibly from one pole to its opposite, as his false ideas proved their lack of fitness to his nineteenth-century environment. Yet, as we shall see, the process of being divested of his hand-me-down clothes forced Adams to tailor some that did fit; the process of reduction in the first half of the narrative, like Thoreau's radical simplification of life in "Economy," provides a base to build on rather than a final answer.

The first section ends in his "failure" as a professor at Harvard, for Adams, himself uneducated, is ill-prepared to educate others. As he retreats from reform into his ineffectual role as a teacher, Adams seems to die into failure; then, in resuming the narrative, he speaks of himself as both "dead" and as beginning a "new" life and education (p. 330). He does not go so far as to speak of a spiritual death and rebirth in the manner of the conversion narrative, but he does alert the reader to the process of self-regeneration that begins in the second half of the narrative.

There, education is no longer preparation for life but life itself. No longer accidental, it is a purposeful quest for a world view with which to replace the myths exposed in the first half. As the narrative proceeds toward its conclusion, it becomes more and more abstract, broadening in scope from the consideration of problems that are primarily American to questions that are universal.[10] Simultaneously, the gap between the narrator and the character gradually diminishes. One result of this tendency is the compression and complication of the central polarities of Adams's thought. That is, whereas in the first half one pole tended to yield to its opposite, in the second, this movement is suspended and the poles are drawn together and juxtaposed in an attempt to reconcile them. By virtue of this movement, the polarities of the first section become true paradoxes in the second. In the end, the second section is not merely iconoclastic but constructive; the manikin emerges as a tailor who creates his new clothes by using scraps and rags of the old ones as well as new material. The Dynamic Theory of History represents the culmination of this process—the intellectual construct or useful fiction in which Adams places his faith. At that point in the narrative, he has exposed his own miseducation and, by implication, the reader's; both are prepared for a vision of the universe that admits its complexity and yet gives man a basis for hope and useful action. The formulation of Adams's synthesis, which, like the Thomistic one, is poised between faith and rationalism, but which substitutes a dynamic world view and relative values for Aquinas's static view and absolute principles,[11] brings most of his paradoxes into sharp focus.

Although these polarities are related to one another and even overlap, it will be convenient to consider them separately. Perhaps the most obvious tension in Adams's thought is what Ernest Samuels has called "the contradiction between the obsessive pose of pessimism and the lurking residue of optimism."[12] Certainly, the *Education*, like all of Adams's prophecy, had as one major goal the overthrow of what he considered to be the complacent optimism of the Victorian era. What some readers fail to see is that he tended to use pessimism as a corrosive agent rather than to *assert* it as a final position. He valued an informed optimism more than a fatalistic pessimism; at least, he left room in his final synthesis for a guardedly optimistic view of the future.

The attack on his youthful optimism gets underway early in the narrative, as the following ironic passage indicates: "Viewed from Mount Vernon Street, the problem of life was as simple as it was classic. Politics offered no difficulties, for there the moral law was a sure guide. Social perfection was also sure, because human nature worked for Good. . . . On these points doubt was forbidden" (p. 33). Adams's experience of Rome, where two great civilizations had failed and which he characterized as a "gospel of anarchy and vice," utterly defied his "orderly, middle-class, Boston-ian, systematic scheme of evolution" (p. 90). Subsequently he embraced Darwinism, but not without a shrewd awareness of the weak points of the theory. Any chance that he would adopt its optimistic social corollary was dashed by the election of the pre-intellectual Grant: "Darwinists ought to conclude that America was reverting to the stone age" (p. 266). However, Adams never adopted an unambiguous pessimism. In spite of his accumulation of evidence of the imminent failure of Western civilization, he evenhandedly asserts that the universe may be "either a supersensuous chaos or a divine unity, which irresistibly attracts, and is either life or death to penetrate" (p. 487). His final position, in "The Law of Acceleration," is similarly equivocal about man's future: ". . . the mind had already entered a field of attraction so violent that it must immediately pass beyond, into a new equilibrium, like the comet of Newton, or suffer dissipation, like meteoroids in the earth's atmosphere" (p. 496). Thus, rather than simply choosing one extreme or the other, Adams struggled to preserve the intellectual respectability of an optimism that took into account the ominous evidence against itself.

Adams desired not to shatter nineteenth-century optimism but to hone it against the hard realities it tended to ignore. For him the real trouble with Victorian optimism was that, like its negative counterpart, it tended to be deterministic; if one attitude was complacent, the other was fatalistic—neither was very useful. Thus, the tension between optimism and pessimism was linked to that between free will and determinism. His nineteenth-century education taught him that the eighteenth-century belief that man was capable of controlling his own destiny and even affecting those of others through benevolent behavior was naive. His autobiography, like the Old World section of Thomas Shepard's, is characterized by a sense of dislocation. From the time when, as a boy, he was marched off to school against his will by his grandfather, his destiny seemed to him to be determined by forces beyond his control and often beyond his comprehension. Episode after episode taught him that personal will was no match for impersonal force. Thus, he was led, in his Dynamic Theory, to portray man as a "feeble atom or molecule" whose thought and action depended on the forces attracting him.

Still, although he could not accept William James's formulation of the will to believe, he was torn, in reading him, between his own "scientific Calvinism" and James's "scientific Arminianism."[13] His own final assessment of the relationship between man and nature asserted not only that man was himself a force but that, uniquely, he was capable of assimilating and reacting to other forces: "These forces never ceased to act on him, enlarging his mind as they enlarged the surface foliage of a vegetable, and the mind needed only to respond, as the forests did, to those attractions" (p. 475). Here Adams subtly combines organic and mechanical metaphors to assume a postion that avoids both optimistic and pessimistic determinism. Reluctant simply to exercise "the will to believe," he nevertheless insists on his right to disbelieve certain nineteenth-century dogmas and reserves a place for the incalculable force of the intellect. He does in fact set forth his own theory of the evolution of the human mind: "Science has proved that . . . the rise of his faculties from a lower power to a higher, or from a narrower to a wider field, may be due to the function of assimilating and storing outside force or forces" (p. 487). The ultimate outcome of the tug-of-war between mind and force was by no means certain: ". . . as the mind of man enlarged its range, it enlarged the field of complexity, and must continue to do so, even unto chaos, until the reservoirs of sensuous or supersensuous energies are exhausted, or cease to affect him, or until he succumbs to their excess" (p. 487). Yet Adams suggested, without proof, that the outcome depended on man's choice and the strength of his reaction. And in his concluding chapters he offered a literary analogue of the process he described; in fact, the entire *Education* is a metaphorical recapitulation of the evolutionary expansion of consciousness.

The question of man's freedom was, of course, related to another dilemma—whether to view history moralistically or naturalistically. Adams's heritage and upbringing were strongly moralistic, and he found even a utilitarian ethic distasteful: "He could not be convinced that moral standards had nothing to do with it and that utilitarian morality was good enough for him as it was for the graceless" (p. 26). However, his historical education exposed the futility of Puritan politics. For example, his diplomatic experience taught him that diplomacy was merely a more genteel theater of the war, not a separate enterprise. Finally, his reform career forced him to the realization that in American politics "the moral law had expired—like the Constitution" (p. 280), leaving him suspended between a moral training which was increasingly anachronistic and a pragmatic education which was amoral.

As the American mind threatened to become merely "an economic thinking machine which could only work on a fixed line" (p. 180), it was imperative for Adams to resolve his dilemma. His solution was more rhetorical that philosophical; nevertheless, it ingeniously allowed him to avoid either extreme of the polarity. His analogies suggest movement from one pole to the other, for a predominance of moral analogies in the first half seems to give way to a predominance of naturalistic ones in the second. For example, among the many biblical references in the first chapter is a punning reference to himself as an "Adam"; this implies choice, responsibility, and judgment. Later in the narrative, however, he naturalizes this allusion, referring to man as a helpless vibrating "atom." Similarly, early in the narrative, his reference to the Fall suggests a moral lapse; later on he translates the concept into physical terms: "After 1500, the speed of progress so rapidly surpassed man's gait as to alarm every one as though it were the acceleration of a falling body which the dynamic theory takes it to be" (p. 484).

Yet Adams does not in fact surrender his moralism to nineteenth-century naturalism. Rather, he reintroduces moral concepts in scientific garb. By using scientific terminology in a metaphorical way, he gains the benefit of intellectual respectability while satisfying his own urge for moral judgment. Thus, while he analyzes the dilemma of the twentieth century in terms like force and acceleration, which seem dispassionate and morally neutral, he clearly conceives of unity and multiplicity, order and chaos as moral as well as conceptual opposites. His viewpoint, then, was an attempt to synthesize a moralistic and naturalistic view of history; each perspective served to illuminate rather than to cancel the other. In the following passage, he uses a naturalistic view to "explain" man's moral failings, but not to excuse them: "He could not deny that the law of the new multiverse explained much that had been most obscure, especially the persistently fiendish treatment of man by man; . . . the perpetual symbolism of a higher law and the perpetual relapse to a lower one" (p. 458). When he compares himself and twentieth-century man to "Adam in the Garden of Eden between God who was unity, and Satan who was complexity, with no means of deciding which was truth" (p. 397), his analogy, though not optimistic, suggests that the fundamental choice was still in man's power to make. In fact, his final synthesis resembles a kind of pseudo-scientific Manicheanism in which man's choices and actions help to determine the course of a perpetual struggle between opposing forces; it is as though he reverted to Augustine's heresy as an escape from a forbidding block universe.

The tension between intuition and scientific rationalism also receives paradoxical treatment in the second half of the narrative. Adams's heritage from the eighteenth century equipped him with both a vestigial religious faith and a trust in scientific method. However, his nineteenth-century education favored scientific rationalism at the expense of intuition in any form—religious, moral, or aesthetic. Furthermore, the death of his sister crushed any remaining faith in a personal deity. In fact, this experience triggered in Adams an intuitive vision of nature as chaos—a kind of parody of the mystic's vision: "For the first time, the stage scenery of the senses collapsed; the human mind felt itself stripped naked, vibrating in a void of shapeless energies" (p. 288). Ironically, science later confirmed what at that moment Adams only intuited. However, scientific education ended by throwing him back on his intuition, for in his understanding, empiricism and rationalism were reaching their limits at the end of the century. The kinetic theory of gases suggested that unity and multiplicity were "the same thing, all forms being shifting phases of matter" (p. 431), and modern psychology indicated that the psyche itself was multiple rather than unified (p. 433). Finally, Karl Pearson's book, *The Grammar of Science*, seemed to exclude from science such concepts as order, reason, beauty, and benevolence and declared that "Chaos was the law of nature; Order was the dream of man" (p. 451).

Ominous as these developments might seem, Adams actually welcomed them and, it must be admitted, exaggerated their significance—first, because they undermined Victorian optimism and second, because the apparent futility of scientific rationalism freed him to use his imagination and intuition. Thus, after coincidence brought him into successive confrontations with the Dynamo and the Virgin, he began to profess "the religion of World's Fairs, without which he held education to be a blind impossibility" (p. 465). Similarly, he exploited science's admission of supersensuous forces as an opportunity to reaffirm within his intellectual system the notion of transcendent values.[14]

In the most important chapter of the *Education*, then, Adams employs both reason and intuition, science and art, in developing his prophetic vision—the Dynamic Theory of History. Lacking any such divine authority as the Transcendentalists' nature, Adams relied on history, in two senses, to be his authority. First, the abstract speculation of his theory was prepared for and supported by the very detailed account of history that his autobiography offers. Second, because he believed history was becoming a predictive science, Adams could, as a "scientific historian," engage in a form of secular prophecy. But in the end, his vision goes beyond both science and history because its ultimate source was his intuition. Having exposed the inadequacies of various nineteenth-century gospels, the heretic was at last ready to offer his own formula for salvation from the determinists' block universe.

The fundamental creative adjustment of Adams's mind was to fuse intuitive and rationalistic epistemologies. The resulting paradoxical vision enabled him to align on the same continuum such diverse entities as the Dynamo and the Virgin. This involved learning, on the one hand, to worship the Dynamo (that is, to perceive it intuitively, as a kind of powerful new god) and, on the other, to measure the Virgin (that is, to consider her now as a force rather than as a divinity). By perceiving each force with the mode of knowledge normally reserved for the other, Adams was able to yoke the two together. The Dynamic Theory, which followed from this initial act of imagination, became the means of plotting the sequential but accelerating movement of history along a supersensuous continuum. The theory provided a climax for Adams's attempt to correct the deficiencies of the American mind, which "shunned, distrusted, disliked the dangerous attraction of ideals, and stood alone in history for its ignorance of the past" (p. 328).

In the late chapters, the polarity between action and contemplation is also compressed into a paradox. Infused with the spirit of "Puritan politics," Adams had since his youth channeled his energy toward the control of power, even if only as a reformer. In contrast, the Adams of the later chapters is apparently resigned to his exclusion from office and the power he once had thought his due. But this apparent dichotomy is complicated by the fact that the younger Adams undergoes the process of education passively, while the older Adams is an active seeker of education. In addition, the late chapters suggest that action and contemplation are interrelated. Thus, chapters consisting largely of abstraction and generalization alternate with chapters which give a running account of John Hay's diplomacy. Because his negotiations are conducted from America's position of increasing world power, they are no longer simply a sideshow to the real battle of forces. Furthermore, they appear to carry to fruition the diplomatic efforts of Adams's ancestors. Finally, since, as a "stable-companion to statesmen," Adams advised Hay on his diplomacy, he could take personal satisfaction in his success. Adams's involvement was indirect and is only hinted at, but it tends to support his feeling that "in the long run, he was likely to be a more useful citizen without office" (p. 323). And Hay's efforts, an unmistakable example of man's ability to control forces and create order out of chaos, gave Adams a rare sense of "possible purpose working itself out in history" (p. 363).

But Adams goes beyond this alternation of action and contemplation to stress the importance of thought for purposeful human action. He perceptively saw that America was still being created —that it was perpetually becoming the New World—and he saw the need for intellectual activity in that world: "The new Americans, of whom he was to be one, must, whether they were fit or unfit, create a world of their own, a science, a society, a philosophy, a universe, where they had not yet created a road or even learned to dig their own iron" (p. 239). The *Education* was Adams's most coherent and sustained effort to participate in and inspire this process.

The Dynamic Theory is not an extraneous but an integral part of the book—an inevitable result of its theme and form. Indeed, Adams is a success as an autobiographer only if the final synthesis seems to follow from the experience detailed earlier; the first part of the narrative is both preparation for the final illumination and autobiographical testimony which gives it validity. Thus, even as the character Adams appears to retreat from the world into contemplation or reflection, the narrator Adams is emerging as a prophet. As he becomes a prophet of force, he learns to exploit the power of prophecy. In part, he develops his cosmology out of a deeply felt need: "Every man with self-respect enough to become effective, if only as a machine, has had to account to himself for himself somehow, and to invent a formula of his own for his universe, if the standard formulas failed" (p. 472). But in sharing it with others, he announced the inadequacies of their myths. Unlike prophets who claimed divine inspiration, he did not pretend to absolute knowledge. In fact, he did not so much urge his new vision on others as he challenged them to adopt it or revitalize their own visions.

If contemplation and action were interrelated, so were self-assertion and self-annihilation. In a sense, Adams had achieved at a stroke, with his use of the third person, what Puritans strove for a lifetime to accomplish—the annihilation of the self. But for Adams, self-annihilation was not a religious duty, and he used this original formal device for quite different reasons. One was to express a sense of discontinuity between his present and his former selves; this was a result not of personal conversion but of the acccleration of history. Another was to facilitate self-depreciation, which reflected both habit and the rhetorical intent of establishing the theme of failure. But, in addition, the device helped create a voice suitable to a prophetic autobiography, which demands a kind of paradoxical fusion of self-assertion and self-effacement: self-assertion because it is, after all, autobiography and expresses deep personal conviction; self-annihilation because it is also prophecy, which means that the self is subordinated to a message expressing the community's highest interests.

Adams's first experience with this paradox was associated with the only elective office he ever won—that of Class Orator at Harvard. This honor he described ironically: "The singular fact remained that this commonplace body of young men chose him repeatedly to express their commonplaces. . . . They saw in him a representative—the kind of representative they wanted—and he saw in them the most formidable array of judges he could ever meet, like so many mirrors of himself, an infinite reflection of his own shortcomings" (p. 168). Typically, he responded to his predicament—and his opportunity—in good Puritan fashion, expressing moralistically his contempt for the world of commerce.[15]

The *Education* is, in a sense, a class oration writ large, whose success also depends on balancing the personal vision with the needs of an audience whom he represents as well as addresses. In some ways, the narrative seems to be a progressive account of the annihilation of the individual self. Impersonally narrated and densely historical from the beginning, the *Education* proceeds toward a broad intellectual synthesis which threatens to swallow up the self, and it includes an account of the destruction of the myth of the unified self by modern psychology. Yet it is in the latter, more abstract portion of the narrative that Adams makes the crucial gesture of self-assertion on which the whole Dynamic Theory depends. Confronted with many powerful and mysterious forces, he realizes that their "common value could have no measure but that of their attraction on his own mind" (p. 383). Ironically, science had taught him that there was no alternative to putting his beleaguered self at the center of his cosmology. Thus, the impersonal and abstract Dynamic Theory was based on a subjectivity and a self-reliance nearly as radical as that of the Transcendentalists.

If, within the *Education*, the Dynamic Theory is the major means of achieving an ordered vision of the world, the writing of the *Education* served this purpose within Adams's life. Therefore, the decision to write an autobiography is itself an important turning point in the narrative.[16] Adams's letters reveal that he approached the task with some trepidation, since he saw autobiography as inevitably diminishing the stature of the subject. He finally undertook it, he suggests, to prevent worse treatment at the hands of a biographer: "After seeing how coolly and neatly a man like Trollope can destroy the last vestige of heroism in his own life, I object to allowing mine to be murdered by anyone except myself."[17] Since he was fond of playing with the notion that biography was literary murder and autobiography literary suicide, his use of the third person, which allows the narrator to treat the life of the subject objectively as finished history,[18] can be seen as the formal equivalent of self-destruction. Nevertheless, the notion of autobiography as taking one's life has another aspect which completes the paradox. As class orator, he had profited from the self-possession Harvard taught; now, as an autobiographer, "he had taken possession, seized his life and put it to use."[19] In both roles, Adams realized himself as a spokesman for a community; only in a large social framework could his experience be properly interpreted and valued.

While Adams had hinted in the *Education* that the largest synthesis was death, and had tended—like a spiritual autobiographer—to anticipate and even rush toward it (p. 402), he chose finally to separate the concept of death from that of the final synthesis. His education, but not his life, ended with the final synthesis of the Dynamic Theory. The creation of that theory was itself evidence that he had managed personally to enact the more optimistic of his theory's predictive possibilities. By embracing contradiction and reacting intellectually to the forces he contemplated, he had attained a dynamic equilibrium between his mind and those forces, instead of succumbing to them and dissipating his energy. This synthesis managed paradoxically to avoid complete self-annihilation.

The inevitable self-annihilation of death is reserved for the last chapter, in which Adams brings his life to a close. His own work and education complete, he begins to contemplate the future with a new detachment. Having made his own contribution to the new education of the twentieth-century American, he rests, attentive to the progress of the "new man" but knowing that his theory can neither be verified nor disproved within his lifetime. Unable, of course, to include his own death in the narrative, he tends to prophesy it in the manner of a spiritual autobiographer. Like Woolman, he substitutes for his own death the exemplary death of a friend. John Hay is portrayed as dying with a sense of accomplishment after having engineered a new international order—a "true Roman pax" (p. 503).

The use of Hay's death helps to give the conclusion of the narrative its surprisingly serene tone. Unable, as a skeptic, to experience a mystical vision of his afterlife, as Woolman, or to anticipate the resolution of the paradoxes of his piety after death, as Edwards, Adams imagines his afterlife as a kind of posthumous education. This would be accomplished by periodic returns to history with his friend Hay: "Perhaps some day—say 1938, their centenary —they might be allowed to return together for a holiday, to see the mistakes of their own lives made clear in the light of the mistakes of their successors; and perhaps then, for the first time since man began his education among the carnivores, they would find a world that sensitive and timid creatures could regard without a shudder" (p. 505). This final passage, though light in tone, is free from irony. And although its optimism surprises many readers, it is consistent with his hopes for the prophetic force of his *Education*. Having, like a revival preacher, disabused his audience of their own ill-founded optimism and convinced them of their apparent helplessness, Adams restores room for hope of salvation with his final gesture.

One suspects that although Adams professed not to be seeking absolute truth, he would have liked to recommend absolute values to young men in the *Education*. The narrative does, of course, tend to reaffirm such traditional values as friendship, honesty, personal responsibility, and intellectual vigor.[20] Nevertheless, its general tendency is to move away from traditional values and absolute principles. Recently, historians have recognized that the whole of American society was undergoing a reorientation of values at the end of the nineteenth century. The rapid transition from a rural to an urban society and from an isolationist nation to a world power necessitated new and more flexible values. Insofar as Adams's implicit values can be aligned with those of any movement of his time, they seem to be compatible with those dynamic and optimistic values Robert H. Wiebe has associated with the Progressive movement. In *The Search for Order*, Wiebe identifies continuity and regularity, functionality and rationality, administration and management as the values of the new, urban, middle-class professionals.[21] Adams clearly favored these values, and the *Education* often draws attention specifically to the problems addressed by the Progressive movement. In "Nunc Age," he declares that the single problem before the public is "to create a society that could manage the trusts" (pp. 500–501), and his desire to reform university education and his role as Hay's adviser suggest his compatibility with the movement's goals.

The point is not that the *Education* is a Progressivist tract, but that, as a prophet, Adams clearly reflected a communal crisis of values. Seeking a middle ground between the callous and anachronistic individualism of the Social Darwinists and the visionary and millenial communism of thinkers like Bellamy, Adams affirmed goals and values like those of the Progressive movement. An important difference is that for Adams these values were more than utilitarian because of the framework in which he conceived of them. Thus, although his notion of economy is far from that of Thoreau and Woolman—for whom it represented a moral duty and offered spiritual fulfillment—he intended it to be more than Franklinian efficiency or Jamesian pragmatism. Economy did not represent short-term mechanical utility; rather, it was a value, dependent on foresight, which worked for communal salvation as it tended to reinforce Order in its Manichean struggle with Chaos. Unable to recommend absolute principles and unwilling to accept mere pragmatism, Adams used his prophetic vision to give a kind of transcendent dimension, if not divine sanction, to values that others might perceive more narrowly as utilitarian. Of course, behind all of these communal values lay Adams's triumphant demonstration of the incalculable force of the mind and the transcendent value of the self.

NINE

Two Prophetic Architects

Louis Sullivan and Frank Lloyd Wright

The contributions of Louis Sullivan and Frank Lloyd Wright to the growth of modern architecture in America are familiar; their achievements as autobiographers are less well known. The similarities between their autobiographies should not be surprising, for the two men had closely linked careers and closely parallel lives. Both cherished their rural childhoods, yet both achieved professional maturity in the raw urban environment of Chicago. Both attributed their success as architects not to their academic education but to the influence of nature and talented contemporaries. Adapting Transcendental theories of art to architecture, they cooperated in the creation of an indigenous, modern, "democratic" architecture. Both disseminated their ideas by lecturing and writing, but as architectural innovators, both suffered, at times, from public neglect or hostility. Thus, in periods of professional inactivity, both wrote autobiographies in which they portrayed themselves as benevolent yet persecuted geniuses dedicated to revitalizing American architecture and society.

The prophetic tendencies of their autobiographies derived from their conception of the architect's role in society, which clearly reflects the new maturity of American architecture and the self-confidence of the American artist in the High Victorian age. Toward the end of the nineteenth century, American visual artists came to think of themselves not merely as independent creative personalities but as cultural leaders and even as interpreters of reality and arbiters of value—as seers whose visions of truth would lead society to greater accomplishments in a progressive evolutionary scheme.[1] This change in the self-concept of the artist was evident when, as their arts matured, painters and architects adopted Transcendental ideas about the artist. Just as the emergence of Sullivan and Wright as architects marks the period during which American architecture began to receive international recognition, their emergence as prophets clearly marks the point at which Transcendental principles were carried over into architecture and into the mainstream of our intellectual life. Sullivan and Wright, like the earlier Transcendentalists, believed man to be innately creative, potentially inspired, and fundamentally in harmony with a unified nature representing divine order. Furthermore, both believed that the development of American society as an ideal democracy was dependent on the establishment of an indigenous, organic architecture.

For our purposes, the most significant similarity between the autobiographies is that both reflect and dramatize the predicament of the architect who is also a Transcendental prophet. More than any other kind of artist, perhaps, the architect needs clients and commissions in order to realize his ideas. To function as an architect, he needs to persuade other people to enable him to give his ideas physical embodiment. As innovative architects, both Sullivan and Wright suffered—personally and professionally—from being ahead of their times. Lacking the academic architect's ability to appeal to hallowed precedent and cultural snobbery, the progressive architect, as Wright put it, "can talk only principle and sense";[2] he has to depend on the integrity of his ideas and the ability of his clients to recognize it. To some extent, then, the prophetic architect is at the mercy of his society; he has to lead while seeming to follow. As latter-day Transcendentalists, Sullivan and Wright endorsed idealistic metaphysics, but as architects they depended on materials to express their ideas. As Wright put it, "a poetic idea . . . had to conquer this stubborn, suspicious, mean, possessive old world—all its refractory materials in between—in order to appear at all . . . " (p. 231). In his autobiography, Louis Sullivan resolved this dilemma in favor of the idea, stressing theory rather than practice. This is appropriate in view of the fact that his theory was more radical than his buildings. Wright—a daring engineer as well as an architect, and a prophet whose social interests were more highly developed than Sullivan's—faced a more difficult predicament, and he resolved it differently. Whereas Sullivan devoted his autobiography to tracing the development of his philosophy of man, of architecture, and of society, Wright concentrated on the difficulties of enacting such a philosophy both in his career and in his personal life.

Louis Sullivan

Louis Sullivan's refusal to accomodate himself to the shift in American taste toward academic eclecticism after the Columbian Exposition of 1893, combined with certain personal problems, led to a precipitous and tragic decline in his professional career after 1900. Written after two decades of increasing poverty and inactivity, *The Autobiography of an Idea* (1924) might have been a bitter and defensive book. To some extent, Sullivan did portray himself as a neglected genius, a victim of the betrayal of American ideals by a group of reactionary architects. But the mood of the narrative is self-celebratory, not self-pitying; its major motives were self-restoration and prophecy, not self-defense and apology. In writing it, he managed to recapture both a sense of his own youthful energy and an optimistic vision of America's destiny. On his deathbed, he regarded this—the last, most consistent, and most readable of his prophetic works—and a companion volume, *A System of Ornament*, as the consummating achievements of his career.

Sullivan's two most important predecessors were, for different reasons, Whitman and Adams. Probably he regarded Whitman less as an autobiographer than as a poet and prophet; "There Was a Child Went Forth" and *Democratic Vistas* were more important for Sullivan than "Song of Myself" and *Specimen Days*. Whitman's influence, then, is less evident in the form than in the content of Sullivan's autobiography. In addition to Transcendental philoso-

phy, Sullivan's strong emphasis on childhood probably derives
from Whitman. Sullivan's idealistic metaphysics may help to account for his unique conception of writing the "autobiography of
an idea," but, as we have noted, neither Thoreau nor Whitman
wrote a chronological narrative of the development of his own
thought. Thus, it is likely that Sullivan's conception of his autobiography owes more to English examples of developmental autobiography. However, Sullivan adapts the developmental form to
his own purposes and to his own philosophy, which is explicitly
opposed to the utilitarianism and Darwinism of most British developmental autobiographers.[3]

Sullivan was similarly aware of the formal model and philosophy of Adams's *Education* and seems to have attempted implicitly
to answer his prophecy with a modern Transcendentalism which
took into account some of the realities Adams claimed the "Concord church" ignored. Sullivan's consciousness of Adams's example is suggested by the fact that Sullivan desired to assign the
royalties from his autobiography to the educational fund of the
American Institute of Architects, just as Adams had given the Institute the rights to his *Chartres*.[4] While Sullivan imitated Adams's
magnanimous gesture, he must have hoped that his own contributions, financial and intellectual, would counteract Adams's perni-
cious "feudal" influence. Similarly, as Sherman Paul has noted,
although Sullivan's formal gesture of adopting the third-person
point of view recalled Adams's method, it served significantly different ends.[5] Perhaps out of deference to Adams, Sullivan acknowledged the shocks of his education and the ominous nature
of modern realities; nevertheless, he boldly asserted his ability to
absorb, organize, and express in plastic forms contemporary social,
economic, and technological forces.[6] Thus, Sullivan acknowledged
Adams's example while refuting his vision of man and history.

Ultimately, *The Autobiography of an Idea* is the spiritual autobiography of a latter-day Transcendentalist, for it narrates the
growth of a religious idea and the nurture of the creative powers
man shares with God rather than the development of an intellectual system or the course of a professional career. Unlike Thoreau
or Whitman, Sullivan offers a chronological narrative of a long portion of his life, but, in contrast to Franklin and Adams, he tends

to suppress historical fact in order to create an aura of myth or legend around his experience. Structurally, the narrative seems to have three main sections. The first and significantly the longest section (chapters 1–8) is devoted to childhood and primary education; the second part (chapters 9–12), to Sullivan's secondary and architectural education; the third (chapters 13–15), to his career and mature thought.

The first section is novelistic in its richly detailed re-creation of sensation and incident, and nostalgic in mood. For the most part, the narrative avoids sentimentality because the nostalgia, evoked by a rural America, establishes a reference point against which to measure subsequent change. Indeed, part of Sullivan's prophetic message, which, like Wright's, is essentially conservative, is that although both the boy and the nation must change, certain qualities of their early stages should be nurtured rather than eclipsed: "To disdain our fertile childhood is precisely equivalent to disdain of our maturity. Hence the illusion that we are no longer the child; the delusion that we are other than grown children."[7] The narrative is to measure not growth from naive childhood into wise maturity but the development of the vision and the latent powers of the child. Growth is not, as it was for Adams, a matter of response to dislocation but of continuous expansion from a stable center.

Childhood for Sullivan, as for Adams, involved a rhythmic alternation between town and country. But Adams used this polarity mainly to establish the theme of the duality of all experience. For Sullivan, the specific content of the polarity became a theme; it was one of the contradictions of nineteenth-century American life he hoped to resolve. Indeed, one manifestation of his growth is his changing attitude toward the city. At first, he perceives it as a prison cutting him off from nature; later, he learns to view it as an environment capable of enlarging his powers; finally, he endeavors to make Chicago truly a "Garden City."

Adams, too, had begun with a description of childhood sensations, but he had quickly moved from a world of the senses and instinct to one of intellect, abstraction, and analysis. He used the third-person narration to suggest the gulf between the narrator and his youthful self, to express his sense of the fragmentation of the psyche, and to exert the pressure of irony on his earlier impressions. Sullivan's use of the third person shares only one motive with Adams's—to thrust his ideas rather than himself into prominence. Otherwise, Sullivan manages to use the same device for very different purposes—to suggest the continuity of experience, the wholeness of the self, and the validity of the child's viewpoint. The third-person narration allows Sullivan to re-create the child's consciousness impersonally, with a minimum of sentimentality. At times, the narrator recalls the child's vision in order to affirm its wisdom, as when he records his perception of a Baptist minister's preaching as a perversion of religion. At other times, Sullivan uses the third-person technique to illustrate the process by which raw sensory data is converted into ideas which can then be tested. One such sequence, in which young Louis learns to appreciate, then to worship, a bridge he had naively mistaken for a monster, serves as a paradigm of American society's adjustment to its new technology.

As was the case with Adams, Sullivan's childhood illusions were often abruptly shattered. The crucial difference is that for Sullivan reality often proved less frightening than illusion. One such beneficial shock occurred when Louis's father revealed to him the nature of visual perspective. This archetypal crisis profoundly disturbed the boy, "for had not that son built up a cherished world all of his own, a world made up of dreams, of practicalities, of deep faith, of unalloyed acceptance of externalities, only now to find that world trembling and tottering on its foundations threatening to collapse upon him, or to vanish before this new and awful revelation from the unseen" (p. 104). The architectural metaphor here is significant, for this experience was crucial to the education of the architect. He not only made a discovery necessary to a draftsman; he also learned to see that reality or truth does not always lie in the apparent or obvious. What seemed an experience destructive of the world of the child eventually enabled him to found his buildings upon a true vision—to realize his creative powers in designs which expressed the latent or "suppressed" functions of a building.

Such shocks were not typical of Sullivan's childhood, which he portrays as characterized by reverie and enjoyment of nature. Much time was spent observing and being absorbed in nature. Sullivan's gardening, his delight in spring, and his excursions to explore and establish—to "possess"—his own domain in the rural countryside are all reminiscent of Thoreau. Building a dam represents not a change in his attitude toward nature but a further development of a natural creative power. His allusion in the following passage suggests that he saw no necessary contradiction between contemplating nature and manipulating it: "Then he loafed and invited his soul as was written by a big man about the time this proud hydraulic engineer was born" (p. 56). Even more characteristic of his invocation of Whitman is his description of his solitary experience of his first sunrise: "Surely the child that went forth every day became part of the sunrise even as this sunrise became forevermore part of him" (p. 61).

Rivalling his experience of nature as he grew older was his schooling, which he found oppressive, and his intuitive response to buildings, which he found liberating: "His history books told him that certain buildings were to be revered, but the buildings themselves did not tell him so, for he saw them with a fresh eye, an ignorant eye, an eye unprepared for sophistries and a mind empty of dishonesty" (p. 117). The climax of this section occurs with Sullivan's decision to become an architect. This event resembles Franklin's adoption of the role of printer because it engages Sullivan in a profession that allowed him to concentrate his powers and employ them in a publicly useful way. It does not resolve the dualities of his childhood, but it suggests a means of their eventual resolution. Furthermore, it gives him a medium for the expression of his prophetic vision.

If the first section focused on Sullivan's unplanned and unconscious experience of nature, the middle section concentrates on his education in institutions, for the boy was in need of having his intuitions translated into ideas and his innate powers disciplined. At Boston English, Moses Woolson taught Sullivan not only the Franklinian lesson that true freedom comes only through discipline of power but also the symbolic language of algebra, which enabled Sullivan to probe the unknown. Sullivan's critical and analytical faculties began to develop alongside his creative ones. Schooling no longer distracted him from nature, but began to make nature's lessons conscious and systematic. Sullivan summarized this crucial phase of his education in a way that contrasts sharply with Adams's comments on his academic education; according to Sullivan, Woolson "had brought order out of disorder, definition out of what was vague . . . [and] made of Louis a compacted personality, ready to act on his own initiative, in an intelligent and purposeful way" (p. 168).

At M.I.T., however, Sullivan became restless with the Beaux Arts method and decided to go "to headquarters to learn if what was preached *there* as gospel really signified glad tidings" (p. 188–89). The main benefits of his time in Europe came not from his education at the École but from his intensive preparation for the exams and from his vacation travel. A mathematics tutor, M. Clopet, who valued only rules so broad as to admit of no exceptions, stimulated Sullivan's quest for an equivalent approach to architecture. Similarly, his study of history and his immersion in European culture led to his discovery of his vocation as a prophet. He came to see history as "a processional of the races and nations, whose separate deeds seemed to flow from their separate thoughts, and whose thoughts and deeds seemed, as he himself progressed, toward them, to coalesce into a mass movement of mankind, carrying the burden of a single thought" (p. 237). His subsequent devotion to the pursuit and expression of that idea reveals that his aspiration was to become a prophet as well as an architect—one who would further the progress of mankind by revealing and realizing the ideals of his society. This new endeavor marks, also, the beginnings of self-education. Armed with his new vision of history, Sullivan quickly became impatient with the architectural training at the École, which he felt offered technique without inspiration.

In the last three chapters, Sullivan sets forth his philosophy and discusses his attempts to realize it in his architecture. At the beginning of "The Garden City," he establishes the nature of the environment in which the idea was finally discovered. He reverts to the fairy-tale tone of the book's opening in order to remove the city from the realm of history into that of myth: "There was a time a city some three hundred thousand strong stood beside the shore of a great and very wonderful lake with a wonderful horizon and wonderful daily moods" (p. 241). According to Sullivan, the city, which had been devastated by a fire, was preparing for recovery and for transformation into a totally new and wholesome environment.

For a time, Sullivan's personal growth, his architectural education, and the growth of the city proceed in parallel fashion. But the narrative focuses not, like a memoir, on the career but, like a spiritual autobiography, on the vision and values of the author. Sullivan's concern is to establish his prophetic stature rather than his professional standing. Only in this chapter does he make explicit what he means by "an idea" and specify what the idea is: "This steadfast belief in the power of man was an unalloyed childhood instinct, an intuition and a childhood faith which never for a day forsook him, but grew stronger, like an indwelling daemon. . . . as he grew on through his boyhood, and through passage to manhood and to manhood itself, he began to see the powers of nature and the powers of man coalesce in his vision into an IDEA *of power*. Then and only then he became aware that this idea was a *new idea,*—a complete reversal and inversion of the commonly accepted intellectual and theological concept of the Nature of man" (p. 248).

It becomes clear, finally, that by "idea" Sullivan means philosophy or even vision, and that the "new idea" consists essentially of the principles of Transcendentalism. The next chapter, "Face to Face," summarizes Sullivan's personal philosophy and uses it as the basis for a prophetic interpretation of human history. Thus, this penultimate chapter corresponds closely in function, though not in content, to Adams's "Dynamic Theory of History." Whereas Adams's vision focused on impersonal forces and made room for man's salvation only by admitting that he too was a force, Sullivan concentrates on making man's latent powers visible to him. In Sullivan's scheme, nature is a beneficent servant of man, who wields impressive powers: "He changes his own situations, he creates an environment of his own" (p. 264).

According to Sullivan, all previous civilizations had been based on delusions and misconceptions—on a tragic underestimation of man's abilities. Sullivan presents his own idea as the successor to two previous "inversions" —the Christian and the Copernican— which had begun to dispel man's self-delusion: "The world of heart and head is becoming dimly sentient that man in his power is Free Spirit—Creator. The long dream of inverted self is nearing its end" (p. 266). In announcing this new and presumably final inversion, Sullivan, of course, assumes the role of a new messiah; the chapter title, which echoes I Corinthians 13, implies that Sullivan's gospel enables man to see himself clearly and hence to realize his divine potential.

Although Sullivan goes on in Whitmanic fashion to enumerate the powers of man and to prophesy the overthrow of "feudalism" in America, his performance is not very convincing. For one thing, his view of history is oversimplified to a point that suggests willful distortion rather than inspired vision. Thus, his optimistic version of the future appears to be without foundation; with regard to history, at least, he seems to have lost his traumatically acquired sense of perspective. Or perhaps his vision was properly graphic and autobiographical rather than prophetic, for, ironically, it is when his idea is presented in bald expository form, divorced from the intuition and experience from which it evolved, that it is least impressive. As his commercial buildings attest, Sullivan's architectural vision was capable of spiritualizing the material, but his autobiographical vision led him to extract an idea from its experiential context and project it upon a vague future. The result seems not, like Adams's synthesis, arduously derived from the minutely detailed history that preceded it but artificially distilled from Sullivan's mythic childhood. The soft focus and latent sentimentality of the earlier chapters are exposed here as liabilities. Instead of revealing man to himself, Sullivan seems to project his own wishes upon nature and to see himself reflected in it—face to face.

If Charles Whitaker, the editor of the *Journal* of the A.I.A. who solicited the autobiography, had not urged Sullivan to add another chapter, the book would have ended on this positive, but false note.[8] Having set forth his idea, or his prophecy, Sullivan had done what he had set out to do, but he had said little about either his architectural theory or his buildings. In a final and somewhat uneven chapter, he dealt with his attempts to enact the idea whose evolution he had traced in the earlier chapters. In doing so, he had to account for the decline of his career and his failure to convert the American public to his viewpoint, either through his writings or his buildings. His solution to this autobiographical problem was to portray himself as a victim of the struggle between "democratic" and "feudal" principles in American civilization.

Sullivan characterizes himself as ignorant of the politics of architectural practice, armed only with the revolutionary concept that form should follow function in architecture—an architectural corollary of the idea of power elaborated in the previous chapter. Thus buildings, like men, were to realize their greatest beauty by making manifest their latent functions or powers. Theoretically, this architectural concept was the seed of an organic architecture which would symbolize the achievement of the final inversion and the arrival of a kind of democratic millenium.

But the new formula for organic architecture, like Sullivan's prophetic writings, failed to transform the contemporary scene. Sullivan quickly sketched in the forces assembling for a showdown between opposing principles within the culture. On the one hand, there were many personalities and technological factors making for vital developments in Chicago architecture in the 1880s, as the city began to recover from the fire of 1871 and the panic of 1873. The rise of the tall office building, with its true skeletal frame, and Sullivan's solution to the problem of expressing it esthetically are prime examples of these creative developments: "The true steel frame structure stands unique in the flowing of man's works; a brilliant expression of man's capacity to satisfy his needs through the expression of his natural powers" (p. 313). On the other hand were the values and activities of men like Daniel Burnham, whose architectural practice embodied for Sullivan the "tendency toward bigness, organization, delegation, and intense commercialism" of the "feudal" trusts (p. 314). Burnham was cast as a traitor and villain because of his deference to the academic eastern architects in the design of the Columbian Exposition of 1893.

The Exposition became the focus of Sullivan's final chapter, as it had been for Henry Adams's "Chicago"; for both, it was an event revealing the destiny of the community. But whereas Adams viewed the attempt "to impose classical taste on plastic Chicago"[9] as a sign of possible improvement in American taste, Sullivan saw signs of cultural regression in the plaster classicism of the fair, which he denounced as "a naked exhibitionism of charlatanry in the higher feudal and domineering culture, conjoined with expert salesmanship of the materials of decay" (p. 322). Similarly, while the bemused Adams found more questions than answers among the fair's exhibits, Sullivan portrayed it as a decisive betrayal of American ideals: "Here was to be the test of American culture, and here it failed" (p. 318).

Sullivan makes his account of the Exposition the occasion for some bitterly satiric writing on eclecticism and commercialism and also for an ironic epitaph for American architecture: "Thus Architecture died in the land of the free and the home of the brave,—in a land declaring its fervid democracy, its inventiveness, its resourcefulness, its unique daring, enterprise, and progress" (p. 325). This interpretation of the significance of the Exposition is, of course, highly personal. As an autobiographer who substitutes an account of the defeat of his revolutionary idea for an account of his personal and professional decline, Sullivan may be accused of shifting the blame from himself to society—of portraying himself, for egotistical reasons, as a genius ignored by an unappreciative public. Still, there is a certain amount of truth to Sullivan's version of events. His career and the development of progressive architecture did suffer from the triumph of academic classicism in the design of the Exposition—a triumph symptomatic of an important shift in taste in the 1890s. Furthermore, the pose of the persecuted genius, in both Sullivan and Wright, is consistent with their portrayal of themselves as prophets. Their exaggeration of public indifference or hostility may derive, not from self-pity or self-delusion, but from their desire to function as prophets in writing autobiography; as prophets, they would inevitably judge society by high ideals. Certainly, Sullivan's indignation and anger seem more authentic than his blandly optimistic prophecy in the previous chapter. His editor's coaxing another chapter out of him seems to have unleashed a power of vituperation latent in the rest of the narrative; Sullivan's performance as a prophet is thus strengthened by his continuation of the narrative.

Still, one remains unsure of Sullivan's motives. While the episode of the Exposition serves as a valuable reminder of the vulnerability of American ideals, it also excuses, without confronting, the subsequent decline of Sullivan's career. Moreover, Sullivan goes on to reassert his faith in America's future, arguing that the masses are withdrawing their consent from the architectural travesty of eclecticism: "Dogma and the rule of the dead are passing. The Great *Modern* Inversion, for which the world of mankind has been preparing purblindly through the ages, is now underway in its world-wide awakening" (p. 328). Sullivan's major motive in his treatment of the Exposition may have been to make the contemporary plight of progressive architecture seem more urgent by citing a recent defeat for its ideals. His own suffering as a result of that failure may make his faith in the final triumph of his ideals more moving to some readers, less convincing to others. Thus, this second reversal may be, to some, evidence of Sullivan's resilience, self-composure, and magnanimity; to others, of his ambivalence toward the American public. One wonders whether he willfully revived his earlier optimism for the sake of consistency, in the hope of pleasing his audience, or out of genuine prophetic conviction.

To unsympathetic readers, Sullivan's subordination of personal experience to the development of his philosophy or vision will seem a ploy for avoiding the unpleasant facts of his later life; to sympathetic readers, it may seem a way of transcending self-concern in order to serve the needs of the community in the manner of the prophetic autobiographer. Another perspective is to view the autobiography as an attempt to resurrect and preserve the self. Unlike some of his predecessors, Sullivan never prophesied his own immortality. Rather, he expressed a sense of self-transcendence which made it superfluous. Thus, he informs the reader that in a moment of spiritual illumination, he had experienced a sense of "peace which is life's sublimation, timeless and spaceless. Yet he never lost his footing on the earth; never came the sense of immortality: One life surely is enough if lived and fulfilled" (p. 298). Still, Sullivan's autobiographical strategy seems calculated to guarantee his immortality in more ways than the obvious and inevitable one. In treating his autobiography as the record of the growth of an idea, rather than as an account of his career, he focused on a contribution—a life-product—which would outlast even his buildings. And, like Whitman, he identified his life with the process of evolution; according to Sullivan, the history of his life simply recapitulated the history of civilization, which is also the autobiography of an idea.

Frank Lloyd Wright

Since Sullivan was the man who most strongly influenced Wright's thought and expression, as well as his design, the connection between their autobiographies is a firm one. Wright discusses their relationship in *An Autobiography* (1932), but its importance to him is even more apparent in a later book, *Genius and the Mobocracy* (1949). In it, he sets out to "right" the art historians' account of their relationship and, in doing so, to write the personal history of that relationship as well. Wright follows the relationship from the beginning, during the crucial period when Sullivan was designing the Auditorium Building, through Wright's dismissal from the firm for violating his contract, to their reunion in Sullivan's declining years. Thus, the book becomes a declaration of allegiance to Sullivan and even a work of confession and atonement. However, Wright portrays himself not as a disciple or imitator but as a co-worker carrying on the master's work. He insists on the mutuality of their relationship, pointing out that at one time Sullivan could not distinguish between their drawings, and claiming that the master owed him as much as he owed the master. Indeed, the relationship between them is so close that the book becomes autobiographical; in concluding, Wright describes it as "neither biograph nor autobiograph but a combination of both."[10] Elsewhere he asserts, "This book is not about him—it is about our work-life and struggle while we were together" (p. 155). More than a biography of Sullivan, the book is finally a meditation on the predicament of the inspired artist in a democracy that has failed to honor individual freedom. Louis Sullivan is the prime example of the tragic fate of a genius in such a society. But, seeing himself in Sullivan, Wright tends to portray his own predicament indirectly.

Yet here, as in the autobiography, Wright is careful to distinguish himself from his master in several respects. Wright argues that he is more aware than Sullivan of the significance of the machine for modern architecture and more sensitive to the nature of materials. Restating Sullivan's dictum more positively as "Form and Function are one," he claims to have refined the master's architectural theory and to have extended its application beyond the treatment of façades. And although his characterization of Sullivan as "untroubled by a social conscience" seems unfair (pp. 53–54), it reflects Wright's sense that he was more concerned than his master with social problems and the function of the institutions for which he designed buildings.

The similarities and differences between them are reflected in their autobiographies. Much of the early part of Wright's reads like a recapitulation of Sullivan's, while the later part reads like its sequel. However, whereas Sullivan fulfilled the role of the prophet explicitly in his writing and implicitly in his architecture, Wright tended to function as a prophet both in his personal life and in his architecture and writing. Sullivan, like Emerson, announced the principles of a radical philosophy; Wright, like Thoreau and Whitman, attempted to explore the implications of these principles by enacting them in his life, which became part of his design. Instead of subordinating his experience to his ideas, Wright chose to treat his experience as a test and demonstration of them; indeed, he calls his book "an autobiographical study of Life-as-Idea and Idea-as-Life."[11] Wright's autobiography is more personal, more concrete, and more inclusive of failure than Sullivan's because, as a self-conscious prophet, he tried to extend his organic principles into a design for his entire society.

Book One of the autobiography is preceded by a "Prelude" which graphically illustrates Wright's sense of his own life. As the nine-year-old Wright and his Uncle John walk across a snow-covered field, the difference between their personalities is revealed by the paths they trace in the snow: "There was the wavering, searching, heedful line embroidering the straight one like some free, engaging vine as it ran back and forth across it" (p. 1). Wright clearly intends to indicate here that although the pattern of his life departs from the purposeful straightness of his uncle's, it does so only because he was seeking for and heedful to a *natural* principle.

The first part of Book One, "Family," is largely devoted to an impressionistic rendering of a rural boyhood. The content and tone of this section are Sullivanesque; minimizing the financial insecurity of his family and the nomadic pattern of his boyhood years, Wright stresses the wholesome influence of nature and the healthy rhythm of farm work. Like Sullivan, he portrays himself as a dreamy, mystical youth susceptible to the influence of music and educated primarily by the "Book of Creation" rather than by school or society: "Something in the nature of an inner experience had come to him that was to make a sense of the supremacy of interior order like a religion to him" (p. 47).

In treating his boyhood, then, Wright portrays not so much its reality as the ideals to which he became devoted. He finds their intellectual sources in his family's Unitarianism and their enthusiasm for what he calls "the transcendentalism of the sentimental group at Concord: Whittier, Lowell, Longfellow, yes, and Emerson, too" (p. 15). But a harsher heritage is implicit in his family's motto, "Truth against the world." Thus, in addition to an appreciation for the beneficence of nature, of rural life, and of the sheltering clan of Welsh relatives within which he lived, Wright, like Thoreau and Adams, acquired a testiness and intolerance for institutions or individuals that threatened his ideals. Even as a youth, he questioned society in the manner of Thoreau: " . . . the boy already wondered why 'culture' . . . shouldn't consist in getting rid of the inappropriate in everything" (p. 57).

Like Sullivan, Wright can record only impatience with his schooling, which he evaluates as an educational blank. His most important architectural lesson came not from his courses in civil engineering at the University of Wisconsin but from witnessing the collapse of a shoddily built section of the state Capitol. This event impressed him with the urgency of structural as well as professional integrity, and provided him with an image of avoidable catastrophe which shaped his professional and prophetic conscience: "The horror of the scene has never entirely left his consciousness and remains to prompt him to this day" (p. 55).

The first real turning point in the narrative comes when, at the end of Part One, Wright runs away from college and family in Madison to seek a practical architectural education in Chicago, "the Eternal City of the West." The significance of this break with

the restrictive influence of his family and school is suggested by
the change from a third-person point of view to a first-person narration: "Here say goodby to 'the boy.' Henceforward, on my own,
I am I" (p. 60). Wright's use of the third person in this section
may be, in part, a gesture of deference to Sullivan's example, but
he uses it largely to distinguish a period of vague memory of dependent childhood from a period of conscious selfhood. At the
point in the narrative at which the character first assumes responsibility for his destiny, the narrator recognizes his identity with
him by means of a simple formal gesture.

If the entire narrative is intended to record an attempt to live a
life according to natural principles, the "Family" section of Book
One establishes Wright's intuitive harmony with nature, while the
"Fellowship" section records the articulation of personal ideals.
Thus, this section of the autobiography, like the middle section
of *The Autobiography of an Idea*, is concerned with the activities
and education of the budding architect—his reading, acquaintances, employers, and the development of his personal taste and
style as a designer. But as his individuality develops, Wright becomes increasingly aware of conventional obstacles to the enactment of his ideas, both in his personal life and his architectural
practice: "I began to see that in spite of all the talk about Nature
'natural' was the last thing they would let you be if they could
prevent it" (p. 88). His relationship with Sullivan became especially important because ". . . the very sense of things I had been feeling as rebellion was—in him—at work" (p. 101). From the beginning
of his architectural career, Wright's sense of himself as an antinomian and heretic in oppostion to the prevailing culture developed
rapidly. Thus, like Thoreau and unlike Whitman, Wright tended
to take a prophetic stance which opposed him to the public. This
tendency helped him to define his prophetic message, but it also
sometimes frustrated his attempts at reform. He simultaneously
thrived on and was thwarted by his antagonistic attitude toward
social conventions.

Book Two, "Work," begins where Louis Sullivan chose to con-
clude his autobiography—with the year 1893. Unlike Sullivan,
Wright did not suffer a personal and professional decline after the
Exposition, and he does not focus on it as a personal and com-

munal catastrophe, as Sullivan had done. However, he does imply that it represented a betrayal of organic principles when he treats "Uncle Dan" Burnham's offer to send him to the École des Beaux Arts as a kind of temptation scene. He portrays himself here as facing a crisis similar to the test Sullivan claimed confronted the nation in the Exposition. But instead of reenacting the communal failure in his personal life, Wright remains true to his and Sullivan's ideals and turns down the offer: "Suddenly the whole thing cleared up before my eyes as only keeping faith with what we call 'America'" (p. 125). Like Sullivan before him, Wright chooses the more difficult route, asserting his faith in the future of America and his own role in bringing about progress.

Unlike Sullivan, Wright includes a detailed account of his career; thus his autobiography seems to display some of the characteristics of the memoir. Yet he resists the impersonality of that form, pointing out that his career cannot be considered separately from his self: "These creations of ours! I see as we look back upon them how we ourselves belong to them" (p. 129). On the other hand, he succeeds, to some extent, in avoiding narrow egocentricity by treating his commissions not as personal achievements but as embodiments of ideals which are, or should be, communal ones: "All true building in our land of the brave and the home of the free is a soul-trying crusade . . ." (p. 24).

During the late 1890s, Wright's dual concern for the family as an institution and for the architectural expression of organic principles came together in his first creative breakthrough—the development of the prairie house.[12] In the autobiography, Wright explains this achievement in terms of the expression of two distinctively American "commodities"—unity and space. In these houses, Wright sought to create an architectural environment which would maximize both a communal sense of shelter and a personal sense of freedom. Like Thoreau, he saw his dwellings not only as embodiments of his spiritual ideals but as environments with regenerative capabilities: "As these ideals worked away from house to house, finally freedom of floor space and elimination of useless heights worked a miracle in the new dwelling place. A sense of appropriate freedom had changed its whole aspect. The whole became different, but more fit for human habitation, and natural for its site" (p. 145). Thus, while Sullivan had tried to translate Whitman's poetic ideals into architectural equivalents, Wright came much closer to fulfilling Thoreau's prophetic architectural program.[13]

Wright was less successful in his attempt to realize in his life the ideal he expressed in the prairie house—an optimum combination of stability and freedom. In 1909, he settled a domestic crisis by choosing individual freedom at the expense of his family's stability, leaving home to go off to Europe with the wife of a neighbor and client. His inclusion of domestic problems introduces a confessional element wholly lacking in Sullivan's autobiography and generally uncharacteristic of American autobiography. There is also an element of the apology in the "sociological tract" concerning marriage, fatherhood, and divorce which serves as the defense of his action. Yet both elements—confession and apology—are still subsumed under his prophetic purpose, for Wright explains his actions as part of an attempt to live a life as true to organic principles as his architecture: ". . . I went out into the unknown to test faith in freedom, test faith in life as I had already proved faith in work" (p. 167).

Hostile publicity about Wright's actions aroused his sense of righteousness and moved him toward the role of an antagonistic prophet. Unable to accept social conventions and reluctant to suffer the consequences of ignoring them, Wright resorted to elitism in his own defense, portraying himself as a genius mistreated by the mob. There is certainly an element of paranoia in Wright's consistent exaggeration of the public's hostility to his architecture and his conduct of his personal life.[14] Yet to some extent, Wright earned his role as a persecuted genius, for he spent more than one night in jail as a result of his unconventional behavior. Furthermore, Wright's predicament stemmed in part from his interpretation of the prophet's role. He was sincere and passionate in his rejection of certain conventions; his devotion to his ideas and his very self-concept demanded a certain amount of public resistance.[15] Yet the dilemma was one he, unlike Woolman, never satisfactorily resolved. Throughout his life he continued to offend the public and to complain of their hostility to his actions and ideas.

The period following this turning point, from 1910 to 1914,

was one of little architectural activity.[16] But Wright's retreat from suburban Oak Park to the rural isolation of Taliesin accomplished some of the benefits for Wright that Thoreau's removal to Walden Pond gained for him. It gave him a self-constructed retreat from which to reexamine and reestablish his personal relationship to society, and it supplied him with an environment suitable to his needs, expressive of his ideals, and conducive to harmony with nature. Moreover, at Taliesin, Wright was able to create an exemplary social unit consisting of "a garden and a farm behind a workshop and a home" (p. 172). He sought both to reenter the world of his youth and to make that world the site of his mature creative development. Like Thoreau, he invoked as an analogue for his change of residence the discovery and settlement of the New World by immigrant pioneers: "I turned to the hill in the Valley as my Grandfather before me had turned to America—as a hope and a haven . . ." (p. 172). There he proceeded to build, at last, a natural house for himself as the site of his future perfect home.

However, once again, Wright's work was opposed by "something not in the reckoning"—this time not a mere temptation but a devastating tragedy: one of his employees at Taliesin went berserk, killing Wright's mistress and six other people and burning down much of Taliesin. Coming two weeks after the outbreak of World War I, this episode marks the nadir of the narrative. In marked contrast to Henry Adams, Wright includes a personal tragedy which might have broken his life in order to show that he had overcome it and kept his life and personality intact. His recovery, which was slow and arduous, began with temporary self-isolation and agonizing self-doubt: "Was this trial for heresy too? Was this trial at some judgment seat . . . to quell a spirit that would not be quelled?" (p. 192). Finally, however, with the activity of rebuilding Taliesin, he felt a sense of self-redemption and triumph.

Nearly as important for his recovery was the time Wright spent in Japan. Japanese culture embodied many of Wright's ideals, both esthetic and religious, and the Japanese print, an indigenous art form based on simplification, was as comforting and inspiring to him as the Gothic cathedral was for Henry Adams. In his autobiography, Wright uses Japan as Adams uses medieval France and Thoreau uses Cape Cod—as cultural ideals with which to reproach and inspire American civilization. Impressed by the physical and spiritual cleanliness favored by the Shinto religion, he declares, "We of the West couldn't live in Japanese houses and shouldn't. But we could live in houses disciplined by an ideal at least as high and true as this one of theirs, if we went about it—for a century or two" (p. 199).

But like Thoreau's Cape Cod, Wright's Japan harbored a threat to his Transcendental philosophy; the earthquake, like the unbridled Atlantic, furnished evidence of potential chaos in nature. Like Thoreau, Wright responded by adapting his organic principles to native conditions, but Wright's trial was more severe since it required not only intellectual accommodation but the creation of a physical construct—a hotel—able to withstand an earthquake. The construction of the Imperial Hotel looms larger in the autobiography than it would in an "objective" biography or an account of his architectural career, because Wright saw this achievement as a supreme and dramatic example of the ability of organic principles of design to transcend natural disasters and of his personal capacity to rise above tragic catastrophe. When the hotel survived an earthquake which flattened much of Tokyo in 1923, Wright's triumph was not only professional but personal, not only real but symbolic.

Wright took advantage of the disappointment in his career and the turmoil in his personal life between 1914 and 1932 to emphasize the difficulty of his struggle to realize his ideals. The stories of certain commissions come to epitomize the lifelong process of conceiving and nurturing an idea. Wright comments with irony but without bitterness on the architect's peculiar predicament, which involves overcoming human as well as material resistance to the force of his idea: "Seeking simplicity in the spirit in which it was sought in La Miniatura, you shall never fail to find beauty—though contractors do betray, workmen botch, all friends backslide, bankers balk, the jaws of heaven open wide to hitherto unsuspected deluge, and all the Gods—but one—be jealous" (p. 250).

Wright did not stint in recording his personal trials during this period. Another fire nearly destroyed Taliesin, but there was no loss of life and a storm quenched the fire before devastation was complete. Wright's recovery was aided by the support of Olgivanna

Milanoff, but his joy in his family was dampened by the harrass-
ment of his estranged and unbalanced wife, Miriam Noel. Interest-
ingly, the interpretive framework of this part of the narrative has
to do with two opposing prophetic principles. One, instilled in him
by his grandfather, is a principle of judgment which Wright associates with Isaiah, the prophet of a severe, masculine deity. The
other represents a principle of acceptance which he associates with
the Welsh prophet Taliesin, the prophet of a deity with the gentle
nature of Adams's Virgin: "Isaiah is the vengeful prophet of an an-
tique wrath. Taliesin is a nobler prophet and he is not afraid of
him. . . . Taliesin loves and trusts—man" (p. 273). Thus, Wright
often interprets favorable events, such as the reconstruction of
Taliesin, as evidence of the strength of the gentler prophet. While
not providential, his framework is teleological, and the struggle
between these opposing principles is reminiscent of the Puritan's
vacillation between forgiving and condemning texts.

Book Three, the final book of the 1932 version of the autobiography, is entitled "Freedom" because the death of Miriam Noel
removed a large obstacle to a free personal life and the resumption
of creative activity. However, the coming of the Depression meant
a lack of construction and hence of commissions. Faced with a
period of professional inactivity, Wright's creative energy, like that
of Sullivan in similar circumstances, expressed itself in a flood of
articles and speeches. Thus, Book Three also records the liberation
of Wright's ideas from the necessity of realization in material form
for paying clients. In a time of national crisis, Wright fully assumed the role of prophet, and his ideas are increasingly presented
in pure expository form. Book Three corresponds, then, to Sullivan's "Face to Face" chapter, for here Wright explicitly states the
essence of his prophetic message.

Freedom is the theme of this somewhat anticlimactic section
in another sense, for the theme of Wright's prophecy is that the
challenge facing America is the reestablishment of freedom in a
designed society. In the 1930s, his thought turned increasingly
to the city, which he thought had been outmoded by modern
communications and transportation. His hope was that decentral-
ization would ruralize Usonia, as he liked to call the United States,
and reestablish the family home as the primary social unit. But in

the meantime, he recognized the need "to mitigate . . . the horror of life held helpless or caught unaware in the machinery that is the city . . . " (p. 324). Thus, he offered his own project for St. Mark's Tower as a humane and organic design for a skyscraper. Although he was generally optimistic about the future, he also felt, like Adams, that American civilization was facing a crisis, and that its salvation might lie in education: "Publicizing organic educational influences, by way of information, may avert the organic disaster that overtook earlier civilizations. It may also precipitate disaster, be it said" (p. 318).

One section of this book, entitled "Journeyman Preacher," describes Wright's travels as an itinerant prophet. One of his goals is to prevent the Chicago World's Fair of 1933, in which he had not been invited to participate, from becoming another setback for organic architecture like the Columbian Exposition. As the title of this section indicates, however, the format for the presentation of his ideas tends to be expository rather than narrative, and the effect is rather flat. In introducing a complete lecture into the text, he admits that the procedure may not seem autobiographical and that the lecture may be skipped, but implies that it ought to be read since it contains "compact, the essence of work and life as philosophy of form, line, material and symbol" (p. 344). Like any prophet, he endeavors to involve the reader by suggesting his inevitable implication in the future of his community: "Let us see what illusions we are cherishing in these prisons for life that we have built, and then see what freedom is possible for us if we will take it" (p. 313). Wright remains optimistic, believing that in his work and his writing he leaves a legacy sufficient to inspire the creation of an organic society. As illustration, one of the final scenes offers an image of Wright's instruction of posterity in the means of their salvation. Describing a game in which he and his five-year-old daughter take turns adding colored blocks to a cooperative construction, he comments: "Always the little form and color exercises would make a good thesis in 'Modern Art.' In fact, that is what I intend them to be" (p. 368).

As Wright brought his narrative to a close, he appeared ready to accept death as part of natural change: "The inevitable is friend to natural order in any true culture founded on this reality. Age,

then, becomes a desirable qualification, . . . death a crisis of
growth" (p. 371). However, although Wright was in his mid-sixties
when *An Autobiography* was first published, he did not die until
1959. Moreover, in the late 1930s, he entered into a new creative
phase which surpassed even his "first golden age" in the first decade of the century. During this time, he continued to write, and
one of his many projects was a continuation of the autobiography.
In the enlarged 1943 edition, he divided Book One into two separate books, "Family" and "Fellowship"; revised "Freedom,"
which now became Book Four; added a fifth book, "Form"; and
suggested in his closing lines that "Broadacres City" be considered
the sixth and final book. This new version of *An Autobiography*
was composed during the early years of World War II, but this
event seems to have had little impact on its content. For Wright,
who was a pacifist and an isolationist, the war would not have
been cause for any cessation of his criticism of the nation. Nor
did he see it as a communal crisis worthy of treatment in his
added book, "Form." It afforded the occasion for this writing
project not because it posed a threat to the community but because it brought about a dearth of commissions. The decisive
historical context for the new version of the autobiography, as
for the old, seems to have been the Depression, with its national
introspection and its experimentation with new approaches to
social problems. In the enlarged autobiography, Wright's concern
for the community is very apparent, for Book Five concentrates
on the Taliesin Fellowship and Book Six explicitly suggests a design for the nation as a whole.

The establishment of the Taliesin Fellowship was, in part, a way
of responding to the professional inactivity caused by the Depression: "No buildings to build at the harrowing moment but, capital-
izing thirty five years of past experience, why not build the
builders of buildings against the time when buildings might again
be built?" [17] But it was also a way of making an institution of
Wright's creative and prophetic self, and once the Fellowship was
established, Taliesin became even more of an "anti-city" on a hill
than it had been when only Wright's immediate family lived there.
With this act, Wright extended his nuclear family into a creative
fellowship which amalgamated elements of Christian pietism, early

monasticism, and Arthurian romance.[18] Thus, the fellowship was a nearly self-sufficient community intended both to inspire the large community by its example and to assume leadership in the process of designing an ideal democratic society. It differed from Thoreau's experiment at Walden in being a group enterprise. Yet a similar effort was made to reconstruct life from the essentials, beginning with the acquisition of materials through activities like logging and lime-burning. The same attempt was made to live a totally designed life. Moreover, like Thoreau, Wright suggests that his experiment is an effort to complete the American Revolution: ". . . this search of ours for democratic FORM is revolutionary. Necessarily. But a Revolution utterly essential to the life of this our country" (p. 416).

In the Taliesin Fellowship, Wright again confronted the dilemma of the genius or prophet in a democracy—how much to anticipate the needs and desires of his people. While the impulse behind the community may have been democratic, the actual arrangements were anything but egalitarian: policy was made rather autocratically by Wright and his wife, and eccentricity seems to have been exclusively Wright's privilege.[19] Certainly, the hierarchical arrangement of the community suggests that Wright developed a community which demanded little self-sacrifice from him and permitted much self-assertion. The fellowship represented an extension, not an annihilation, of Wright's self. The dichotomy between individual freedom and social order was one he was never able to resolve comfortably or consistently; as Robert Twombly has observed, "His own life-style extolled the one, his intellectual constructs the other."[20]

The relationship between the fellowship and the commissions executed by Wright in this period is complex. Detractors have argued that Wright exploited his apprentices in order to rebuild his practice; in the sense that the fellowship supplied cheap assistance which multiplied Wright's efforts, it *was* a means toward an architectural end-product. But the commissions also provided both a creative and a financial stimulus to the fellowship; thus, they were a means toward the end of sustaining and developing the community. Ultimately, of course, both were means of releasing Wright's creative and reform energies.

Among other commissions Wright chose for inclusion in this section is the Administration Building for the Johnson Wax Company in Racine, Wisconsin (1936). This building, which he describes as "a socio-economic interpretation of modern business at its top and best" (p. 472), was a kind of counterpart of Taliesin for a commercial community. As with Taliesin, the ideal embodied was conservative in that the building gave clear architectural expression to the administrative hierarchy of this small, paternalistic firm. In a period when unemployment was high and the value of work was being undermined by programs like National Relief, Wright deliberately sought to create a visual symbol of the therapeutic power of work. Like its predecessor, the Larkin Building, this building was intended to reaffirm the quasireligious gospel of work: "Organic architecture designed this great building to be as inspiring a place to work in as any cathedral was in which to worship" (p. 472).

The story of the construction of this building, which required some novel engineering devices, brings Wright back to the theme of testing his ideas. In the manner of a Transcendentalist, he develops a mundane fact into a comprehensive autobiographical symbol: "Nearly every structure I have built, large or small, required some test. Or many. . . . Frequently one test would require others. One experience would lead to the next until the building process extending back over a period of forty-five years resembles the continuous test to which life itself subjects the architect himself" (p. 478). The tests demanded by bureaucratic building commissions reflect their distrust or incomprehension of the genius's designs. But Wright learns to welcome them for two reasons. First, they are a good experimental way of discovering nature's inherent tolerances and equilibriums—which building codes merely attempt to estimate on the basis of conventional building methods. As natural methods of learning natural laws, they are a means of self-education. Second, the tests offer Wright a way of proving himself to skeptics. Thus, they are a means of educating the public about organic design; as a means of communication, they can help to close the gaps between the designer, the contractor, the client, and the commissions.

Book Five might have properly concluded the autobiography,

since it portrayed Wright's life as combining the values of the previous four books—family, fellowship, work, and freedom—in a happier form than ever before. But as if to answer questions raised by his critics, Wright chose to add another book, which he introduces in this fashion: "I wish to build a city for Democracy: the Usonian city that is nowhere yet everywhere. Since this search for FORM ends there, the Usonian City, Broadacres, will be the sixth book of 'An Autobiography.' The natural Conclusion" (p. 560). Thus, Wright decided to end this enlarged version of the narrative as he had the earlier one, with speculative prophecy rather than retrospective autobiography.

As its interpreters have been quick to point out, Broadacres City is not a city at all. Rather, it is a section of a national scheme that attempts to resolve the urban-rural polarity with a mix of residential, industrial, agricultural, and service areas in a uniformly populated county. It is not relevant to discuss the plan in detail here, but it is worthwhile to point out that it belongs not in the tradition of Franklin's projects for urban improvement, but in the tradition of the cooperative communities which proliferated in the United States beginning in the mid-nineteenth century. As its name suggests, it was a bit of a conundrum—a paradoxical resolution of some of the polarities of American civilization that had concerned Wright. He was vague about the nature of its economic and political systems, and he failed to specify how the scheme could be realized. But it was not really intended to be practicable; Wright was not interested in the specific economic and social arrangements but in the values and the pattern of life they encouraged.[21] Historically, the plan represents a conservative ideal, for it perpetuates many of the qualities of the rural America he and Sullivan had known as youths. Mythically, it represents a kind of timeless ideal beyond history and yet worth striving for, a combination of two Christian images of Paradise—heaven as a garden and heaven as a strong city.[22]

As a conclusion for the autobiography, it is appropriate in several respects. First, it is self-revelatory. Its comprehensiveness and its prophetic nature reveal Wright's desire to design a total society rather than unrelated buildings. Also, its installation of the architect as the highest authority exposes his personal and professional self-esteem. But it is also a statement about the possibilities of the self in general; it is a scheme designed to ensure that the individual would remain in wholesome contact with his essential powers and in control of his destiny. In Norris Kelly Smith's words, it is "an assertion . . . about Wright's own self and, in general, about a kind of sacred and central selfhood which he believed is being obliterated in the present-day world."[23] Finally, it is a statement about responsibility and self-reliance; like Thoreau, Wright communicates the individual's responsibility to account for himself by the exemplary act of creating his own ideal world.

TEN

Gertrude Stein

The Making of a Prophet

Like Benjamin Franklin, Gertrude
Stein is an exceptional figure who tests the concept of prophetic
autobiography. Certainly *The Autobiography of Alice B. Toklas*
would seem to have no place in the tradition we have traced, for
it was not apparently written from a prophetic impulse. Indeed,
Gertrude Stein's attitude toward America and toward history
would seem to preclude her writing prophetic autobiography. As
an expatriate, she seems primarily concerned with a group of avant-
garde artists of many nationalities, rather than with the American
community. As an autobiographer, she displays little sense of history as crisis; she acknowledges it when it intrudes upon her creative circle in the form of a world war, but she does not invoke it
as the context for, or an analogue of, her own experience. She
casts her experience in an aesthetic, not a mythic framework; instead of attempting to replace the myths the twentieth century
had rendered obsolete, she seeks to develop new techniques for
expressing consciousness itself. Thus, *The Autobiography* seems
merely an idiosyncratic version of the memoir or reminiscence; it
is best known for its gossipy anecdotes and witticisms. Like Franklin's *Autobiography*, it seems too playful to be prophetic, and it
too is vulnerable to the charge that it is merely a form of self-ad-

vertisement—a devious way of popularizing herself and her contributions to modern literature.

Still, writing autobiography was for Gertrude Stein a complex act, involving conflicting motives. All of her autobiographical work is concerned with the relation of the genius to society, and although she did not identify the genius with the prophet as readily as did her contemporary, Frank Lloyd Wright, she moved perceptibly closer to a prophetic role in her successive autobiographies. Although *The Autobiography* lacks a truly prophetic impulse, she makes prophetic gestures in it; in fact, she poses as a prophet of modern art—a genius who makes life in the twentieth century possible by creating new forms of expression for modern consciousness. The impulse to be prophetic, lacking or latent in this book, becomes more obvious and authentic in the sequels to it. Although the title, *Everybody's Autobiography* (1937), is not altogether justified by her achievement, it nicely epitomizes her desire to write collective or inclusive autobiography in the prophetic mode. Finally, in *Wars I Have Seen* (1945), special circumstances—the pressure of threatening historical forces—enabled and encouraged her to assume a fairly traditional stance as a prophet.

In assessing the prophetic features of Stein's autobiographies, Whitman's example provides a good foil for her theory and practice, for the two writers shared certain personal concerns and aesthetic beliefs. For both, creative activity was impelled by the unavoidable fact of death and the eroding effect of time. Both saw the isolated self or the externally defined identity as an obstacle to the act of creation and hence to full self-realization. In their theories of creativity, self-transcendence was crucial. Both sought in literature to transcend the self in two ways: to escape the narrow viewpoint of the individual self and to rise above its vulnerability to time.

However, an essential difference between them on the issue of transcendence helps account for the differences between their autobiographies. For Whitman, self-transcendence depended on his belief in the existence of a supernatural reality and in human immortality; it was a mystical experience, but one he considered to be available to all men. For Stein, art was the sole medium for such an experience, and in practice it was available only to a few geniuses like her; furthermore, even the artist rose above time only temporarily in the creative act. For Whitman, art was a medium for achieving communion with those not in his physical presence, but it was meant to simulate a union that was more literal than literary; Whitman identified himself, body and soul, with his poetry. For Stein, the primary goal of creation was insight or expression rather than communication; the created object was to evoke an imaginative response linking the audience to the artist, but the act of creation depended on total detachment from the needs and expectations of the audience.[1] Thus, Stein's gestures toward transcendence and prophecy were restrained and circumscribed; her temperament and philosophy prevented her from fully assuming a Whitmanic role as seer, namer, and prophet.

Still, Gertrude Stein's autobiographical writing has strong similarities to Whitman's. Like his, it was innovative and experimental in form because, like him, she used autobiography as a way of getting outside the self. For both writers, autobiography—conventionally the history of an individual's growth in time—tended to be written in the present tense and to become collective, or inclusive of others' experience. And both writers portray themselves not merely as creative artists but as prophets. If Whitman was the prophet of a new religion, enjoying a mystical union with the Creation, Stein was a prophet presiding over the creation of twentieth-century art and literature. If Whitman offered everybody a new vision and through it a new life, Stein showed herself influencing the vision of her contemporaries and initiating Alice Toklas into a "new full life." If Whitman offered to become everybody's autobiographer, Stein actually did become Alice Toklas's. Of course, whereas Whitman shaped his experience to make it universally available, Gertrude Stein presumed to write the autobiography of one whose life she had already profoundly changed.

The Autobiography, then, was not simply self-advertisement. In part, it grew out of Stein's experimentation with literary portraiture and her exploration of consciousness, which she considered to be the ultimate reality. It also served private needs; she sought to regenerate herself after a decline in creative energy by exploring her past without becoming mired in it.[2] In her first attempt at autobiography she did not completely solve the problem of escaping time and memory, of writing autobiography in the complete actual present, but she did manage to subvert any conventional sense of chronology. Most of the book is chronologically arranged, but narrative sequence is interrupted by non sequiturs, digressions, and associational leaps. The content of the narrative is inescapably memories of the past, yet the reader is exposed not to a chronological sequence of static memories but to the ongoing process of reminiscing. The constant revision and digression, the conversational tone, and the anecdotal style treat the reader as a physical presence, or create the narrator in the present. Thus, the narrative represents Stein's present consciousness of her past, rather than a record of it. But her achievement is different from Whitman's. While her book seems to be written in a continuous present, Whitman's autobiographical writing seemed to represent life *lived* in the eternal now.

Stein's attempt to rise above individual identity is perhaps more successful than her rebellion against the tyranny of time. Underlying, and perhaps justifying, the flow of her anecdotes is the portrayal of the development of modern art as a cooperative enterprise—a process in which egos compete and conflict but finally, perhaps unconsciously, collaborate. Gertrude Stein not only documents but exemplifies this collaboration among artists and writers. She portrays herself not only as a creative writer but as one capable of releasing the creative energy in others: "She understands very well the basis of creation and therefore her advice and criticism is invaluable to all her friends."[3] Furthermore, Stein's concern with the nature of artistic influence, the mingling of creative minds, leads her at times to blur the distinctions between individual artists.

The best example of this is the story of Picasso's portrait of Gertrude Stein. According to Stein, Picasso was unable to finish her portrait satisfactorily even after many long sittings, because her unconventional essence eluded capture by existing techniques. Eventually, having acquired a twentieth-century technique appropriate to his subject, Picasso completed the portrait without even looking at Stein. Stein, then, forced Picasso to a new style; her role in the creation of the portrait was an active one. The reciprocity of the process is such that even as Picasso completes Gertrude

Stein on canvas, he is completed by her as a cubist. Furthermore, as she is being made into twentieth-century art, she is busy creating twentieth-century literature in her head. Picasso and Gertrude Stein, subject and object, art and literature, art and life, are seen to be involved in a web of mutual influence.[4]

Later disagreements between Picasso and Stein illustrate how difficult it was to sustain such a creative symbiosis, how tenuous self-transcendence was even for a pair of geniuses. Thus, although this relationship may be exemplary, it does not broaden the autobiography very much. Nor does Stein's inclusion of a multitude of other artists make *The Autobiography* a communal narrative in the prophetic mode. For one thing, Stein's contacts with these artists lack the intensity of Whitman's receptive and uncritical identification with his "specimens." For another, Stein locates herself at the center of the artistic ferment: "It was an endless variety. And everybody came and no one made any difference. Gertrude Stein sat peacefully in a chair and those who could did the same, the rest stood" (pp. 123–24). The book's portrayal of Gertrude Stein as the high priestess of a shrine at which others are converted to modern art seems less prophetic than self-serving.[5]

Traditionally, as we have seen, the prophetic autobiographer associates his experience in some way with that of his audience. Protective of her vulnerable sense of identity and wary of the public, Gertrude Stein made a more limited gesture; she made her autobiography that of an intimate friend who becomes a surrogate for the audience she desired. Although Stein refers to it in the last sentences of the book as a simple, even casual decision, her assumption of the task of writing Alice Toklas's autobiography was a complex act, highly presumptuous and charged with risk. The form of the narrative has aggressive implications, in its usurpation of another's prerogative, and potential for condescension, in its implication that Gertrude Stein, having given significance to Alice Toklas's life, is better equipped to write her autobiography. But Stein successfully avoids these pitfalls. The form itself suggests the intimacy of the relationship and even hints confessionally at its emotional and sexual dimensions. Stein's use of Alice Toklas's viewpoint does not lead to caricature or condescension; rather, Stein's compassionate portrayal of Alice Toklas, her faithful approximation of her style in the narrative, and the frequent use of the first-person plural pronoun combine to emphasize the interdependence of the two women and the mingling of their consciousnesses.

Alice Toklas is seen not only as the intimate friend but also as the ideal reader and virtual collaborator. Thus, while the emotional aspect of the relationship is only suggested, the intimacy achieved through art is acknowledged. As Stein's companion, proofreader, and typist, Alice Toklas comes to have a special relationship to her work: "You cannot tell what a book is until you type or proofread it. It then does something to you that only reading can never do" (p. 113). As proofreader, editor, and finally publisher, Alice Toklas facilitates, and even participates in, the creative process. The mutuality of the relationship is developed in the latter half of the autobiography, for even as Gertrude Stein presents Alice Toklas to the world by writing her autobiography, Alice Toklas is seen to be presenting Gertrude Stein to the world by publishing her books.

In the end, the book's unique form expresses the intimacy between the two women and suggests Stein's transcendence of her individual ego through a virtual merging of identities with Alice Toklas. One has the sense that writing Alice Toklas's autobiography was finally neither a way of solving an aesthetic problem nor a devious way of writing her own autobiography; rather, the book's form and its creation reflect the loving relationship that existed in reality. Ultimately, then, the creation of the book was not an act of aggression but a gesture of love and tenderness, a recognition and reenactment of the life the two women shared.

While the book is more than mere self-advertisement, it is less than fully prophetic. Certainly it offers no prophetic interpretation of communal experience to the reader. Yet its rather single-minded concentration on art reflects values Stein wishes to urge on her audience, perhaps especially on the American public which had neglected her. More important than Stein's relationship with Picasso, her relationship with Alice Toklas stands as an example of an ideal, mutually fulfilling relationship between writer and reader, artist and audience. Finally, although Gertrude Stein offers no prophetic vision in *The Autobiography*, she does, like a prophetic autobiographer, demand an adjustment of vision in the reader. For just as she draws Alice Toklas to her through the medium of art—the confusing vernissage of the independents and the unsettling paintings in her atelier—Stein plunges her readers into a narrative whose structural principles and techniques are unfamiliar. Like Alice Toklas and like Picasso, the reader must discard conventional perspectives if he is to perceive Gertrude Stein properly; in doing so, he adapts his vision, all unconsciously, to the conditions of modern life. In this way, Gertrude Stein tricks the reader into entering the century she and her fellow artists were already inhabiting.

Ironically, the popular success of *The Autobiography* posed a threat to Stein's sense of identity. Her sense that she had, to some extent, compromised her artistic principles in writing the book depressed her. And she felt that having exposed herself, however obliquely, to the public, she had sacrificed a sense of privacy and freedom that was essential to her creative life: "The minute you or anybody else knows what you are you are not it, you are what you or anybody else knows you are. . . ."[6] One of her responses to this predicament was to retreat into private meditations. However, the popularity of the book also resulted in her triumphal tour of America in 1934–35. Following that, she wrote *Everybody's Autobiography*, a sequel to *The Autobiography* which dealt with its aftermath and the American trip. In addition to turning to meditation, then, Gertrude Stein sought to confront and perhaps resolve the problems of the first autobiography by writing a sequel.

Unsatisfied with her earlier response to the tyranny of the past, she determined to master the problem this time. Her innovation here was to supplement the conversational voice of the reminiscing narrator with the more immediate interior monologue of the remembering and meditating mind. The structure of the book is roughly chronological, and the content of the interior monologue is usually memory, but the narrator takes even greater liberty with chronology in her digressions than she had in *The Autobiography*. Speaking in her own person, Stein indulges in a more personal and idiosyncratic "narrative"; her mind ranges forward and backward in time with even greater mobility. Her new attempt at writing autobiography in the present tense was, as Richard Bridgman has suggested, her attempt "to proclaim the adequacy of the present moment,"[7] in spite of the emptiness of the universe. But it is ultimately less satisfying than the earlier book because it lacks the concrete conversational presence of the narrator; in her place we have a disembodied remembering mind.

The title of the book is in part ironic, for this is the autobiography of Gertrude Stein after she allowed herself to become everybody's (and thus lost possession of herself) by writing *The Autobiography*. But it also suggests a Whitmanic conception of autobiography and reflects her attempt to resolve her dilemma by meeting her audience face to face in America. The early chapters, which dwell on her predicament after the first autobiography, are the least focused; they range associationally into her past in a confessional manner, as though the inclusion of material left out of the earlier book could somehow reinforce her sense of herself. Only the long fourth chapter, "America," justifies the book's title, for her trip to America was both a delightful return to her native land and a test of her ability to be herself despite public exposure —to rediscover herself in America and to rediscover America in herself.

Gertrude Stein gives *Everybody's Autobiography* an American theme by identifying publicity, or the lack of privacy, as part of the democratic way of life. Noticing that shutters on American houses were always open, she remarks, ". . . well as everybody is a public something and anybody can know anything about any one and can know any one then why shut the shutters and the curtains and keep any one from seeing, they all know what they are going to see so why look" (p. 183). Thus, in America, she finds her experience characterized by association with "everybody": "Everybody speaking to you everybody knowing you, everybody in a hotel or restaurant noticing you everybody asking you to write your name for them . . . " (p. 178). Confronting this in person, Stein learned to enjoy her public recognition as a fact of her life as an American rather than a violation of her privacy as a writer.

The American section of the autobiography finds her making prophetic gestures—including strangers in her autobiography and assuming, to some extent, a prophet's role in visiting her native

land. Her delight in the commonplace as she traversed America
is especially reminiscent of Whitman, and the similarity did not
go unnoticed. Her friend Bernard Faÿ wrote encouragingly: "I
feel that what is going on now in America, what this trip of yours
is doing is tremendously important in the mental life of America.
What you bring them, nobody had brought them since Walt Whitman . . . and they know it."[8] In Whitmanic fashion, she sketches
"specimen" characters such as Chicago policemen, South Side
Negroes, marathon dancers, mechanics, railroad conductors, jour-
nalists, and people who greeted her on the streets. And like Whitman, she finds confirmation of her art in the boundless landscape,
especially as seen from a plane: "It made it right that I had always
been with cubism and everything that followed after" (p. 192). In
the flush of her popularity, her thought sometimes follows Whitmanic channels. Thus, she defines her genius in relation to the
development of her nation and its need for a spokesman: "After
all a genius has to be made in a country which is forming itself to
be what it is not yet" (p. 92). Perhaps most reminiscent of Whitman is her pleasure in the opportunity to strike up a dialogue with
America en masse.

But there remains an element of self-protective individualism
which prevents Stein from fully assuming a prophetic role. She
lacks Whitman's egalitarian urge to merge with others, and sometimes retreats to a Wrightian elitism: "I used to say that I would
not go to America until I was a real lion, a real celebrity at that
time of course I did not really think I was going to be one. But
now we were coming and I was going to be one. In America
everybody is but some are more than others. I was more than
others" (p. 168). Similarly, she persists in being more interested
in the individual than in social groups and in art than in history.
Thus, she criticizes Robert Maynard Hutchins's and Mortimer
Adler's concept of the great ideas because of its bias toward politics: "Government is the least interesting thing in human life,
creation and the expression of that creation is a damn sight more
interesting . . . the real ideas are not the relation of human beings
as groups but a human being to himself inside him and that is an
idea that is more interesting than humanity in groups" (p. 206).

In a revealing sentence, Gertrude Stein explained the nature of the collectiveness of her second autobiography: "If this Every-body's Autobiography is to be the autobiography of everyone it is not to be of any connection between anyone and anyone because now there is none" (p. 99). Here Stein was articulating her belief that since the modern world is completely covered with people, the old tribal or national bonds are no longer valid. But this state-ment also serves to distinguish the sequel from the first autobiog-raphy. *The Autobiography* had become collective and expressed the possibilities of self-transcendence through its recognition of the strong bonds between Gertrude Stein and Alice Toklas, and the weaker, but still creative, bonds between Stein and her artistic friends. *Everybody's Autobiography* may be more democratic in its inclusion of the common man, but the intensity of the earlier contact between Gertrude Stein and others is lacking. Although she makes prophetic gestures, she again offers no prophetic vision or message; rather, she simply revels in her apparently egalitarian interaction with her audience, offering at best a prophetic pres-ence. Too often, her collection of specimens seems motivated by superficial curiosity: "I like to know the name and occupation and what their father did or does and where they were born about anyone" (pp. 203-4). Thus, the narrative is everybody's autobi-ography only in a nominal way. Lacking a religious basis, her egalitarianism was qualified and did not imply the possibility of self-transcendence through actual human contact. In broadening her autobiography, Stein was perhaps attempting to transcend the bounds in which she usually defined herself and in which her gen-ius operated, but, in doing so, she entered an area where self-trans-cendence was not available to her.

It was only in her last attempt at autobiography, *Wars I Have Seen*, that Gertrude Stein's circumstances enabled her to function as a prophetic autobiographer in the traditional sense. Her relative security during World War I had allowed her to portray that con-flict as a temporary disruption of the normal creative life of her Paris circle. Her precarious circumstances during World War II led her to treat it very differently. Against the advice of friends and French officials, Gertrude Stein and Alice Toklas decided to re-main in the French countryside rather than flee to Switzerland or some other refuge. As Americans and Jews, they took a consid-

erable risk; on more than one occasion German troops spent the
night in their house. Begun as a journal in 1943, *Wars I Have Seen*
is a record of the last fifteen months of this uncertain existence.
The divisions among the separate entries are not indicated in the
published text, so the effect is of one uninterrupted monologue
which incorporates consecutive events into an ongoing present.
Thus, it displays much of the immediacy and spontaneity of *Specimen Days*, especially the Civil War section. In addition, as a narrative of occupation, its structure resembles that of the captivity and
slave narratives.

The book begins as a kind of autobiographical meditation on
war. In the early chapters Stein alludes to other wars she had seen
and the way they had affected her earlier life. In doing so, she employs a common strategy of the prophetic autobiographer: she attempts to find analogies between her own experience and historical
events. Although her childhood passed without any major wars,
she notes that inner or psychological wars and wars she read about
gave her some vicarious experience of violence. The relevance of
war to her adolescence was also more psychological than historical;
she finds the anxiety and fear of dissolution she experienced as an
adolescent to be typical of the communal experience in wartime.
This section of the book is loosely organized, repetitive, and ruminative—less a chronological narrative than an introspective and
retrospective meditation. For the most part, she fails to find significant links between her personal experience and historical conflicts.

However, as she moves on to ponder the meaning of World
War II—the most threatening war she had seen—she found its
redeeming feature to be that it finally "killed" the nineteenth
century by utterly discrediting its belief in progress, peace, and
harmony. The war, then, was to permit the development of a truly
modern consciousness and enable men to live fully in the present.
An important feature of this interpretation of the war was that it
enabled Stein to find an objective validation of her career in a
historical event. Thus, her situation parallels that of Whitman, who
was able to realize his imagined self and confirm his role as the
prophet of union in his response to the Civil War. The following
passage marks Gertrude Stein's discovery of the personal relevance

of the war: "And now, except Germany there is really nothing left of the nineteenth century and when that will be exterminated then the nineteenth century is over and the twentieth century has come to stay. I belong to the generation who born in the nineteenth century spent all of the early part in escaping from it, and the rest of it in being the twentieth century yes of course."[9]

This realization allows her henceforth to focus on the progress of the war, which becomes a struggle for liberation on many levels. Most obviously, there is the liberation of the French from the prison that their occupied nation had become. Gertrude Stein often expresses the communal wish to be free, and many of her observations concern the details of the daily adjustment to occupation. But liberation has special personal significance as well. The narrative records the liberalization of the narrator, whose growing admiration for the maquis causes her to change her previously conservative political views. More important, the arrival of the American troops finally liberates her not only from the danger of discovery by the Germans but from an isolation from her appreciative American public.

The prophetic qualities of the book result from a central tension between her dual loyalties during the war, for Stein had obligations and strong ties both to the citizens of occupied France and to her native land. Her security among the Germans depended on the community's silent conspiracy to protect her anonymity, and her liberation depended on the American troops. The necessary sacrifice of her visibility and the suppression of her individuality enabled her to assume a prophetic stance toward the local community. In person, she shared their plight sympathetically and reassured them of their eventual liberation by her compatriots; in her diary, she became their spokesman and historian. In person, she spoke to the local community for the not-yet-present liberation forces; in her diary she spoke for the community to a not-yet-available American audience.

For her fate as a prophet, the crucial fact of her predicament was that the communal crisis broke down conventional barriers and involved her intensely for the first time with a small, permanent community of common people. She describes how the situation allowed this narrative to become collective autobiography in a way that *Everybody's Autobiography* had not: "Everything is dangerous and everybody casually meeting anybody talks to any-body and everybody tells everybody the history of their lives, they are always telling me and I am always telling them and so is every-body, that is the way it is when everything is dangerous" (p. 121).

Although the book is prophetic in more profound ways, one of its persistent concerns is with prophecy as prediction. Natural-ly, the community is obsessed with the war's effect on their des-tiny and, as the Allies grow stronger, with the timetable of the invasion. Stein found her most reliable guide to the future in the prophecies of Saint Odile, a fifteenth-century saint whose general-ized predictions concerning "the worst war of all," when properly interpreted, seemed to fit World War II history with uncanny ac-curacy. The numerous references to and restatements of these optimistic predictions make them a kind of leitmotif of the book. Although she never offers any prediction of her own, Gertrude Stein does assert that this prophetic faculty is universal and varies only in degree: "And it is true we can all prophesy to a certain extent depending upon our knowledge of people and things, some can prophesy from day to day, some the life time of some one, and Saint Odile for five hundred years that's all. Believe it or not it is very simple, it is the same thing only a little longer" (p. 68).

Gertrude Stein's functions as a local prophet go deeper than prediction. She becomes a kind of communal historian, recording incidents involving local people or the conversations through which she learns to penetrate the communal mind and to appreci-ate its folk wisdom. The narrative becomes everybody's autobiog-raphy in an almost literal sense, for an extraordinary number of. sentences have the word "everybody" as their subject. In *Every-body's Autobiography*, "everybody" was really a kind of imper-sonal medium, a collection of strangers, into which Stein ventured in an experiment in self-definition. Here, "everybody" is truly a collective entity consisting of a community linked by bonds made stronger by crisis. Of all her autobiographical books, this is the first in which her interpretation of events has a communal focus, for in addition to her own idiosyncratic responses, she respectfully includes the opinions of others and faithfully captures the com-munity's mood. Furthermore, this is the only book that depends on her exemplary response to a communal crisis. Here, her presence itself is risky, and she endeavors, even as she masters her own fear, to reassure others in her motherly way.

This aspect of her role is complicated by the fact that her prophetic stature depends on her being *in* the community but not entirely *of* it. Thus, while she records the collective mood of "everybody" in her diary, in daily life she sometimes speaks as a representative American in defense of the American conduct of the invasion: "I get impatient and I say you French you have such old fashioned ideas of war, you just think about land fighting and taking places but we Americans we believe in destroying the production of the enemy. . . . I tell what I always told them that Americans like a long preparation and then when they are really ready then something does happen" (p. 159). As the Allied invasion proceeds and American troops approach her region, a perceptible transfer of allegiance occurs in the narrative. More than previously, she reports division in the French community between those who support the maquis and the reactionaries who are outraged by its seizure of power. Simultaneously, in preparation for the arrival of the American troops, which carried special significance for her, she advises the French on how to welcome them and weeds her terrace "so when the American army gets here it can sit comfortably on it" (p. 203).

Gertrude Stein acknowledged the division of her loyalties as an expatriate and patriot, particularly in wartime: "I have lived in France the best and the longest part of my life and I love France and the French but after all I am an American . . . one's native land is one's native land you cannot get away from it" (p. 132). Here her anticipation is related to that expressed in the early chapters of *Everybody's Autobiography* where she found that as the time of the trip approached, America "was certainly just now coming nearer that is to say it was getting more actual as a place where one might be" (p. 111). Now, however, she found America coming to her, and its arrival on a "day of days" was a joyful event: "In the last war we had come across our first American soldiers and it had been nice but nothing like this, after almost two years of not a word with America, there they were. . . . How we talked last night, they just brought all America to us every bit of it" (pp. 245–46). Aware that the arrival of the American troops meant an opportunity for her book to reach its intended audience, she had Alice Toklas begin to type the manuscript, previously kept in Gertrude Stein's illegible handwriting for security reasons.

The arrival of the American troops also promised to emancipate Gertrude Stein from a condition of enforced anonymity. Hence, she aggressively sought out the first soldiers to arrive and, in announcing herself, resumed her identity as the American writer and celebrity. However, her emergence from anonymity did not end her role as a prophet; rather her deliverance allowed her to express herself as a prophet in new ways. First, it made possible the publication of the book that recorded her achievement of prophetic stature within the French community. Second, it allowed her to function as a spokesman for her native land in a new prophetic way. Thus, the narrative ends with her being asked "to go with them to Voiron to broadcast with them to America on Sunday" (p. 246).

The "Epilogue" concludes with the substance of her radio message, which is an idiosyncratic yet inspirational interpretation of what it means to be an American. Here she reiterates her idea that America is "the oldest country in the world" because it was the first to enter the twentieth century, the era of cheap mass production. But she goes on to argue that one of the most significant American achievements since the last war has been to make their borrowed language their own: "Yes in that sense the Americans have changed, I think of the Americans of the last war, they had their language but they were not yet in possession of it, and the children of the depression as that generation called itself was beginning to possess its language but it was struggling but now the job is done, the G.I. Joes have this language that is theirs, they do not have to worry about it, they dominate their language and in dominating their language which is now all theirs they have ceased to be adolescents and have become men" (p. 259).

According to Stein, then, the war completed a process of cultural maturation: the liberation and possession of its language by the American people. It is an odd index by which to measure the war's significance, but it is one appropriate to the theme of liberation. More important, the creation of a truly American language is an achievement to which Gertrude Stein could feel she had contributed, for she had exported that language to France, experimented with it in private, shared it in conversation with American soldiers, and presented her native land with a purer, more American version of it in her writing.

In a sense, Gertrude Stein's autobiographies record the making of a prophet. *The Autobiography* portrayed her as a prophet of modern art and recorded self-transcendence achieved through a special intimate relationship. *Everybody's Autobiography* dealt with her ambivalent relationship as a celebrity with the public and recorded the prophetic gestures she made toward them. Finally, *Wars I Have Seen* revealed a kind of prophecy and self-transcendence that depended not on her creative powers or her celebrity status but on her human sensitivity and her involvement in a community in crisis. But even with this book, she had not finished exploring the significance of the war, nor had she completely expressed her prophetic message. Its epilogue had begun: "Write about us they all said a little sadly, and write about them I will" (p. 249). The promise was fulfilled only in her last book, *Brewsie and Willie* (1946), which Richard Bridgman has described as a record of "the new Americans talking about the faults they see in the world they have inherited, and how to improve it."[10] In this book, Stein tried to express, in their own language, the G.I.s' concerns about postwar America. This in itself reflects a prophetic impulse, but in its epilogue Stein spoke prophetically in her own voice: "I am sure that this particular moment in our history is more important than anything else since the Civil War. We are there where we have to fight a spiritual pioneer fight or we will go poor as England and other industrial countries have gone poor, and dont think that communism or socialism will save you, you just have to find a new way, you have to find out how you can go ahead without running away with yourselves, you have to learn to produce without exhausting your country's wealth, you have to learn to be individual and not just mass job workers. . . . find out the reason why of the depression, find it out each and every one of you and then look facts in the face. We are Americans."[11] Having emerged as an American prophet from her successive attempts at autobiography, Gertrude Stein was evidently reluctant to relinquish the role.

ELEVEN

Three Contemporaries

Malcolm X, Norman Mailer, and Robert Pirsig

To establish the place of *The Autobiography of Malcolm X* in the tradition traced in the preceding chapters, one might suggest the following series of parallels. Like Thomas Shepard, Malcolm X created a narrative whose first half shows him as part of a persecuted minority and whose second half portrays him as a member of a religious and political community which offered him a new life and virtually a new identity. Like Increase Mather, he functioned as the spokesman of a colonized people and struggled, sometimes unsuccessfully, to avoid the egocentric temptations of the prophet's role. Like all the Puritan autobiographers, he considered conversion to be a crucial event in his life, viewed history as teleological, and wrote out of a strong concern for the special destiny of a tribe of the chosen. Like Woolman, he recorded his travels in the service of his ministry, which was concerned at once with the consolidation of a religious community and the raising of its consciousness. Like Franklin, he wrote a kind of success story which was an autobiographical analogue of the liberation of a colonized people. Like Douglass, he denounced psychological and spiritual as well as legal slavery and devoted much of his life to abolishing American racism. Like Thoreau, he was imprisoned in Concord, and he declared his personal

independence from a corrupt nation. Like Whitman, he recorded
a conversion experience which involved a new sense of the brotherhood of man. Like Adams, he narrated his progression through
various ready-made world views until, in the context of overwhelming rapid change near the end of his life, he attempted to create
his own philosophical synthesis. Like Louis Sullivan, he wrote his
autobiography, in part, as the history of the development of a liberating vision, and, like Frank Lloyd Wright, he included the details of his frustrated attempts to enact that vision. In summary,
like all of them, he functioned—in writing autobiography—as a representative, interpreter, and shaper of the history of his community.

It was probably inevitable that Malcolm X's autobiography
would display the characteristics of the prophetic mode, for, as
his biographer has pointed out, Malcolm's essential role was not
that of an original thinker or even a strategist but that of a "revolutionary of the spirit"—a prophet.[1] His awareness of his prophetic
role in life is obvious in the narrative, and evidence in his collaborator's epilogue suggests that he was aware that tact and delicacy
were required for the successful treatment of that role in autobiography.[2] He strove to resist the temptation to attribute too much
importance to himself and to write an exemplary and didactic narrative in which his own experience of family instability, poverty,
unemployment, and discrimination would stand for the plight of
all American blacks.

Ironically, however, the power and the complexity of the narrative result from the frustration of Malcolm's original intentions.
This irony and the evolving form of the autobiography are best
understood in the context of his predicament as an autobiographer. When the book was begun in 1963, Malcolm was still a member
and faithful minister of the Nation of Islam; the original dedication was to Elijah Muhammad, and the proceeds were to go to the
Black Muslims.[3] Malcolm saw himself more as a prophet or propagandist than as an autobiographer. Instead of exploring the inconsistencies in the Black Muslim ideology, Malcolm wished simply to
convey its powerful message. The autobiography was conceived,
then, wholly within an orthodox framework. Just as he frequently
prefaced remarks in his speeches with a conventional formula at-
tributing his ideas to "the Honorable Elijah Muhammad," Malcolm

chose, as an autobiographer, to ascribe the coherence and significance of his life to Elijah or Allah. His conception of his role as a
passive agent of God encouraged him to cast his autobiography
in the form of a spiritual autobiography with the emphasis on
his conversion and his ministry. Thus, his collaborator, Alex
Haley, reported that in the early stages his notebook "contained
nothing but Black Muslim philosophy, praise of Mr. Muhammad,
and the 'evils' of 'the white devil.' He would bristle when I tried
to urge him that the proposed book was *his* life."[4] At this point,
Malcolm seems to have been reluctant to consider his personal
identity as separate or separable from the corporate identity provided by the Nation. Had this conception of his identity and role
been realized, the autobiography would have been a one-dimen-
sional polemic. Paradoxically, as events frustrated Malcolm's
original prophetic impulse, the book became not only a multidi-
mensional self-portrait but more compelling prophecy.

Two significant developments complicated the process of writing and thus enriched the book. First, Haley, impatient with Malcolm's singlemindedness, probed his almost compulsive misogyny
until he touched its source—Malcolm's pity and anger toward his
mother, who had broken down under the strain of managing her
family alone. This breakthrough released Malcolm into preconver-
sion life, not only his nightmarish childhood but also his career as
a ghetto hustler. In doing so, it freed him from the confining role
of the didactic autobiographer. While the retrospective interpretation of these years is that of the doctrinaire ideologue, the nostalgic treatment of some episodes belies this. For even as the sober
Black Muslim minister narrated his escape from a misguided
youth, the private Malcolm recaptured some of the sensations and
emotions of those years. Notably, he delighted in recalling the
music, re-creating the language, and reliving the uninhibited danc-
ing he enjoyed in his early days as a hustler. As spontaneous memory competed with detailed analysis, the pleasure in the retelling
conflicted with the didactic interpretation.[5] Thus, with Haley's
prompting, the self-styled prophet became a reminiscent autobiographer, and the autobiography was individualized and deepened.

A second complication stemmed from Malcolm's growing disenchantment with Elijah Muhammad and his sudden excommunica-

tion from the Nation. Although this development actually paralleled and reinforced the first, Haley did not welcome it, for it changed Malcolm's perspective on events already recorded and thus threatened to invalidate the form the narrative had taken. For Malcolm, of course, it did more than that; it threatened his sanity by depriving him of the source of his sense of identity. Ultimately, however, this unexpected dislocation, which complicated Malcolm's life and autobiography simultaneously, forced him out of conventional autobiographical forms and toward a new prophetic vision. The stature of the book, finally, derives from the fact that its composition coincided with a crisis that demanded a radical reexamination of his ideas and a redefinition of himself.

The finished narrative divides Malcolm's life into four fairly distinct periods: his childhood and adolescence (chapters 1 and 2), his hustler phase (chapters 3 to 10), his career as a Black Muslim (chapters 11 to 15), and his life after excommunication (chapters 16 to 19). The first section is characterized by a strong didacticism, which locates the origins of his later activities and uses his experience to expose American racism; for example, he describes his family's condition when they were wards of the state as "legal modern slavery" (p. 21). The second section combines nostalgic reminiscence and titillating confession with an initiation narrative (as Malcolm gives up his naive assimilationist ambitions and enters the underworld of the black community) and a parodic success story (as he gains status and power in his new environment). However, the framework that orders and controls the narrative, even in this evocative section, is that of the didactic conversion narrative. This becomes clear in the middle of the book—at its structural and thematic center—when Malcolm X, in prison, is converted to the Nation of Islam. His exposure to the Black Muslim myth of black supremacy came at an opportune moment when his mind was prepared for illumination and his soul for salvation. The new ideology explained and excused Malcolm Little's troubled life and provided him with a new sense of himself: "I still marvel at how swiftly my previous life's thinking pattern slid away from me, like snow off a roof. . . . I would be startled to catch myself thinking of my earlier self as another person" (p. 170). This conversion also gave a new impetus and a new focus to a self-education already begun in the

prison library. Investigating history in search of a communal past
and probing the dictionary in quest of a new voice and language
appropriate to a new vision, Malcolm unwittingly prepared himself
for his role as a Black Muslim minister and prophet. In fact, even
before his release from prison and his formal acceptance into the
faith, he began to proselytize among his fellow inmates.

Malcolm notes ironically that the most liberating experience of
his life thus far had occurred in prison. Yet he is less successful at
communicating the sense of this experience than he had been at
re-creating his previous life. The narrative of Malcolm's previous
life certainly makes his conversion credible, and there is no doubt
of its sincerity and significance. But the reader is given no sense
of the experience which suggests that it consisted of more than an
intellectual and emotional commitment to an ideology which offered him a redeeming self-image and a useful mythology. Nor
does Malcolm acknowledge at this point the possibility that his
experience of liberation had made him, in a sense, a prisoner of
a racist ideology. Instead of indicating the provisional nature
of his conversion, he lets it stand as a crucial, if imperfectly communicated experience.

Upon leaving prison in 1952, Malcolm immediately purchased
new glasses, a suitcase, and a watch—symbols of his new vision, his
new vocation, and his new time-consciousness. As part of his initiation into the Nation, he also acquired an "X" in place of his last
name—to signify both the things he was no more (a Christian, for
example) and the unknown quantity he now represented to the
white man.[6] Malcolm X then became a Black Muslim minister—a
faithful servant of and eventually the spokesman for Elijah Muhammad. Because of his responsible position and his positive and
stable self-image, this section lacks the exciting incidents and
rapid role changes of the previous section. Rather, it becomes a
mixture of clerical memoir and political testament as Malcolm
seeks to recount his achievements as a Muslim organizer and to
communicate the essence of Muslim ideology. This section, then,
records not personal growth but the growth of the Nation, not
self-education but the enlightenment of the black masses.

The narrative does recount another Franklinian rise to prominence and power—now within an administrative hierarchy rather than the fluid and treacherous society of the underworld. But Malcolm's didacticism, previously limited to the commentary upon events, now becomes the *content* of the narrative as he sets forth the prophetic myth of the Black Muslims. As a result, in this section the expositon of doctrine not only supplements but also displaces narrative. There is much precedent for this in Thoreau, Adams, Sullivan, and Wright, and the tendency derives naturally from a prophetic impulse. Yet this section, which most closely corresponds to Malcolm's original intentions, is the least compelling part of the book; the narrative's polemical extreme does not provide its climax.

Nor does this section deliver what it promises. Although Malcolm claims to have acquired a radically new vision of himself and of history, the narrative fails to demonstrate this. As Carol Ohmann has observed, he continued to be more interested in objectively measurable achievements than in subjective experience.[7] Just as his ideology, like a mirror image of white racism, reverses some elements while others remain the same, Malcolm remains interested in power over others, for different reasons. Similarly, his vision of society is still that of a jungle, although individual competition has been replaced by racial struggle. Thus, although his goals and his cosmology are new, his consciousness does not seem essentially different, and his prophetic vision, however revolutionary, is secondhand and somewhat simplistic. Furthermore, while Malcolm has clearly grown as a *man*, he seems to have retreated, as a *narrator*, from a complex, ambivalent viewpoint to a monocular, orthodox one.

The final chapter of this section, "Icarus," concludes with a pledge of loyalty to the movement that had rescued, defined, and ordained him: "I silently vowed to Allah that I would never forget that the wings I wore had been put on by the religion of Islam. That fact I have never forgotten . . . not for one second" (p. 287). Yet Malcolm found that his role as the dynamic organizer of new temples and as spokesman for the movement to the world inevitably drew attention to himself and away from the reclusive leader of the Nation. Inevitably, too, his mind became impatient with the orthodoxy, and engaged by the paradoxes, of Black Muslim ideology. Soon he was accused of personal ambition and insubordination—in effect, of forgetting that he was a humble servant of Elijah Muhammad.

More than a clash of personalities, the friction between Malcolm X and Muhammad was a manifestation of power politics within the Nation: Malcolm's aggressive efforts as an organizer and proselytizer threatened Muhammad's control of the movement even as they expanded his power base. But the friction also stemmed from Malcolm's growing tendency to distinguish between Allah and Elijah and to assert his right to interpret Allah's will for himself. To put it another way, he was beginning to resolve the inconsistencies in Black Muslim ideology in his own way.

Thus certain tensions, suppressed in the early part of the narrative, begin to surface: those between the Black Muslims' disciplined bourgeois morality and their revolutionary rhetoric; between their policy of nonengagement in politics or protest and their militant posture; between the claim that the Nation was a brotherhood and the fact of its strict hierarchical organization; between the religious and secular aspects of the movement; and finally, between the indictment of American racism and the adoption of a mythology of reverse racism.[8] Malcolm's personal tendency was to secularize the ideology and move toward a more activist stance than that endorsed by Muhammad. By degrees, he diverged from an almost Calvinistic dependence on God to deliver his people and began to assume a more Arminian position that held black people responsible for achieving their own liberation. (In this respect, his development recalls Franklin's secularization of Puritan and Quaker myths and Douglass's movement from a providential framework of interpretation to an acknowledgment of his own initiative in his "conversion.") Although he stopped short of recommending violence or revolution, he posed a threat both to the authority of Muhammad and to the vested interests of the Nation.

The chapter entitled "Out" records Malcolm's silencing and his excommunication from the church that had saved him. The narrative takes on yet another conventional form—that of the apologia —as Malcolm attempts to defend himself against the Nation's portrayal of him as a heretic and traitor. His brief against this accusation consists of the argument that he was more faithful to the Nation's true ideals than were its other established leaders, that if he erred it was only through an excess of zeal: "If I harbored any personal disappointment whatsoever, it was that privately I was convinced that our Nation of Islam could be an even greater force in the American black man's overall struggle—if we engaged in more *action*" (p. 289). Although this apologia is sincere, it is not entirely convincing, for the narrative has revealed in him an eagerness, a determination, a willfulness, and a degree of personal initiative that would threaten such an autocracy as that of the Nation. The reader can understand his ouster without sympathizing with it; it is easier to side with Malcolm than it is to accept his careful self-defense.

More important than the real reasons for his expulsion from the Nation was its effect on Malcolm's life. He confesses that it was a traumatic experience for him: "I felt as though something in *nature* had failed, like the sun or the stars" (p. 304). Deprived of all communal support from the institution that had offered him a new identity and provided his entire frame of reference for over a decade, Malcolm had to refashion his thought and his self-conception simultaneously: ". . . after twelve years of never thinking for as much as five minutes about myself, I became able finally to muster the nerve and the strength to start facing the facts, to think for myself" (p. 306). The expulsion did not negate his conversion: he could still cling to his faith in Allah. Yet it instantly deprived him of the institutional and ideological security of the Nation. Carrying on his work meant generating new organizations and new programs and revising his ideology even as he attempted to redefine himself. In effect, he had to re-create both the authority and the content of his prophecy.

The rest of the narrative is dominated by his attempt to reconcile the sometimes divergent secular and religious aspects of his thought. This tension is obvious in his need to create two institutions in order to further his goals. On the one hand, he founded the Muslim Mosque, Inc., which he hoped would attract some converts from the Nation of Islam and provide a broader religious base for economic, political, and social programs. On the other hand, the Organization of Afro-American Unity was to have its base in a more secular sense of international racial brotherhood. Both were intended to free him from the restrictions of Black Muslim orthodoxy on his thought and action. Yet the OAAU represents a new dimension in his thought, an international perspective on the race problem, while the Muslim Mosque reveals his desire to maintain some continuity with his past.

The establishment of the Muslim Mosque may also be seen as part of an attempt to maintain a claim to religious legitimacy, for his excommunication had threatened to deprive him of his prophetic stature. His new inquiry into orthodox Moslem religion and his eventual pilgrimage to Mecca also helped reestablish this sense of himself, but the new conversion he experienced on his pilgrimage further complicated his predicament. Among pilgrims of many races at Mecca, Malcolm X experienced a novel kind of color-blind tolerance and underwent at least a partial liberation from the Black Muslims' narrow race-consciousness to a more universal, more humanistic set of values: "Everything about the pilgrimage atmosphere accented the Oneness of Man under One God" (p. 330). In part, this conversion may be accounted for by the special treatment afforded him when he was recognized as a celebrity among the pilgrims and by the much-needed feeling of acceptance into a community; in part, by his consciousness that he needed to build a wider base of support in the United States. But at its core was a spontaneous awakening to a point of view that judged men not by their color but by their deeds.

This pilgrimage seems to have afforded him a rare but necessary moment of respite, tranquility, integration, and growth, and this conversion, more than his first one, was a truly liberating experience. Like John Woolman, he found that extending his geographical horizons extended his moral ones as well. Yet like his first conversion, this one is passed over rather quickly and superficially; we are told about rather than allowed to share in the change that occurred. Again, the spiritual or emotional dimension of his experience is sacrificed to the business of translating it into power. Once he is converted, as El-Hajj Malik El-Shabazz, he devotes himself to working out the ramifications of this potent new ideology for the resolution of racial problems. His "American-style thinking" is concerned with the application of public relations methods to the promotion of his new faith. Thus, although his pilgrimage did provide him with a momentary release from the opportunistic ethos which had dominated his experience, his new spiritual energy was soon diverted into secular channels,[9] as though the sources of his new consciousness were not as worthy of attention as were programs designed to give it political expression.

Whatever tranquility and new assurance Malcolm experienced while on his pilgrimage and during his triumphal tour of Africa was challenged immediately upon his return to America, where he was beset by the everyday pressures of the life of a protest leader. The last chapter of the book portrays a prophet overwhelmed by the need to develop new organizations and tactics while still trying to assimilate his new vision. During this period of his life, the paradoxes of his predicament tended to become irresolvable contradictions. Even as he sought to establish his personal authority, he recognized that his new movement should have a more democratic organization than the Nation of Islam. In addition, his new sense of human brotherhood tended to evaporate amidst rumors that his life was in danger. Yet his fundamental problem was one of translating a less racist ideology into programs that would more effectively combat white racism, for his sense of the ideal unity of man did not alter his knowledge of the actual oppression of American blacks. In order to achieve broad-based support, he needed media coverage, but the media had stereotyped him as a militant racist and were not equipped to register his more subtle new ideology.[10]

Malcolm's predicament as an autobiographer was also difficult, for his excommunication had invalidated the viewpoint that had governed most of the narrative. Nor did his second conversion yield a simple formula according to which the narrative could be continued or revised. Alex Haley discouraged Malcolm from revising the autobiography to make it an anti-Muhammad polemic in response to his own ouster; such a revision would sacrifice suspense and drama, he argued.[11] After some hesitation, Malcolm accepted this viewpoint, arguing that a revision would, in a way, falsify his experience of his career as a Black Muslim; but he did insert material that criticized Muhammad and telegraphed the split. Deprived of his didactic narrative formula, Malcolm came to see the impossibility of writing an autobiography that would be a true equivalent of continual growth; events steadily outran the viewpoints they generated. He expressed his frustration in a note to Haley: "How is it possible to write one's autobiography in a world so fast-changing as this?"[12]

Like *The Education of Henry Adams, The Autobiography of Malcolm X* is weighted in favor of the later years; the chapter "Out" comes about three-quarters of the way through, so that nearly a quarter of the book is dedicated to the last years of his life. Thus, in spite of the impossibility of his task, Malcolm continued, and he succeeded in conveying a sense of the desperation and hope of his final year. Increasingly, he sensed that his time was limited, but he did not abandon the autobiography to save languishing projects. Rather, as the threats against him escalated, he devoted more of his energy and dwindling time to his book, which he hoped would carry on his prophetic mission. One strong motive for continuing was to ensure that the book would include his second conversion and thus prevent his exploitation as a symbol of race hatred after his death. This intention was only partly realized, for Malcolm never fully assimilated his new vision, and the effect of the last chapter is one of groping, stumbling growth—of a man attempting to find adequate expression for a vision he found at once liberating and frustrating.

The indecision of this final period and the incompleteness of the autobiography have made it possible for members of various groups to claim, on the basis of partial evidence, that Malcolm was becoming one of them. It is truer to state that in his last years he was simply absorbed in the process of *becoming*; in spite of the dramatic changes that had already characterized his life, the text suggests that in his final phase the most profound transformation of all was under way. Thus, the book's power as prophetic autobiography lies not in its blunt exposition of Black Muslim ideology but in its bold portrayal of a prophet deprived of both his stature and his vision; its value as prophecy is not in the vision it contains but in the one it moves toward and prophesies.

As I have noted, the book displays features of many conventional autobiographical forms—success story, reminiscence, apology, and conversion narrative. But just as Malcolm X's identity could not be long confined to a single social role—even that of the Black Muslim minister whose ideology seemed to freeze his previous roles in a teleological progression—so his autobiography finally outruns the forms he retrospectively imposed upon his experience. The narrative was finally completed, as well as cut off, by Malcolm's death, for the final stretch of the narrative, which seems so formless, is definitively shaped by an event which had not happened. The knowledge that his future was going to be taken from him, as his past had been, impelled Malcolm's efforts to make his life whole in autobiography. As he refused, in his last year, to be defined by others, so he avoided conventional formulas in bringing his life up to date.

Finally, his impending death becomes the crucial event of the book. His assassination gives the narrative symmetry, for its end recalls its beginning. Just as the dual role of his father as Baptist minister and Garveyite organizer is reflected in Malcolm's attempt to reconcile the religious and secular aspects of his thought at the end of his life, so the death of his father anticipates Malcolm's fate. Now, however, the perpetrators of the violence are not white bigots but, apparently, Black Muslims unwilling to tolerate a heretic and competitor. Malcolm's anticipation of his imminent death in the final pages recalls his days as a hustler, but his courage is now based on faith rather than drugs. Living each day resigned to death and struggling to complete a book he does not expect to read in finished form, he recalls the attributes of the traditional spiritual autobiographer. In his book, as in his life, his devotion was to the defeat of racism, and if he failed to destroy "the racist cancer . . . in the body of America" (p. 382), he did at least achieve an exemplary victory over it in his own soul. The price of that victory was his life, for Malcolm was destroyed by men who thought he had betrayed them, when in fact he had prophesied their liberation.

Norman Mailer

If during the tumult of the 1960s Malcolm X found it difficult, at first, to justify taking time away from political action to write an autobiography, Norman Mailer found it equally difficult to justify taking time away from writing fiction to participate in protest marches. Both men eventually committed their energies to autobiographical writing about the revolution, but Malcolm, already an influential black leader, struggled to minimize his own significance, whereas Mailer, who was merely a literary celebrity, tended to magnify his own importance in order to validate his viewpoint and make an impact on history. In this phase of his career, Mailer, like Malcolm, made a significant contribution to the tradition of prophetic autobiography in American literature. For, in different ways and to varying degrees, *Armies of the Night*, *Miami and the Siege of Chicago*, *Of a Fire on the Moon*, and *A Prisoner of Sex* all employ the prophetic autobiographer's strategies of using the imagination to mediate between the self and history, seeking analogies between individual and communal experience, and examining both in such a way as to offer a new vision to his audience.

Equipped with hindsight, we can see Mailer rehearsing for these performances in earlier books, particularly *Advertisements for Myself* (1959) and *Presidential Papers* (1963). In *Advertisements*, Mailer used annotations, or "advertisements," which are confessional as well as critical, to portray himself as a prophet concerned about the declension of American democracy into a totalitarian and conformist society: "The sour truth is that I am imprisoned with a perception which will settle for nothing less than making a revolution in the consciousness of our time."[13] With a historical imagination informed by the Holocaust, Mailer feared what he saw as a kind of subtle fascism in the representative cultural climate of the 1950s. However, caught up as he was in tumultuous developments in his personal life, Mailer confessed that he was not yet ready to command an army of moral and social revolutionaries. In "The White Negro," he did, however, preach a kind of existentialism he felt would protect individuality and creativity—authentic self-hood—against repressive forces.

Mailer identified his "megalomaniacal God" as "energy, life, sex, force" (p. 351), and he affirmed violent antisocial behavior in His service, arguing that it was potentially self-redemptive and preferable to the violence of repression by the state. But in a later interview, he portrayed his deity not as an anarchic force unleashed by the individual but as a God bound up in a covenantal relationship with groups of people. Unlike the Christian God, Mailer's is not omnipotent; rather, "He exists as a warring element in a divided universe, and we are part of—perhaps the most important part— of His great expression, His enormous destiny; perhaps He is trying to impose upon the universe His conception of being against other conceptions of being very much opposed to His. Maybe we are in a sense the seed, the seed-carriers, the voyagers, the explorers, the embodiment of that embattled vision; maybe we are engaged in a heroic activity, and not a mean one" (pp. 380-81).

If *Advertisements* was a "muted autobiography" announcing a prophetic vision of the self, of God, and of America, *The Presidential Papers*, which escalates Mailer's imaginative engagement with history, moved closer to prophetic autobiography. Mailer's theory was that a hero who could expose the paradoxes of his age by personifying them might be able to rescue the nation from its cultural schizophrenia; his intent was to make John F. Kennedy that culture hero. However, from his attempts to bring about the election of the man he hoped would become an existential politician—a kind of hipster president—Mailer acquired a sense of personal responsibility for Kennedy's policies; this special bond with the president made him a writer existentially engaged with history rather than merely a journalist commenting on current events. Furthermore, believing that his imagination could almost magically influence history, Mailer tended to become the existential hero of his own account of events.

This tendency culminated in Mailer's "new journalism" of the late 1960s and early 1970s. When, in his view, the stream of American politics converged with the nation's dream life, the new historical reality demanded new modes of perception and expression, and Mailer was not too modest to nominate himself to succeed the assassinated president as the salvific culture hero. Mailer's most sustained and convincing performance as a prophetic autobiographer was his first one—in *Armies of the Night*. But there is some question as to whether the book can properly be described as autobiography. Its temporal scope is extremely short and, in some ways, its affinities would seem to be with the memoir, which narrates not the development of the individual but a sequence of historical events to which he was a privileged witness. However,

insofar as Mailer becomes an active participant as well as an observer, the book tends to become at least an installment in a continuing autobiography. Like Thoreau, he relies on crucial episodes
of short duration to make up his autobiography.

The most obvious literary category for the book would be that
of journalism, but Mailer, contemptuous of mere reporters, chose
to conceive of it as a creative fusion of history and the novel, arguing that the two major sections combine the two modes of writing in complementary ways. His "aesthetic" is at times valuable,
especially as it illuminates the way the two genres may reinforce
each other, but it fails to describe entirely or accurately the differences between Book One and Book Two. The claim of having
created a new form is also somewhat misleading, for, as Warner
Berthoff has noted, the book "grows into its power or eloquence
. . . by adopting or reinventing a classic American literary mode:
the exploratory personal testament in which the writer describes
how he has turned his own life into a practical moral experiment."[14] The book illustrates in a new and intense way the impulses at work in the long tradition of American prophetic autobiography.

For Mailer, journalism was one of the totalitarian forces hostile
to both the perception and the expression of authentic selfhood,
and in *Armies* he attempted to transcend the limitations of the
reporter's vision in two ways. First, as a celebrity participating in
the March on the Pentagon, he struggled to disentangle his self-
image from the distorted accounts of his behavior published in the
mass media.[15] Second, as a witness, he tried to offer a demonstra-
bly superior version of the event. Both purposes are served by the
book's opening, in which Mailer offers the reader an alternative to
Time's account of his speech to the demonstrators at the Ambas-
sador Theater. The background of his participation in the march,
a confession of his mixed and uncertain motives, an exposition of
the inner workings of his mind which supplements his own report
of the wanderings of his tongue as he gave his speech—this context establishes the complexity of his personality and the sophis-
tication of his method of reporting. As his narrative departs from
the conventional journalistic account to enter the realm of autobiography—of confession and apology—it exploits fictional tech-

niques: flashbacks, detailed description, interior monologue, and even invented dialogue. The impulses toward self-revelation and self-creation reinforce each other in Mailer's attempt to embarrass journalism and to offer a prophetic interpretation of the march.

Mailer's strategy of opening the book with his own performance on stage is not only appropriate—since he was an important participant—but inevitable, because his concept of reporting made it autobiographical. Like Thoreau, he confesses to the essential egotism of his book: "So if the event took place in one of the crazy mansions or indeed the crazy house of history, it is fitting that any ambiguous comic hero of such a history should be not only off very much to the side of the history, but that he should be an egotist of the most startling misproportions, outrageously and often unhappily self-assertive, yet in command of a detachment classic in severity. . . . Once history inhabits a crazy house, egotism may be the last tool left to History."[16] But unlike Thoreau, Mailer omitted the "I" and employed a variation of Adams's third-person narrative. Like Adams, Mailer liked to insist on the divided nature of his self, which included multiple personalities and assumed various roles; both saw the contradictory and inconsistent quality of the self as an accurate mirror of events and hence as an appropriate medium for their reflection.[17] However, more than Adams, Mailer used the third-person point of view to gain a certain distance from the events; to the immediacy of the account of his participation, the third person adds a detached perspective. This is evident even in the first episode, for Mailer, aware of how poorly he had communicated in his speech, attempts in his narrative to rectify his own failure as well as *Time*'s. In reporting his actions, he seeks to relate them both to an interior context—his own motivations, the vision impelling him into action—and to an external context—the larger arena of the demonstration. In reporting, criticizing, and justifying his own performance as a speaker, Mailer is establishing the pattern of the narrative, which will be both an account of and a commentary on events that are at once real and symbolic. Mailer reveals that, in both the event and the report, he is acting out a role in a highly imaginative drama which has both private and prophetic significance.

One of the roles Mailer imaginatively assumes in the course of the march is, inevitably, that of a general whose troops are engaged in a kind of civil war, an existential revolution against the military-industrial complex of "technology land." This imaginative dimension is momentarily realized and Mailer's heroic pretensions are deflated when he is caught up in a panicky retreat from the military police. However, he attempts to restore his sense of self-esteem by resolving to get arrested right away; in turn, this resolve brings a new sense of vitality: "He felt immediately much more alive—yes, bathed in air—and yet disembodied from himself as if indeed he were watching himself in a film where this action was taking place" (p. 129). Then, at the dramatic moment of his arrest, he admits, in a long authorial intrusion, that he was in fact being filmed—by an English film crew making a documentary on him. Thus, at the moment of his confrontation with the enemy, he self-consciously introduces a complication; at the "moment of truth," he reveals an element of artifice which forces the reader to question whether historical events were being passively recorded or whether those events were following a dramatic script. Mailer very candidly includes this confession at the moment when it might do the most damage to his credibility. However, ultimately, like Franklin, he gains rather than sacrifices the reader's confidence by allowing him to peek behind the scenes. Eventually, he returns from a digression on filmmaking to report that the moment of his arrest brought him a sense of importance, integration, and the confirmation of his self-hood. Perhaps because of, rather than in spite of, the overlapping of the spotlights of history and art, the moment of confrontation is one of inner illumination.

Throughout the rest of Book One, "History As a Novel," Mailer's sense of engagement in the events alternates with one of disembodied detachment; this oscillation provides one of the central dynamics of the narrative, just as the modes of history and fiction provide its aesthetic poles. A characteristic strategy is to move from the particulars of his experience to the general predicament of the community. For example, although he admits that it is "a great deal to read on the limited evidence before him," he professes to see the madness of America in the faces of the hostile federal marshalls (p. 174). Thus, his prophetic vision is aided by his novelist's license. Rhetorically more extravagant is his interpolation of his theory of the nation's involvement in Vietnam into the account of his stay in jail; the excuse for this expository digression is that it reflects and elaborates his thoughts as he listened to a Leninist haranguing the other prisoners. Functioning here explicitly as an interpreter of communal history, Mailer argues that an illogical extension of a Christian crusade against communism has led to a violation of the nation's Christian ideals. In fact, Mailer finds this paradox typical of the American mind, which believes both in the mystery of Christ and in technology, which denies all mystery—"two opposites more profoundly apart than any previous schism in the Christian soul" (p. 188). Increasingly, Mailer—one of America's most prominent Jewish writers—employs imagery and terminology typical of the traditional spiritual autobiography as he attempts to resolve the communal dilemmas.

The public climax of Book One is Mailer's delivery of a Sunday sermon on the meaning of the war to the assembled reporters and cameramen as he emerges from prison. Privately, the narrative culminates with his sense of grace at having survived his brief ordeal with a minimum of destructive fear and capitulation: "He felt one suspicion of a whole man closer to that freedom from dread which occupied the inner drama of his years, yes, one image closer than when he had come to Washington four days ago. . . . this very nice anticipation of the next moves of life itself . . . must mean, indeed, could mean nothing else to Christians, but what they must signify when they spoke of Christ within them" (p. 213).

In an authorial intrusion inserted between the two major sections of the narrative, Mailer discusses the book's "aesthetic." He offers the following as a description of the genesis and nature of Book Two: "In writing his personal history of these four days, he was delivered a discovery of what the March on the Pentagon had finally meant, and what had been won, and what had been lost, and so found himself ready at last to write a most concise Short History, to elucidate the mysterious character of that quintessentially American event" (p. 216). Book Two is "historical" in its use of other eyewitness accounts and secondary sources; in its restrained, at times impersonal, style; and in its attempts to analyze the whole phenomenon of the march in a larger perspective. This longer view of the event is made possible, Mailer argues, by the biased and particular account which has preceded it. The earlier, "novelistic" book, which he compares to a crooked tower equipped with warped telescopes for viewing the horizon, prepares the reader for the "historical" book by acquainting him with Mailer's idiosyncratic viewpoint; upon reaching Book Two, the reader is able to compensate for the distortions caused by Mailer's biases.

The metaphors are clever and sometimes apt, but Mailer's distinctions between his role as a Novelist in "History as a Novel" and as a Historian in "The Novel as History" are often misleading and reflect a rhetorical as well as a conceptual failure. First, the attempt to portray the first book as a mere scaffolding to support the second is undermined by the somewhat anticlimactic effect of the second book. Moreover, the impulse to distinguish between the two parts is misguided because their virtue is to complicate rather than to clarify the relationship between art and life and between fiction and history—to make the reader understand the ways in which they may overlap and reinforce each other, to make him aware that the historian's detachment is itself a fiction. Finally, in appending an essay on the historical significance of the event, Mailer fails to take credit for having illuminated it in his earlier account of its personal significance. Having successfully conflated the private and public dimensions of the event in the manner of the prophetic autobiographer in Book One, having combined the modes of fiction and history, Mailer is wrong to pretend to be able to disentangle them in Book Two.

This conceptual confusion is partially offset by the clear indication that the impulse behind the narrative is prophetic rather than narcissistic. To initiate the reader into the collective psyche of the demonstrators, Mailer shifts the focus from himself to others; as in traditional spritual autobiography, a strategy of self-examination leads eventually to self-annihilation and the subordination of the individual's experience to the community's history. As Warner Berthoff has put it, "the basic movement of the narrative . . . is from pugnacious personal comedy to prophetic witness and litany, with 'the Protagonist' . . . increasingly subordinated to the high historical occasion."[18]

In any event, Mailer maintained an impersonal detachment in Book Two only as long as he was describing the long foreground of the event—analyzing the coalitions of leftist groups, the motives and strategy of the demonstrators, and the negotiations in preparation for the march. Finally, after offering the reader an aerial view of the march itself and of the actions of various groups, he zoomed in for another close-up of the confrontation, dropped his historian's detachment, and resumed using the tools of the novelist: "The difference is that the history is interior—no documents can give sufficient intimation: the novel must replace history at precisely that point where experience is sufficiently emotional, spiritual, psychical, moral, existential, or supernatural to expose the fact that the historian in pursuing the experience would be obliged to quit the clearly demarcated limits of historic inquiry. So these limits are now relinquished" (p. 255). Finding that he cannot understand the event without indulging in speculation and cannot communicate its significance without employing novelistic techniques, Mailer supplements his sources with personal intuition.

He finds the ultimate significance of the event in the ordeal suffered by the hard core of demonstrators who chose to keep a night-long vigil outside the Pentagon—while he languished in jail. Ruminating on their experience, he compares it to other trials in American history, notably that suffered by the Pilgrims—"the rite of passage on which the country had been founded" (p. 280). This vigil, a kind of communal analogue of his own arrest and imprisonment, signifies, like his experience, a kind of conversion: "One has voyaged through a channel of shipwreck and temptation, and so some of the vices carried from another nether world into life itself (on the day of one's birth) may have departed, or fled, or quit; some part of the man has been born again, and is better" (pp. 280–81). The final focus of the narrative is on the last survivors of the vigil, the Quakers who practiced noncooperation in jail. Here, Mailer suggests that their ordeal had redemptive implications not only for them but for the whole nation: "But if the end of the March took place in the isolation in which these last pacifists suffered naked in freezing cells, and gave up prayers for penance, then who was to say they were not saints? And who was to say that the sins of America were not by their witness a tithe remitted?" (p. 287).

In these final pages, Mailer's writing recaptures some of the power it lost in the transition to Book Two, proving that it does not depend on a naked display of ego for its impact. Rather, it assumes an almost Quakerly quality of self-effacement in this passage. The paean to Quaker piety is a fitting conclusion to a book that performs, in modern circumstances, many of the functions of the traditional spiritual autobiography. Not for nothing does the book end with a hortatory message. The final image of America is that of a nation in labor. Biblical allusions suggest that the country is struggling to deliver a messianic savior, but the nature of the offspring is very much in doubt.[19] Like Adams and others of his predecessors, Mailer refuses to predict the course of history; rather, he exhorts his audience to rescue the nation from its crisis: "God writhes in his bonds. Rush to the locks. Deliver us from our curse. For we must end on the road to that mystery where courage, death, and the dream of love give promise of sleep" (p. 288).

Mailer's invocation of historical precedents for the martyrdom of the Quaker pacifists points to his deep imaginative involvement with American history. One could go back beyond the Quakers in search of an analogue to Mailer's vision of God and America, for his metaphysics present a mirror image of Calvinistic theology. Whereas the Puritan's God saved man, Mailer's God depends—in his Manichean struggle with the Devil—on man's assistance. But despite his Arminianism and Manicheanism, Mailer shares with the Puritan spiritual autobiographer a sense of the individual's implication in a communal covenant with God. And for Mailer, as for the Puritan, the compelling obligation to act morally—that is, to enact God's will—is complicated by the difficulty of accurately perceiving it.

In his mystical existentialism and his positive assessment of man's moral freedom, he shares much with the Transcendentalists. In his combative individualism and his affirmation of civil disobedience, he recalls Thoreau. But unlike Thoreau, he seeks an event with which to involve himself, rather than an uninhabited environment in which to define himself. In this he recalls Whitman, who also embraced the underside of American society and attempted to write the interior history of a civil conflict.[20] (In fact, *Armies* is studded with allusions to the Civil War.)

Probably, however, Mailer's autobiographical practice is closest to that of another Harvard man—Henry Adams—with whom he shares ambition for high office, a sense of the multiplicity of the self, and the ability to confess failure in an arrogant way. Certainly, Mailer's preoccupations are those of Adams: politics (in *Armies* and *Miami and the Siege of Chicago*), technology (in *Of a Fire on the Moon*), and sex (in *A Prisoner of Sex*). Furthermore, collectively, these books chronicle Mailer's progress through a modern version of Adams's pilgrimage to successive world's fairs. Like Adams, he is attracted to events that promise to reveal or to affect the nation's destiny. And like Adams's mind, Mailer's thrives on paradoxes and polarities like those between God and the Devil, nature and technology, and creativity and waste. Thus, as Michael Cowan has suggested, "like *The Education of Henry Adams*, Mailer's most recent work is in important ways a poet's search for a metaphorical structure that will at last bring the illusion of order to the multiplying contradictions of modern experience."[21] Of course, unlike Adams, Mailer fears an excess of order more than he fears chaos, but, like Adams, he is concerned with "a period in our history where nothing is nailed down. All the American faiths, one by one, are being exploded."[22] Like Adams, he is as much a myth-breaker as a myth-maker; failing to become president, both nominate themselves in times of crisis to be our imaginative spokesmen—arbiters of our values and interpreters of our history.

Robert Pirsig

If there is a paradox inherent in Robert Pirsig's *Zen and the Art of Motorcycle Maintenance*, it is not the one suggested by the title—Zen is no more incompatible with motorcycle maintenance than it is with archery—but by the conflict between the idea of Zen and the idea of autobiography. As Eugen Herrigel notes in *Zen in the Art of Archery*, the book upon whose title Pirsig plays, "descriptions of the way and its stations are almost entirely lacking in Zen literature."[23] The Zen adept views talk of the self and its progress as incompatible with Zen because he recognizes that insight into the way is not his to give. Both writers, Western professors interested in philosophy, pursued a mystical end—transcendence of the subject-object duality—but their circumstances and temperaments

channeled their pursuits into different forms. Herrigel mastered
Zen only by losing himself and escaping his philosophical training
in six years of instruction in the art of archery; to communicate his
experience without betraying it, he concentrated on the essentials
of his training in his narrative. Pirsig did not attempt to master
Zen, but he did achieve a condition in which motorcycle maintenance became for him what archery was for Herrigel: an "artless
art" which brought the mind into contact with ultimate reality.
He reached this goal only after a relentless, egotistical, philosophical inquiry ended in the loss of self through insanity. As a result,
his narrative is heavily intellectual and frankly confessional—an
autobiography of intellectual passions. It has to do with a concept
related to Zen, but not with Zen practice; in its form and content,
it belongs entirely to the Western tradition.

This idiosyncratic and unpredictable book gives the impression
of being artful because it reads at times like fiction. In order to
re-create the quality of his experience and make it yield the maxi-
mum meaning, Pirsig, like Mailer, treats his material with a novelist's license: he withholds certain information from the reader to
create suspense, uses flashbacks freely, and weaves together several
narrative threads. Yet the "Author's Note" states: "Although
much has been changed for rhetorical purposes, it must be regarded in its essence as fact."[24] Elsewhere he suggests that although the
essay would be the most natural form for his ideas, he prefers to
express them in an autobiographical narrative, which presents the
speaker as an individual rather than as a disembodied voice (p. 166).
As an autobiography, the book is less artful than archeological,
for Pirsig undertakes to piece together a fragmented life in order
to understand its significance. In doing so, as he admits, he strays
far from both Zen and motorcycle maintenance, but he does so in
response to an impulse which is prophetic as well as autobiographical. His concerns, his themes, and even his unusual narrative form
link his book more closely with the prophetic autobiography than
with fiction or the literature of mysticism.

It is no accident that *Walden* is among the few books Pirsig carries with him on his journey. If his list of basic equipment for a
motorcycle trip is reminiscent of Thoreau's list of life's essentials
in "Economy," and if the description of his slow, deliberate read-

ing of *Walden* recalls Thoreau's advice in "Reading," it is because Pirsig is acutely aware of Thoreau's example as an autobiographer and social critic. Pirsig shares many attitudes, ideas, and goals with Thoreau. He endeavors to fuse Eastern and Western philosophy; he is concerned with recovering lost dimensions—intellectual, aesthetic, and spiritual—of our daily activities; and he believes that social reform must begin with the individual: "The place to improve the world is first in one's own heart and head and hands, and then work outward from there" (p. 291). Yet Pirsig finally finds *Walden* "tame and cloistered" (p. 219); Thoreau offered no solution to Pirsig's dilemma because Thoreau retreated from the developing technology of his day toward a union with nature. Like so many American writers, Pirsig finds technology to be involved in the crucial problems of his time, but, uniquely, he seeks not only to confront it directly but to reconcile man with it. Whereas Thoreau found a repository of value and an analogue of the self at Walden Pond, Pirsig finds these things in his motorcycle: "The real cycle you are working on is a cycle called yourself. The machine that appears to be 'out there' and the person that appears to be 'in here' are not two separate things" (p. 319). Pirsig sets out to do for technology what Thoreau did for nature—discover the spirit within it and achieve peace with it: "The way to resolve the conflict between human values and technological needs . . . is to break down the barriers of dualistic thought that prevent a real understanding of what technology is—not an exploitation of nature, but a fusion of nature and the human spirit into a new kind of creation that transcends both" (p. 284).

Pirsig's narrative recounts not a sojourn but an excursion that becomes a pilgrimage. Among Thoreau's books, its form most resembles that of *A Week on the Concord and Merrimack Rivers*; the narrative of a brief journey with a relative (Pirsig's son Chris) is interrupted by long digressions—largely expository passages which purport to reflect the thoughts of the narrator while traveling. As in *A Week*, the interpolated passages often overshadow the travel narrative, but in *Zen* the inner and outer journeys are much more closely related. Although the reader is allowed only gradually to sense the strong connections between the two basic elements of the book, the inner journey is ultimately revealed as crucial to the

autobiographical narrative. The apparent digressions, in the form
of lectures addressed directly to the reader, seem at first to arise
from the immediate circumstances of the motorcycle trip from
Minnesota to the West Coast. But they are also an attempt to
make a coherent philosophy out of the ideas of a person he calls
Phaedrus, who, it is revealed, is actually Pirsig's former self—a man
whose personality had been annihilated by electroshock after society judged him insane.

This revelation clarifies the autobiographical nature of the
"Chautauquas" and reveals the similarity between *Zen* and the autobiographies of Louis Sullivan and Henry Adams. As the lectures
recapitulate Phaedrus's pursuit of an elusive concept he calls
"Quality" (which turns out to be identical with Reality, Truth,
and Goodness), *Zen* becomes an autobiography of that single idea,
the story of a lifelong education which causes Pirsig to challenge
the orthodoxy of his day. Whereas Sullivan saw his idea as a prod-
uct of the progress of civilization, Phaedrus discovered his to be an
idea discarded by the ancient Greeks; only by reaching back to the
source of the original philosophical conception which mistakenly
divided the universe into subjects and objects can he resolve the
contemporary dilemma posed by technology. Thus, like Adams,
Pirsig views Western civilization as a failure and presumes to offer
an original intellectual synthesis to replace the discredited myths
of his culture. Like Adams, Phaedrus adopted the role of a heretic,
mounting a deliberate, passionate attack on the dominant ideas of
his day. However, while Adams had only played with the conception of autobiography as literary suicide, Phaedrus actually committed a kind of intellectual suicide by following his ideas to their
conclusions; when his criticism of Western rationality carried him
beyond the cultural mythos entirely, he exhibited symptoms of
insanity and his very identity was taken from him.

The reconstruction of Phaedrus's intellectual system holds certain dangers for Pirsig. To follow Phaedrus is to risk getting lost in
"the high country of the mind"—to lose touch with concrete
things and other people. Because the recovery of the prophetic
vision entails personal risk, Pirsig's prophetic and autobiographical
motives are not always in harmony; it is easier to deal with Phaedrus-as-idea than with Phaedrus-as-identity. Desiring to retrace

Phaedrus's steps without reenacting his fate, Pirsig treats him gingerly and objectively. He draws upon an analogy between his own trip and the westward movement of the previous century to distinguish between his two selves. Thus, Phaedrus is portrayed as an individualistic explorer or pioneer who opens up new territory in a daring, but messy way, while Pirsig functions as a farmer who moves in afterward to cultivate the land.

For protection from abstraction and isolation, of course, Pirsig can always turn to his motorcycle and his son. The motorcycle functions on several levels and in several ways: it is the vehicle of both the outer and inner journeys and a focus for two visions that need to be reconciled. As the vehicle for the physical journey, it carries Pirsig into the "secondary America" of back roads, front porches, orchards and lawns which he prefers to the "primary America " of freeways and jet flights; furthermore, unlike an automobile, it immerses him in the "hereness and nowness" of the scene. Yet the long hours of riding also free his mind to meditate on Phaedrus's ideas and fate; through the medium of the book he is able to expose this interior monologue directly to the reader. Similarly, in the "Chautauquas," motorcycle *riding* illustrates a romantic approach to reality, which emphasizes the appreciation of sensations and surfaces, while motorcycle *maintenance* demonstrates a classical vision, which attends to underlying forms. Thus, while the motorcyle trip allows time for intellectual speculation, the machine itself provides Pirsig with a concrete reference for his ideas when they threaten to become too abstract. The machine, then, unites the inner and outer worlds of the book—the realms of mind and of matter. The narrative's rhythmic alternation between the two journeys not only simulates a real experience, it also illustrates the intellectual and spiritual predicament of modern man. For, according to Pirsig, a healthy culture depends on a view of technology that reconciles romantic and classical visions. Insofar as the two threads of the narrative appear at times unrelated, the book imitates the community's dilemma; insofar as they prove to be aspects of one story, the form of the book achieves the resolution the content suggests.

Clearly, the motorcycle in this book carries a heavy burden. In addition to Pirsig's intellectual baggage, it carries his son, a troubled and troublesome child. The excursion is intended, of course, to strengthen the relationship between the father and the son, who shows signs of incipient mental illness. But the noise of riding makes communication difficult, and Pirsig's preoccupation with Phaedrus makes him even more remote. Unfortunately, the further he follows Phaedrus, the more the inner journey dominates the outer one and the further the father gets from his sulky son. Aware of this, Pirsig likens his situation to that in Goethe's ballad, "The Erlkönig"; he feels that, like the father in the poem, he may lose his son to the threatening specter—in this case, that of his insane former self. Yet in spite of this fear, he cannot resist probing deeper into his personal past in order to understand it and exorcise the ghost of Phaedrus.

In Part I, Pirsig begins by characterizing himself as a prophet who hopes to deepen the channels in which the national consciousness flows. The couple who accompany Pirsig and his son to Montana represent the American dilemma: the inability to perceive the machine in the garden properly. Viewing technology romantically rather than classically, they become troubled by what they imagine to be the "force that gives rise to technology; something undefined, but inhuman, mechanical, lifeless, a blind monster, a death force" (p. 16). Their response is to flee it—ironically, on motorcycles. Pirsig's failure to win them over to his own more comprehensive view of technology recalls Thoreau's failure to convert John Fields in *Walden*. Indeed, in response to his failure, Pirsig, like Thoreau, seeks to take on the cultural malaise and resolve it for the community in his autobiography. He withdraws from them, but not from the problem; he uses the medium of his interior monologue to reach a more extensive audience with a more fully developed message.

Pirsig invokes Phaedrus's ideas as relevant to this problem, for he, too, had seen "a sick and ailing thing happening and he started cutting deep, deeper and deeper to get at the root of it" (p. 73). At first, however, Pirsig conceals Phaedrus's identity, thus burying the deepest autobiographical vein of the narrative; Pirsig appears to be merely reconstructing the fragmented vision of an eccentric friend and translating it into socially useful terms. However, the confession of Phaedrus's identity restores the autobiographical dimension. Henceforth, Pirsig appears to be a strange kind of vision-ary or prophet himself, with a mysterious source of inspiration: "In seeing these sudden coalescences of vision and in recall of some strange fragment of thought whose origins I have no idea of, I'm like a clairvoyant, a spirit medium receiving messages from an-other world" (p. 84).

In Part II, Pirsig fuses Phaedrus's classical vision with his own understanding of motorcycles to explore the close relationships among technology, art, science, and religion. He attributes intel-lectual respectability to motorcycle maintenance, analyzing a motorcycle as a system, and arguing that mechanics use scientific method, at least intuitively, in doing repairs. Similarly, he attrib-utes a religious dimension to motorcycle maintenance; for Pirsig, routine jobs like tuning take on the ritualistic function Zen arch-ery assumed for Herrigel. This sense of the common foundation of art, science, and religion had once been a source of confusion rath-er than reassurance; Pirsig notes that Phaedrus's religious devotion to science, in his undergraduate days, had led him to a crisis of faith. As a science major he had been pleased, at first, to discover that the most mysterious aspect of scientific method—the formula-tion of hypotheses to account for phenomena—came easily and in-tuitively to him. But as he sensed the implications of the rapid proliferation of hypotheses, he began to question the validity of scientific method: "The more you look the more you see. Instead of soliciting one truth from a multitude you are *increasing the multitude*. What this means logically is that as you try to move toward unchanging truth through the application of scientific method, you actually do not move toward it at all. You move *away* from it!" (p. 110). Scientific truth, then, was not absolute dogma, eternal in duration, but an explanation of phenomena which proved convenient at a given time.

Although this crisis is the result of rather naive preconceptions in a modern undergraduate, it is worth noting that in "The Gram-mar of Science" Henry Adams had identified a similar crisis as cen-tral to the dilemma of twentieth-century man. For Pirsig, too, the shock was both personal and cultural; he renounced the religion of science to become a heretic who excoriated Western rationality as "emotionally hollow, esthetically meaningless and spiritually empty" (p. 110). Although this crisis blocked his intellectual development for some time, it later stimulated an attempt, like Adams's, to correct the education he inherited.

As the outer journey brings Pirsig and his son into Montana, the inner journey moves forward in time to Phaedrus's sojourn as a college teacher in Bozeman. Here, among old friends and acquaintances, Pirsig has to impersonate the lost self he both fears and longs for. Autobiography is always, in a sense, self-impersonation and self-creation, but this is doubly true of *Zen*, which records episodes in which Pirsig had to imagine his former self in order to create an impression of continuity rather than disjunction between periods of his life. This contributes to the book's fictive feeling; however, Pirsig's role-playing is not in the service of art but of self-discovery and self-preservation.

Speaking in a prophetic, Phaedrus-inspired vein at a party, Pirsig succeeds only in confusing everyone, including himself. At this point in his experience, Pirsig has not earned the right to fuse the two halves of his identity. The character's monologue, prematurely voiced to a live audience, fails to convert or even enlighten them. Again, the narrator's interior monologue, like Mailer's, attempts to compensate for the character's failure. And turning from public utterance to self-exploration, Pirsig finds that the trail of Phaedrus's ideas leads back, through a flood of memories released by his former haunts, toward the reality of Phaedrus, which he desires but hardly dares to confront.

As if to provide relief from the tensions of the book as autobiography, Part III emphasizes its prophetic function; in it, we find the clearest articulation and application of Phaedrus's ideas. Pirsig's geographical analogue for his mental journey takes on a different, but even more Thoreauvian, form here—that of a mountain climb—as Pirsig and Chris take a side trip by themselves. While their ascent corresponds to Phaedrus's pursuit of the ghost of rationality into ethereal realms of thought, their descent parallels Pirsig's attempt to demonstrate the relevance of Phaedrus's lofty abstractions to everyday life.

Phaedrus had viewed his own discovery of the significance of Quality as a Copernican revolution in consciousness. But realizing the megalo- and monomanical nature of Phaedrus's quest, Pirsig leaves open the question of the truth and originality of Phaedrus's philosophical synthesis. He tries to salvage some of Phaedrus's ideas and rehabilitate them as prophecy, converting private illumination into enlightenment for the community. According to Pirsig, technology seems alien to the humanities only because our mode of rationality has a rigid subject-object duality built into it. His remedy for alienation from technology establishes a sequence (reminiscent of Shaker thought) in which each element gives rise to the next: peace of mind, right values, right thoughts, right actions, and work which is a material reflection of spiritual reality.

The testament delivered in Part III is somewhat disappointing—in its oversimplification—as a solution to the contemporary communal crisis. But a more alarming deficiency of the book lies in the lack of a real connection, in spite of contrived analogies, between the two journeys. On foot now, and alone with his son, Pirsig lacks the usual pretexts for his Chautauquas—adjustments to his motorcycle and conversations with adult companions. The two threads of the narrative diverge dangerously; absorbed in thought, Pirsig pays insufficient attention to his demanding son. Nevertheless, the submerged autobiographical dimension of the narrative develops in a strange dream involving Pirsig, Chris, and a ghostly other.

In response to his deteriorating relationship with his son, Pirsig turns his attention to his personal predicament in Part IV and comes to terms with his dream. Although their moods often correspond, there seems to be an impassable gulf between father and son, symbolized in the recurrent dream by a glass door which separates them. In terms of the inner journey, this shift in the narrative represents Pirsig's attempt to see if his new value system will apply to the relationship between himself and his son as well as it does to that between him and his cycle. In fact, Pirsig is more easily frustrated by a sulky son than by a balky cycle, in part perhaps because he approaches them in the same way. The father has given so much energy to reconciling himself with technology that he threatens to cut himself off from intimate personal relationships, as Phaedrus sacrificed them to his pursuit of ideas. In fact, the form of the narrative, in which the interior monologue tends to dominate the narration of the outer journey, serves as a reminder of the danger that Pirsig may reenact Phaedrus's fate of isolation followed by a breakdown. At the beginning of this section, Pirsig makes an advance in his understanding of his dream; at first perplexing, this unexpected revelation opens the way to reconciliation. This time, he sees that the specter which prevents him from opening the glass door and reuniting with his family is himself; hence, the dreamer must be Phaedrus. This reversal of his earlier assignment of these roles strengthens his fear that his travels have reawakened and revitalized the ghost of his former self.

However, just as he had earlier pursued, in his Chautauquas, the force his friends had fled, now he resumes the narrative of Phaedrus's intellectual quest and pushes it to its conclusion. This section bogs down somewhat in the account of Phaedrus's amateurish but fanatical critique of Western thinking. But here the focus is on Phaedrus-as-identity rather than Phaedrus-as-idea; the impulse is more autobiographical than prophetic. Whereas earlier, Pirsig stressed the value of Phaedrus's discoveries, now he emphasizes their cost. Pirsig comes to see that Phaedrus had known how his pursuit of Quality would end: "Insanity is the *terra incognita* surrounding the mythos. And he knew! He knew the Quality he talked about lay outside the mythos" (p. 345). Seeking a cure for twentieth-century lunacy, Phaedrus committed himself to a position his society could only pronounce insane; he condemned himself, consciously, to execution by electroshock.

Following his account of Phaedrus's end, Pirsig makes an important confession, admitting the hypocrisy of lecturing on overcoming subject-object dualities even as he ignores his own son. Yet before Pirsig can be reconciled with his son, he must be reconciled with Phaedrus. Thus, the climax of the book is not the prophecy of Part III but the self-recognition of Part IV. It is Chris's reproachful presence that pushes Pirsig to this crucial perception: "What I am is a heretic who's recanted, and thereby in everyone's eyes saved his soul. Everyone's eyes but one, who knows deep down inside that all he has saved is his skin. . . . If I hadn't turned on Phaedrus I'd still be there, but he was true to what he believed right to the end. That's the difference between us, and Chris knows it. And that's the reason I sometimes feel he's the reality and I'm the ghost" (p. 396). Thus as they reach the western limit of their journey—the Pacific coast—the father and son finally confront one another. Only then does Pirsig recognize the true import of his dream: it is not Phaedrus who stands between Pirsig and Chris but Pirsig who stands between Chris and the father he once loved. Chris does not fear his father's former self; rather, he mourns for him. Recognizing the cost of his cowardice, Pirsig affirms his identity with Phaedrus, confirming Chris's belief in Phaedrus's sanity and his love for his family.

Because the prophet has given way to the autobiographer, the books ends not with a broad intellectual synthesis but with a poignant reunion between father and son. Still, there is a connection between the two elements. The forging of the synthesis draws Pirsig closer to Phaedrus and helps facilitate the reconciliation; this in turn serves to validate the new philosophy. Like Thoreau, Pirsig achieves a kind of regeneration at the shore of America, but Pirsig, like a Puritan autobiographer, uses his immediate posterity to stand for the larger community he hopes will adopt his vision and values.

Even when it is written in the first person, as it conventionally is, autobiography demands a degree of detachment from oneself, for the "I" serves as both subject and object. For Henry Adams, autobiography issued from his sense of the historical gulf between the I-now and the I-then; hence his adoption of the third-person viewpoint. But by allowing him to treat himself objectively, autobiography also enabled him to complete his experience—to possess it, finish it, and make it available to others. Pirsig's sense of self-division has a more radical source, for his former self and his former life had been taken from him by society. Pirsig's division of self into subject and object is no literary conceit; it is a painful, mysterious fact of his life.

Insofar as he fears the emergence of his former identity (because he accepts society's valuation of it), he welcomes the inevitable self-objectification of autobiography. But insofar as he longs to rediscover his previous life and fuse his existence into one continuum, his wishes are frustrated by the literary convention of treating his former self as Phaedrus. As he needs, in life, to reconcile his two selves, he needs, in his autobiography, to make the first-person narrator and the third-person character truly one person. Instead of disowning, repressing, or exorcising his former self, Pirsig must embrace him. In the end, the narrative's most significant allusion may be, not to Goethe's "Erlkönig," but to another more universal ghost story. In spite of all the philosophical and technical material, the book's basic plot is the story of a father, a son, and an unholy ghost. Phaedrus is, of course, the spirit of a man who had messianic pretensions and who suffered (or enjoyed) a martyr's fate. Finally, however, Pirsig must treat him not as a savior or even a prophet, but rather as the *man* he used to be. Only this recognition will bring about the atonement of the father and the son. This event at once fulfills the book as prophecy and completes it as autobiography.

EPILOGUE

Prophetic Autobiography

and Prophetic Behavior

Because the Old Testament prophets were, in some sense, the models for out first autobiographers, this study began with a biblical scholar's definition of the prophet. But although prophetic autobiography was first conceived of, in America, within the context of Judaeo-Christian mythology, it has not been wholly contained by that framework. Thus, it may be appropriate to conclude by considering a somewhat broader view of the prophet. For the anthropologist, the prophet's function is to offer his society a vision or a visionary experience which revises the culture's traditional mythology in such a way as to resolve a communal crisis. If his vision is judged insane and he is ignored, he proves a false messiah; his effect then is merely to reinforce the established order. If his vision gains credence, perhaps giving rise to a crisis cult, it may, at the very least, create an illusion of change and thus bring relief by easing psychological tensions. It may do more; its imaginative power may be such that it will in fact reshape society and alter its history—not necessarily in the literal image of the vision but in a way made possible by revision of the culture's mythology.[1] In extreme circumstances, the vision of the prophet may be extravagant, even apocalyptic, and the changes in the social order drastic, even disastrous. More often, especially in complex societies, the phenomenon takes a more subtle form.

Among our autobiographers, those who most obviously participate in this more broadly defined phenomenon are the charismatic leaders: Shepard, Mather, Edwards, Douglass, and Malcolm X. For them, prophecy was a career as well as a way of writing autobiography. Puritanism was itself a crisis cult—a hugely successful one— and much of American Puritan literature can be described as prophecy inspired by the crisis of emigration and adaption to the new continent. Thomas Shepard's reassuring testimony suggests that emigration was a regenerative rite and that the community's problems could be solved by allegiance to the ideals that impelled it. While Increase Mather did not function as a prophet in writing his autobiography, his private lobbying with God reveals his sense that he could wield an almost magic power over the destiny of the colony. Unlike his predecessor's autobiographies, Edwards's slights his role as the leader of a crisis cult; indeed, its obsessive focus on his mystical growth in grace anticipates his withdrawal from the movement he inspired. On one level, his narrative prophesies the millenium; on another, it merely foreshadows his removal to Stockbridge.

In the cases of abolitionism and the Nation of Islam, the alteration of the prevailing mythology by the prophet of the oppressed is quite clear. Douglass's *Narrative* is both original and subtle in its exploitation of the morphology of conversion. With that gesture, he not only translated his own experience into widely understood terms, making the experience of slavery palpable to his free white audience; he also brought the power of Christian mythology to bear on the peculiar American institution in an effective way. The original prophets of the Black Muslim movement were W. D. Fard and Elijah Muhammad, who revised the culture's dominant mythology in such a way as to alter the historical relationship of blacks and whites. During his tenure as a Black Muslim minister, Malcolm X was less a prophet than a priest. But in his last years, he struggled to achieve prophetic stature; while he failed to consolidate a crisis cult around him before his death, the publication of his book established his power as a prophet.

While the style of Quakerism in the eighteenth century did not encourage charismatic leadership, John Woolman came close to achieving such stature. Clearly, the course of his life was altered by his sense of his implication in the well-documented communal crisis of 1755. And his journal certainly records signs of prophetic behavior: obscure visions, excessive emotions, eccentric acts, and psychosomatic illnesses. His predicament as a prophet stemmed from the subtlety of his vision: he stressed not visible signs of distinction but subtle inward changes of attitude as the salvation of the community.

The prophetic stature of many of the other writers is less obvious because, unlike the charismatic leaders, they became prophets only as autobiographers. Nevertheless, many of them lived their lives with conscious prophetic intent. Whitman, of course, made a curative vision the substance of his great autobiographical poem: his persona consciously aspires to heal the nation's illness. During the Civil War, he undertook the task of healing in a literal, practical way—nursing the soldiers of America one by one. In a similar but less obvious way, Franklin, Thoreau, Wright, and Sullivan used their autobiographies to recommend values and principles of design calculated to solve communal problems. Norman Mailer viewed with some skepticism the attempt of a crisis cult to work magic on the Pentagon, yet his own response to the march depended on a similar faith in the power of the imagination to change reality. Indeed his own performance was so dramatic, his style so energetic, because he had to compete with the extravagantly prophetic behavior of the counterculture. Autobiography offered Mailer a way of creating himself as a prophet. His speeches and actions as a protester, while also prophetic in intent, can be comic in their ironies; only autobiography enabled him to reach a wide audience and to complete his participation in historical events. Thus, literary prophecy can be a substitute for, as well as a supplement to or record of, prophetic behavior; words can compensate for or capitalize on failures in deed, and certain of the book's readers may become the equivalent of a crisis cult. In our culture, autobiography has often been the medium chosen for such prophecy.

Possibly the most extreme prophet we have encountered is

Phaedrus, who deliberately pursued a quest which led him out of the cultural mythos in search not of personal sanctuary but of a cure for the culture's illness. When the Church of Reason denounced him as a heretic, the high priests of rationality—court-appointed psychiatrists—diagnosed him as insane and he was reintegrated into the community by means of a technological ritual—electroshock treatments. Pirsig compensates, in a way, for Phaedrus's failure, rescuing him from obscurity and insanity. But while Pirsig seems to have cured incipient insanity in his son by fusing the alienated halves of his own identity, his prophetic vision of technology and Western reason seems tame. For all we know, it is only a pale version of what Phaedrus intuited.

There are few intimations of the apocalypse in this tradition, perhaps because our crises have rarely seemed so threatening as to inspire such dire prophecies. Nor do many of these books appear to be visionary. Aside from "Song of Myself," which is all vision, and Woolman's *Journal*, which records several visions, the texts may seem uninspired. But prophetic vision always combines the old and the new, the shared and the idiosyncratic. In prophetic autobiography, the traditional, shared element is supplied by the historical content itself. What is new and intuited by the individual is the significance of the shared experience. The vision, then, depends on the form and the content—on the shape the autobiographer gives history and the values he distills from it. The traditional elements or symbols of the dominant mythology are resistant to change, but each autobiography rearranges them, revising the mythology in subtle ways which correspond to tensions felt by the writers. The texts make history intelligible, and because they are themselves events, the books enter and alter the stream of history. Thus, finally, in a literate culture, writing a prophetic autobiography becomes a prophetic act, and reading one brings the reader into contact with a spirit who perceives his historical situation in a different and redemptive way.

That we continue to read these books after their particular crises have passed suggests their success as prophecy. For they speak to the perpetual crisis of being American, of living with the contradictions of that identity. Furthermore, in addition to being prophets as autobiographers, these writers have served as prophets *of* autobiography. If literary genres can become institutions, then autobiography has become an important American institution, one with a rich tradition. Like our best institutions, it is flexible and democratic: it welcomes participation. These writers have persistently urged autobiography upon their audiences as a valuable means of self-examination, self-creation, and self-regeneration, and they have demonstrated its usefulness in the process of imagining and bringing into existence America and Americans from the Puritans to the present. In addition to examining themselves and their communities' history, they have explored the meaning of autobiography itself, and their formal experiments and innovations have ensured its continued vitality.

The ultimate ideal toward which the tradition points is, I suppose, like that of the Old Testament prophets, a community in which prophecy is no longer necessary because each individual is his own prophet. The Transcendentalists, especially, insisted that American democracy requires its citizens to be, in effect, prophets. Until that time, the institution will be necessary. But while it deserves our respect, there is a danger in excessive reverence for it. For it must not become, as the Puritan jeremiad did, a substitute for reform. We must not pay it so much attention that we substitute the activity of retelling our story for the task of making our history.[2]

NOTES

Chapter One

1. Ross Miller has attributed this characteristic to the autobiographies of Franklin, Adams, and Malcolm X. See "Autobiography as Fact and Fiction," *Centennial Review* 16, no. 3 (1972): 221-32.
2. Robert F. Sayre, *The Examined Self* (Princeton: Princeton University Press, 1964); James M. Cox, "Autobiography and America," *Virginia Quarterly Review* 47, no. 2 (1971): 252-77; William C. Spengeman and L. R. Lundquist, "Autobiography and the American Myth," *American Quarterly* 17, no. 3 (1965): 501-19; Daniel B. Shea, Jr., *Spiritual Autobiography in Early America* (Princeton: Princeton University Press, 1968); Perry Miller, "Jonathan Edwards to Emerson," *New England Quarterly* 13, no. 4 (1940): 589-617; Sacvan Bercovitch, *The Puritan Origins of the American Self* (New Haven: Yale University Press, 1975); Hyatt H. Waggoner, *American Poets* (Boston: Houghton Mifflin, 1968); Richard Chase, *The American Novel and Its Tradition* (Garden City, N.Y.: Doubleday and Co., 1957).
3. Robert H. Pfeiffer, *Religion in the Old Testament*, ed. Charles Conrad Forman (New York: Harper and Brothers, 1961), pp. 117-18. For a more complete discussion of the Old Testament prophets, see Ibid., pp. 117-58.
4. Sacvan Bercovitch, "Cotton Mather," in *Major Writers of Early American Literature*, ed. Everett Emerson (Madison: University of Wisconsin Press, 1972), p. 101.
5. Sacvan Bercovitch, *The Puritan Origins of the American Self*, pp. 89-90.
6. Ibid., pp. 42-43, 114.
7. Waggoner, *American Poets*, p. 94.
8. Shea, *Spiritual Autobiography*, p. xi.

9. Waggoner, *American Poets*, p. xv.

10. Barrett John Mandel, "The Autobiographer's Art," *Journal of Aesthetics and Art Criticism* 27, no. 2 (1968): 217.

11. Ibid., p. 219.

12. Francis R. Hart, "Notes for an Anatomy of Modern Autobiography," *New Literary History* 1, no. 3 (1970): 488.

Chapter Two

1. Owen C. Watkins, *The Puritan Experience* (New York: Schocken Books, 1972), p. 238.

2. Kenneth B. Murdock, *Literature and Theology in Colonial New England* (Cambridge: Harvard University Press, 1949), p. 117.

3. Daniel B. Shea, Jr., *Spiritual Autobiography in Early America* (Princeton: Princeton University Press, 1968), p. 91.

4. For a discussion of the Puritans' "tribalism," see Edmund S. Morgan, *The Puritan Family*, rev. ed. (New York: Harper and Row, 1966), pp. 168-82.

5. For a discussion of the full-life narrative, see Shea, *Spiritual Autobiography*, pp. 111-51.

6. Paul Delany, *British Autobiography in the Seventeenth Century* (New York: Columbia University Press, 1969), p. 56.

7. Written between 1646 and 1649, it was first published by Nehemiah Adams as *The Autobiography of Thomas Shepard*, Boston, 1832, and in 1846 was included by Alexander Young in *Chronicles of the First Plantation of the Colony of Massachusetts.*

8. Shea, *Spiritual Autobiography*, pp. ix, 139-57.

9. Michael McGiffert, Introduction, *God's Plot: The Paradoxes of Puritan Piety, Being the Autobiography and Journal of Thomas Shepard*, ed. Micheal McGiffert (Amherst: University of Massachusetts Press, 1972), pp. 3-4.

10. Shea, *Spiritual Autobiography*, p. 111.

11. Shepard, "My Birth and Life," p. 68. Hereafter the page numbers will be cited in the text.

12. Murdock, *Literature and Theology*, p. 122.

13. Larzer Ziff, *Puritanism in America* (New York: Viking, 1973), p. 216.

14. Robert Middlekauff, *The Mathers* (New York: Oxford University Press, 1971), p. 114.

15. Ibid., pp. 173-74.

16. Shea, *Spiritual Autobiography*, pp. 152-53.

17. "The Autobiography of Increase Mather," ed. M. G. Hall, *Proceedings of the American Antiquarian Society* 71, part 2 (1961): p. 277. Hereafter the page numbers will be cited in the text.

18. For a succinct definition of this term, see Perry Miller, *The New England Mind: The Seventeenth Century* (1939; rpt., Boston: Beacon, 1961), p. 8.

19. Although it was apparently not intended for publication, Samuel Hopkins did publish it in his *Life and Chronicles of Jonathan Edwards* in 1765. Shea, *Spiritual Autobiography*, p. 188.

20. Ibid., p. 182.

21. Jonathan Edwards, *Personal Narrative*, in *Jonathan Edwards: Representa-*

tive Selections, ed. Clarence H. Faust and Thomas H. Johnson (1935; rpt., New York: Hill and Wang, 1962), p. 60. Hereafter the page numbers will be cited in the text.

22. Edward M. Griffin, *Jonathan Edwards* (Minneapolis: University of Minnesota Press, 1971), p. 35.

Chapter Three

1. John Woolman, *The Journal and Major Essays of John Woolman*, ed. Phillips Moulton (New York: Oxford University Press, 1971), p. 31. Hereafter page numbers will be cited in the text.
2. Frederick B. Tolles, *Quakers and the Atlantic Culture* (New York: Macmillan, 1960), pp. 21–22.
3. Owen C. Watkins, *The Puritan Experience* (New York: Schocken Books, 1972), p. 177.
4. Luella M. Wright, *The Literary Life of the Early Friends, 1650–1725* (New York: Columbia University Press, 1932), p. 116.
5. Watkins, *Puritan Experience*, pp. 182–87.
6. Daniel B. Shea, Jr., *Spiritual Autobiography in Early America* (Princeton: Princeton University Press, 1968), pp. 5–7.
7. Sydney V. James, *A People Among Peoples* (Cambridge, Mass.: Harvard University Press, 1963), pp. 164–69.
8. Frederick B. Tolles, *Meeting House and Counting House* (Chapel Hill: University of North Carolina Press, 1948), p. 230.
9. Paul Rosenblatt, *John Woolman* (New York: Twayne, 1969), p. 115.

Chapter Four

1. David Levin, "*The Autobiography of Benjamin Franklin*," *Yale Review* 53, no. 2 (1963): 261–62.
2. Frederick B. Tolles, *Meeting House and Counting House* (Chapel Hill: University of North Carolina Press, 1948), pp. 247–48.
3. *The Autobiography of Benjamin Franklin*, ed. Leonard W. Labaree et al. (New Haven: Yale University Press, 1964), p. 44n. Hereafter page numbers will be cited in the text.
4. Robert F. Sayre, *The Examined Self* (Princeton: Princeton University Press, 1964), p. 23.
5. Alfred Owen Aldridge, *Benjamin Franklin and Nature's God* (Durham: Duke University Press, 1967), pp. 250–51.
6. Daniel B. Shea, Jr., *Spiritual Autobiography in Early America* (Princeton: Princeton University Press, 1968), p. 244.
7. John William Ward, "Who Was Benjamin Franklin?" *American Scholar* 32, no. 4 (1963): 544.
8. James M. Cox, "Autobiography and America," *Virginia Quarterly Review* 47, no. 2 (1971): 261.
9. Sayre, *Examined Self*, p. 33.
10. Ibid.
11. Shea, *Spiritual Autobiography*, pp. 234–35, 248.

Chapter Five

1. For a discussion of the influences on the slave narrative, see Stephen Butterfield, *Black Autobiography in America* (Amherst: University of Massachusetts Press, 1974), pp. 32, 47–48.
2. Sidonie Smith, *Where I'm Bound* (Westport, Ct.: Greenwood Press, 1974), p. 10.
3. Frederick Douglass, *My Bondage and My Freedom* (1855; rpt., Chicago: Johnson Publishing, 1970), p. 129.
4. Richard Slotkin offers an illuminating discussion of the relationship between the slave narrative and the captivity narrative, which employs the structure of the conversion narrative, in *Regeneration through Violence* (Middletown: Wesleyan University Press, 1973), pp. 441–42.
5. Frederick Douglass, *Narrative of the Life of Frederick Douglass* (1845; rpt., New York: New American Library, 1968), p. 25. Hereafter page numbers will be cited in the text.
6. See Sidonie Smith for a discussion of the rites of masking, flight, naming, and mastery, pp. 14–22.
7. Butterfield, *Black Autobiography*, p. 27.
8. Smith, *Where I'm Bound*, p. ix.
9. Ibid., p. 10.
10. *The Liberator* (Boston: Little, Brown, 1963), p. 5.

Chapter Six

1. Lawrence Buell, *Literary Transcendentalism* (Ithaca: Cornell University Press, 1973), p. 20.
2. Ibid., p. 222.
3. Ibid., p. 268.
4. *The Writings of Henry David Thoreau*, I, *A Week on the Concord and Merrimack Rivers* (Boston: Houghton Mifflin, 1906), pp. 347–48.
5. Joseph J. Moldenhauer, "The Rhetorical Function of Proverbs in *Walden*," *Journal of American Folklore* 80 (1967): 156–58.
6. Henry D. Thoreau, *Walden*, ed. J. Lyndon Shanley (Princeton: Princeton University Press, 1971), pp. 18–21. Hereafter page numbers will be cited in the text.
7. Daniel B. Shea, Jr., *Spiritual Autobiography in Early America* (Princeton: Princeton University Press, 1968), p. 259.
8. Jonathan Edwards, "Personal Narrative," in *Jonathan Edwards: Representative Selections*, ed. Clarence H. Faust and Thomas H. Johnson (New York: Hill and Wang, 1962), p. 63.
9. William J. Wolf, *Thoreau* (Philadelphia: United Chruch Press, 1974), p. 79.
10. Stanley Cavell, *The Senses of Walden* (New York: Viking, 1972), p. 113.
11. Paul Lauter, "Thoreau's Prophetic Testimony," *Massachusetts Review* 4, no. 1 (1962): 122.
12. Richard Slotkin, *Regeneration through Violence* (Middletown: Wesleyan University Press, 1973), p. 526.
13. *Writings*, I, p. 61.

14. James M. Cox, "Autobiography and America," *Virginia Quarterly Review* 47, no. 2 (1971): 267.
15. Cavell, *Senses of Walden*, pp. 7–11.
16. John J. McAleer, "Thoreau's Epic *Cape Cod*," *Thought* 43, no. 169 (1968): 234.
17. For an extended discussion of this chapter, see James McIntosh, *Thoreau as Romantic Naturalist* (Ithaca: Cornell University Press, 1974), pp. 216–35.
18. *Writings*, IV, *Cape Cod and Miscellanies*, pp. 6–7. Hereafter page numbers will be cited in the text.

Chapter Seven

1. Lawrence Templin, "The Quaker Influence on Whitman," *American Literature* 42, no. 2 (1970): 166–67.
2. F. O. Mathiessen, *American Renaissance* (1941; rpt., New York: Oxford University Press, 1968), p. 538.
3. Walt Whitman, "November Boughs," in *Prose Works* (Philadelphia: David McKay, n.d.), pp. 464–65 n., 455.
4. Henry Seidel Canby, *Classic Americans* (New York: Harcourt, 1931), p. 324.
5. Walt Whitman, *Specimen Days* (Boston: David R. Godine, 1971), p. 103. Hereafter page numbers will be cited in the text.
6. Paul Rosenblatt, *John Woolman* (New York: Twayne, 1969), p. 30.
7. For a discussion of this term, see Mutlu Konuk Blasing, *The Art of Life* (Austin: University of Texas Press, 1977), p. 30.
8. Walt Whitman, "A Backward Glance O'er Travel'd Roads," *Leaves of Grass: The Comprehensive Reader's Edition*, Deathbed Edition, ed. Harold W. Blodgett and Sculley Bradley (New York: W. W. Norton, 1965), pp. 573–74.
9. Horace Traubel, *With Walt Whitman in Camden* (New York: Mitchell Kennerley, 1914), III, p. 355.
10. Hyatt Waggoner, *American Poets* (Boston: Houghton Mifflin, 1968), p. 155.
11. There may be a tenuous thread of influence from Woolman to Whitman through Elias Hicks, whose liberal faction drew their inspiration from Woolman in the schism of 1827–1828. See Phillips Moulton, Introduction, *The Journal and Major Essays of John Woolman* (New York: Oxford University Press, 1971), p. 11.
12. Daniel B. Shea, Jr., *Spiritual Autobiography in Early America* (Princeton: Princeton University Press, 1968), pp. 251, 159.
13. Quoted in Owen C. Watkins, *The Puritan Experience* (New York: Schocken Books, 1972), p. 12.
14. Whitman, *Leaves of Grass*, lines 30–34 of "Song of Myself." Hereafter line numbers will be cited in the text.
15. *Selections from Ralph Waldo Emerson*, ed. Stephen E. Whicher (Boston: Houghton Mifflin, 1957), p. 157.
16. James M. Cox, "Autobiography and America," *Virginia Quarterly Review* 47, no. 2 (1971): 267.

17. Lawrence Buell, *Literary Transcendentalism* (Ithaca: Cornell University Press, 1973), p. 330.
18. Frederick P. Hier, Jr., "The End of a Literary Mystery," *American Mercury* 1 (1924): 472.
19. Gay Wilson Allen, *The Solitary Singer* (New York: New York University Press, 1967), pp. 493, 501.
20. In fact, one of Whitman's tendencies in revising "Song of Myself" over the years was to add autobiographical and historical facts to it; the effect of these revisions is to render the mythic persona into a historical figure. Blasing, *Art of Life*, p. 46.
21. Alfred Kazin, Introduction to *Specimen Days*, p. xx.
22. J. Middleton Murry, "Walt Whitman: The Prophet of Democracy," in *"Leaves of Grass": One Hundred Years After*, ed. Milton Hindus (Stanford: Stanford University Press, 1966), p. 137.
23. Allen, *Solitary Singer*, p. 334.
24. "A Backward Glance . . ." in *Leaves of Grass*, p. 570.
25. Allen, *Solitary Singer*, p. 419.

Chapter Eight

1. Quoted in Ernest Samuels, *The Young Henry Adams* (Cambridge: Harvard University Press, 1948), p. 58. Hereafter to be referred to as Samuels, I.
2. Henry Adams, *Mont-Saint-Michel and Chartres* (1905; rpt., New York: Doubleday, 1959), p. 8.
3. John Conder, *A Formula of His Own* (Chicago: University of Chicago Press, 1970), p. 188.
4. Henry Adams, *The Education of Henry Adams*, ed. Ernest Samuels (1918; rpt., Boston: Houghton Mifflin, 1974), p. 63. Hereafter page numbers will be cited in the text.
5. Ernest Samuels, *Henry Adams: The Major Phase* (Cambridge: Harvard University Press, 1964), p. 220. Hereafter to be referred to as Samuels, III.
6. Robert F. Sayre, *The Examined Self* (Princeton: Princeton University Press, 1964), p. 110.
7. Ibid., pp. 91–92.
8. J. C. Levenson, *The Mind and Art of Henry Adams* (Boston: Houghton Mifflin, 1957), p. 191.
9. Ernest Samuels, *Henry Adams: The Middle Years* (Cambridge: Harvard University Press, 1958), p. 330. Hereafter to be referred to as Samuels, II.
10. Melvin Lyon, *Symbol and Idea in Henry Adams* (Lincoln: University of Nebraska Press, 1970), p. 226.
11. Sayre, *Examined Self*, p. 133.
12. Samuels, III, p. 362.
13. Samuels, II, p. 230.
14. Samuels, III, pp. 378–79.
15. Samuels, I, p. 50.
16. Sayre, *Examined Self*, p. 129.

17. Letter to Hay, 23 January 1883. *The Letters of Henry Adams,* ed. Worthington C. Ford, I (Boston: Houghton Mifflin, 1930), p. 347.
18. James M. Cox, "Autobiography and America," *Virginia Quarterly Review* 47, no. 2 (1971): 271.
19. Sayre, *Examined Self,* p. 129.
20. Ibid., p. 135.
21. Robert H. Wiebe, *The Search for Order, 1877–1920* (New York: Hill and Wang, 1967), passim.

Chapter Nine

1. Alan Gowans, *Images of American Living* (New York: J. B. Lippincott, 1964), pp. 356, 416–17.
2. Frank Lloyd Wright, *An Autobiography* (New York: Longmans, Green, 1932), p. 162.
3. For a discussion of developmental autobiography, see Wayne Shumaker, *English Autobiography* (Berkeley: University of California Press, 1954), pp. 85–88.
4. Willard Connely, *Louis Sullivan As He Lived* (New York: Horizon Press, 1960), p. 304.
5. Sherman Paul, *Louis Sullivan* (Englewood Cliffs, N. J.: Prentice-Hall, 1962), p. 133.
6. Albert Bush-Brown, *Louis Sullivan* (New York: George Braziller, 1960), p. 7.
7. Louis Sullivan, *The Autobiography of an Idea* (1924; rpt., New York: Dover, 1956), p. 175. Hereafter page numbers will be cited in the text.
8. Paul, *Louis Sullivan,* p. 135.
9. Henry Adams, *The Education of Henry Adams,* ed. Ernest Samuels (1918; rpt., Boston: Houghton Mifflin, 1974), p. 340.
10. Frank Lloyd Wright, *Genius and the Mobocracy* (1949; rpt., New York: Horizon, 1971), p. 166. Hereafter page numbers will be cited in the text.
11. Wright, *Autobiography,* p. 314. Hereafter page numbers will be cited in the text.
12. Robert C. Twombly, *Frank Lloyd Wright* (New York: Harper and Row, 1973), pp. 26, 32–33.
13. Theodore M. Brown, "Thoreau's Prophetic Architectural Program," *New England Quarterly* 38, no. 1 (1965): 20.
14. Twombly, *Frank Lloyd Wright,* pp. 132–33.
15. Ibid., pp. 132, 216.
16. Ibid., p. 112.
17. Frank Lloyd Wright, *An Autobiography* (New York: Duell, Sloan, and Pearce, 1943), p. 389. Hereafter page numbers will be cited in the text.
18. Norris Kelly Smith, *Frank Lloyd Wright* (Englewood Cliffs, N. J.: Prentice-Hall, 1966), p. 124.
19. Twombly, *Frank Lloyd Wright,* p. 173.
20. Ibid., p. 177.
21. Smith, *Frank Lloyd Wright,* pp. 148–52.
22. Ibid., p. 162.
23. Ibid., p. 170.

Chapter Ten

1. Allegra Stewart, *Gertrude Stein and the Present* (Cambridge: Harvard University Press, 1967), pp. 195-99.
2. Richard Bridgman, *Gertrude Stein in Pieces* (New York: Oxford University Press, 1970), pp. 203-4.
3. Gertrude Stein, *The Autobiography of Alice B. Toklas* (New York: Random House, 1933), p. 77. To be referred to as *The Autobiography;* page numbers to be cited in the text.
4. For an illuminating discussion of this episode and for the relationship between the autobiography and cubist practice, see Earl Fendelman, "Gertrude Stein among the Cubists," *Journal of Modern Literature* 2, no. 4 (1972): 487-89.
5. John Malcolm Brinnin, *The Third Rose* (Boston: Little Brown, 1959), p. 270.
6. Gertrude Stein, *Everybody's Autobiography* (New York: Random House, 1937), p. 92. Hereafter page numbers to be cited in the text.
7. Bridgman, *Gertrude Stein in Pieces*, p. 279.
8. Quoted in Brinnin, *The Third Rose*, p. 342.
9. Gertrude Stein, *Wars I Have Seen* (New York: Random House, 1945), p. 80. Hereafter page numbers to be cited in text.
10. Bridgman, *Gertrude Stein in Pieces*, p. 335.
11. Gertrude Stein, *Brewsie and Willie* (New York: Random House, 1946), p. 113.

Chapter Eleven

1. Peter Goldman, *The Death and Life of Malcolm X* (New York: Harper and Row, 1973), pp. 396, 398.
2. Alex Haley, "Epilogue," *The Autobiography of Malcolm X*, by Malcolm X with the assistance of Alex Haley (New York: Grove Press, 1965), pp. 392, 395. Hereafter citations from the text of the autobiography will be identified in parentheses.
3. George Breitman, *The Last Years of Malcolm X* (New York: Merit, 1967), p. 4.
4. Haley, "Epilogue," p. 388.
5. David P. Demarest, Jr., *"The Autobiography of Malcolm X,"* *CLA Journal* 16, no. 2 (1972): 183.
6. C. Eric Lincoln, *The Black Muslims in America*, rev. ed. (1963; rpt., Boston: Beacon Press, 1973), p. 115.
7. Carol Ohmann, *"The Autobiography of Malcolm X,"* *American Quarterly* 22, no. 2, part 1 (1970): 133-35.
8. These tensions are evident in most discussions of the movement. In addition to Lincoln, see Louis E. Lomax, *When the Word is Given* (New York: World, 1963), and Archie Epps, "The Paradoxes of Malcolm X," in *The Speeches of Malcolm X*, ed. Epps (New York: William Morrow, 1968), pp. 15-112.
9. Ohmann, *"The Autobiography of Malcolm X,"* pp. 147-48.
10. Goldman, *Death and Life of Malcolm X*, p. 292.

11. Ibid., pp. 412–14.
12. Quoted in Ibid., p. 408.
13. Norman Mailer, *Advertisements for Myself* (New York: G. P. Putnam's Sons, 1959), p. 5. Hereafter to be referred to as *Advertisements*; citations to be identified in the text.
14. Warner Berthoff, "Witness and Testament," in *Fictions and Events* (New York: E. P. Dutton, 1971), p. 301.
15. Earl Barry Fendelman, "Toward a Third Voice," (diss. Yale, 1971), p. 213.
16. Norman Mailer, *Armies of the Night* (New York: New American Library, 1968), p. 54. Hereafter to be referred to as *Armies*; citations to be identified in text.
17. Fendelman, *Toward a Third Voice*, pp. 210, 207.
18. Berthoff, "Witness and Testament," p. 307.
19. Raymond A. Schroth, "Mailer and His Gods," *Commonweal* 90, no. 8 (1969): 229.
20. For an extended parallel, see Nathan A. Scott, Jr., "Norman Mailer—Our Whitman," in *Three American Moralists* (Notre Dame, Indiana: University of Notre Dame Press, 1973), pp. 19–97.
21. Michael Cowan, "The Americanness of Norman Mailer," in *Norman Mailer*, ed. Leo Braudy (Englewood Cliffs, New Jersey: Prentice-Hall, 1972), p. 153.
22. Quoted in Laura Adams, "Existential Aesthetics," *Partisan Review* 42, no. 2 (1975): 205.
23. Eugen Herrigel, *Zen in the Art of Archery*, trans. R. F. C. Hull (1953; rpt., New York: Random House, 1971), p. 11.
24. Robert M. Pirsig, *Zen and the Art of Motorcycle Maintenance* (New York: Bantam, 1974). Hereafter to be referred to as *Zen*; page numbers to be cited in parentheses.

Epilogue

1. For a discussion of the anthropologist's view of the prophet, see Eleanor Wilner, *Gathering the Winds* (Baltimore: Johns Hopkins University Press, 1975), pp. 15–40.
2. For an illuminating discussion of the fate of the Puritan jeremiad, see David L. Minter, *The Interpreted Design* (New Haven: Yale University Press, 1969), p. 63.

SOURCES

Adams, Henry. *The Education of Henry Adams*, edited by Ernest Samuels. 1918. Reprint. Boston: Houghton Mifflin, 1974.
——. *Letters of Henry Adams*, edited by Worthington Chauncy Ford, vol. 1, 1858–1891. Boston: Houghton Mifflin, 1930.
——. *Mont-Saint-Michel and Chartres*. 1905. Reprint. New York: Doubleday, 1959.
Adams, Laura. "Existential Aesthetics: An Interview with Norman Mailer." *Partisan Review* 42, no. 2 (1975): 197–214.
Aldridge, Alfred Owen. *Benjamin Franklin and Nature's God*. Durham, North Carolina: Duke University Press, 1967.
Allen, Gay Wilson. *The Solitary Singer: A Critical Biography of Walt Whitman*. New York: New York University Press, 1967.
Asselineau, Roger. *The Evolution of Walt Whitman*, I, *The Creation of a Personality*. Cambridge: Harvard University Press, 1960.
Bercovitch, Sacvan. "Cotton Mather." *Major Writers of Early American Literature*, edited by Everett Emerson, pp. 93–149. Madison: University of Wisconsin Press, 1972.
——. *The Puritan Origins of the American Self*. New Haven: Yale University Press, 1975.
Berthoff, Warner. "Witness and Testament: Two Contemporary Classics." *Fiction and Events: Essays in Criticism and Literary History*. New York: E. P. Dutton, 1971.
Blasing, Mutlu Konuk. *The Art of Life: Studies in American Autobiographical Literature*. Austin: University of Texas Press, 1977.
Breitman, George. *The Last Years of Malcolm X: The Evolution of a Revolutionary*. New York: Merit, 1967.
Bridgman, Richard. *Gertrude Stein in Pieces*. New York: Oxford University Press, 1970.

Brinnin, John Malcolm. *The Third Rose: Gertrude Stein and Her World.* Boston: Little, Brown, 1959,

Brown, Theodore M. "Thoreau's Prophetic Architectural Program." *New England Quarterly* 38, no. 1 (1965): 3-20.

Buell, Lawrence. *Literary Transcendentalism: Style and Vision in the American Renaissance.* Ithaca: Cornell University Press, 1973.

Butterfield, Stephen. *Black Autobiography in America.* Amherst: University of Massachusetts Press, 1974.

Bush-Brown, Albert. *Louis Sullivan.* New York: Braziller, 1960.

Canby, Henry Seidel. *Classic Americans.* New York: Harcourt, 1931.

Cavell, Stanley. *The Senses of Walden.* New York: Viking, 1972.

Chase, Richard. *The American Novel and Its Tradition.* Garden City, N.Y.: Doubleday and Co., 1957.

Conder, John. *A Formula of His Own: Henry Adams's Literary Experiment.* Chicago: University of Chicago Press, 1970.

Connely, Willard. *Louis Sullivan As He Lived.* New York: Horizon Press, 1960.

Cowan, Michael. "The Americanness of Norman Mailer." *Norman Mailer: A Collection of Critical Essays,* edited by Leo Braudy, pp. 143-57. Englewood Cliffs, N. J.: Prentice-Hall, 1972.

Cox, James M. "Autobiography and America." *Virginia Quarterly Review* 47, no. 2 (1971): 252-77.

Delany, Paul. *British Autobiography in the Seventeenth Century.* New York: Columbia University Press, 1969.

Demarest, David P., Jr. "*The Autobiography of Malcolm X*: Beyond Didacticism." *CLA Journal* 16, no. 2 (1972): 179-87.

Douglass, Frederick. *My Bondage and My Freedom.* 1855. Reprint. Chicago: Johnson Publishing, 1970.

——. *Narrative of the Life of Frederick Douglass.* 1845. Reprint. New York: New American Library, 1968.

Edwards, Jonathan. *Jonathan Edwards: Representative Selections,* edited by Clarence H. Faust and Thomas H. Johnson. Rev. ed. New York: Hill and Wang, 1962.

Emerson, Ralph Waldo. *Selections from Ralph Waldo Emerson,* edited by Stephen E. Whicher. Boston: Houghton Mifflin, 1957.

Epps, Archie. "The Paradoxes of Malcolm X." *The Speeches of Malcolm X,* edited by Archie Epps, pp. 15-112. New York: William Morrow, 1968.

Fendelman, Earl. "Gertrude Stein among the Cubists." *Journal of Modern Literature* 2, no. 4 (1972): 481-90.

——. *Toward a Third Voice: Autobiographical Form in Thoreau, Stein, Adams, and Mailer.* Ph.D. dissertation, Yale University, 1971.

Franklin, Benjamin. *The Autobiography of Benjamin Franklin,* edited by Leonard W. Labaree, Ralph L. Ketcham, Helen C. Boatfield, and Helen Fineman. New Haven: Yale University Press, 1964.

Goldman, Peter. *The Death and Life of Malcolm X.* New York: Harper and Row, 1973.

Gowans, Alan. *Images of American Living: Four Centuries of Architecture and Furniture As Cultural Expression.* New York: J. B. Lippincott, 1964.

Griffin, Edward M. *Jonathan Edwards*. Minneapolis: University of Minnesota Press, 1971.

Hart, Francis R. "Notes for an Anatomy of Modern Autobiography." *New Literary History* 1, no. 3 (1970): 485–511.

Herrigel, Eugen. *Zen in the Art of Archery*. Translated by R. F. C. Hull. 1953. Reprint. New York: Random House, 1971.

Hier, Frederick P., Jr. "The End of a Literary Mystery." *American Mercury* 1 (1924): 471–78.

James, Sydney V. *A People among Peoples: Quaker Benevolence in Eighteenth-Century America*. Cambridge: Harvard University Press, 1963.

Lauter, Paul. "Thoreau's Prophetic Testimony." *Massachusetts Review* 4, no. 1 (1962): 111–22.

Levenson, J. C. *The Mind and Art of Henry Adams*. Boston: Houghton Mifflin, 1957.

Levin, David. *"The Autobiography of Benjamin Franklin:* The Puritan Experimenter in Life and Art." *Yale Review* 53, no. 2 (1963): 258–75.

Lincoln, C. Eric. *The Black Muslims in America*. Rev. ed. 1963. Reprint. Boston: Beacon Press, 1973.

Lomax, Louis E. *When the Word Is Given: A Report on Elijah Muhammad and the Black Muslim World*, New York: World Publishing, 1963.

Lyon, Melvin. *Symbol and Idea in Henry Adams*. Lincoln: University of Nebraska Press, 1970.

McAleer, John J. "Thoreau's Epic *Cape Cod.*" *Thought* 43, no. 169 (1968): 227–46.

McIntosh, James. *Thoreau As Romantic Naturalist: His Shifting Stance toward Nature*. Ithaca: Cornell University Press, 1974.

Mailer, Norman. *Advertisements for Myself*. New York: G. P. Putnam's Sons, 1959.

———. *Armies of the Night: History As a Novel, the Novel As History*. New York: New American Library, 1968.

———. *Miami and the Siege of Chicago: An Informal History of the Republican and Democratic Conventions of 1968*. New York: World Publishing, 1968.

———. *The Presidential Papers*. New York: G. P. Putnam's Sons, 1963.

Malcolm X. *The Autobiography of Malcolm X*, with the assistance of Alex Haley. New York: Grove Press, 1965.

Mandel, Barret John. "The Autobiographer's Art." *Journal of Aesthetics and Art Criticism* 27, no. 2 (1968): 215–26.

Mather, Increase. "The Autobiography of Increase Mather," edited by M. G. Hall. *Proceedings of the American Antiquarian Society* 71, part 2 (1961): 271–360.

Mathiessen, F. O. *American Renaissance: Art and Expression in the Age of Emerson and Whitman*. 1941. Reprint. New York: Oxford University Press, 1968.

Middlekauff, Robert. *The Mathers: Three Generations of Puritan Intellectuals, 1596–1728*. New York: Oxford University Press, 1971.

Miller, Perry. "Jonathan Edwards to Emerson," *New England Quarterly* 13, no. 4 (1940): 589–617.

———. *The New England Mind: The Seventeenth Century.* 1939. Reprint. Boston: Beacon Press, 1961.

Miller, Ross. "Autobiography As Fact and Fiction: Franklin, Adams, Malcolm X." *Centennial Review* 16, no. 3 (1972): 221–32.

Minter, David L. *The Interpreted Design As a Structural Principle in American Prose.* New Haven: Yale University Press, 1969.

Moldenhauer, Joseph J. "The Rhetorical Function of Proverbs in *Walden.*" *Journal of American Folklore* 80 (1967): 151–59.

Morgan, Edmund S. *The Puritan Family: Religion and Domestic Relations in Seventeenth-Century New England.* Rev. ed. New York: Harper and Row, 1966.

Murdock, Kenneth B. *Literature and Theology in Colonial New England.* Cambridge: Harvard University Press, 1949.

Murry, J. Middleton. "Walt Whitman: The Prophet of Democracy." *"Leaves of Grass": One Hundred Years After*, edited by Milton Hindus. Stanford: Stanford University Press, 1966.

Ohmann, Carol. "*The Autobiography of Malcolm X*: A Revolutionary Use of the Franklin Tradition." *American Quarterly* 22, no. 2, part 1 (1970): 131–49.

Paul, Sherman. *Louis Sullivan: An Architect in American Thought.* Englewood Cliffs, N. J.: Prentice-Hall, 1962.

Pfeiffer, Robert H. *Religion in the Old Testament: The History of a Spiritual Triumph*, edited by Charles Conrad Forman. New York: Harper, 1961.

Pirsig, Robert M. *Zen and the Art of Motorcycle Maintenance: An Inquiry into Values.* New York: Bantam, 1974.

Rosenblatt, Paul. *John Woolman.* New York: Twayne, 1969.

Samuels, Ernest. *Henry Adams: The Major Phase.* Cambridge: Harvard University Press. 1964.

———. *Henry Adams: The Middle Years.* Cambridge: Harvard University Press, 1958.

———. *The Young Henry Adams.* Cambridge: Harvard University Press, 1948.

Sayre, Robert F. *The Examined Self: Benjamin Franklin, Henry Adams, Henry James.* Princeton: Princeton University Press, 1964.

Schroth, Raymond A. "Mailer and His Gods." *Commonweal* 90, no. 8 (1969): 226–29.

Scott, Nathan A. *Three American Moralists: Mailer, Bellow, Trilling.* Notre Dame: University of Notre Dame Press, 1973.

Shea, Daniel B., Jr. *Spiritual Autobiography in Early America.* Princeton: Princeton University Press, 1968.

Shepard, Thomas. *God's Plot: The Paradoxes of Puritan Piety, Being the Autobiography and Journal of Thomas Shepard*, edited by Michael McGiffert. Amherst: University of Massachusetts Press, 1972.

Shumaker, Wayne. *English Autobiography: Its Emergence, Materials, and Form.* Berkeley: University of California Press, 1954.

Slotkin, Richard. *Regeneration through Violence: The Mythology of the American Frontier, 1600–1860.* Middletown: Wesleyan University Press, 1973.

Smith, Norris Kelly. *Frank Lloyd Wright: A Study in Architectural Content.* Englewood Cliffs, N. J.: Prentice-Hall, 1966.

Smith, Sidonie. *Where I'm Bound: Patterns of Slavery and Freedom in Black American Autobiography*. Westport, Ct.: Greenwood Press, 1974.

Spengeman, William C., and Lundquist, L. R. "Autobiography and the American Myth." *American Quarterly* 17, no. 3 (1965): 501-19.

Stein, Gertrude. *The Autobiography of Alice B. Toklas*. New York: Random House, 1933.

——. *Brewsie and Willie*. New York: Random House, 1946.

——. *Everybody's Autobiography*. New York: Random House, 1937.

——. *Wars I Have Seen*. New York: Random House, 1945.

Stewart, Allegra. *Gertrude Stein and the Present*. Cambridge: Harvard University Press, 1967.

Sullivan, Louis H. *The Autobiography of an Idea*. 1924. Reprint. New York: Dover, 1956.

Templin, Lawrence. "The Quaker Influence on Walt Whitman." *American Literature* 42, no. 2 (1970): 165-80.

Thoreau, Henry David. *Walden*, edited by J. Lyndon Shanley. Princeton: Princeton University Press, 1971.

——. *The Writings of Henry David Thoreau, IV, Cape Cod and Miscellanies*. Boston: Houghton Mifflin, 1906.

——. *The Writings of Henry David Thoreau, I, A Week on the Concord and Merrimack Rivers*. Boston: Houghton Mifflin, 1906.

Thomas, John L. *The Liberator: William Lloyd Garrison, A Biography*. Boston: Little, Brown, 1963.

Tolles, Frederick B. *Meeting House and Counting House: The Quaker Merchants of Colonial Philadelphia, 1682-1763*. Chapel Hill: University of North Carolina Press, 1948.

——. *Quakers and the Atlantic Culture*. New York: Macmillan, 1960.

Traubel, Horace. *With Walt Whitman in Camden*, III *(1888-1889)*. New York: Mitchell Kennerley, 1914.

Twombly, Robert C. *Frank Lloyd Wright: An Interpretive Biography*. New w York: Harper and Row, 1973.

Waggoner, Hyatt H. *American Poets: From the Puritans to the Present*. Boston: Houghton Mifflin, 1968.

Ward, John William. "Who Was Be nin Franklin?" *American Scholar* 32, no. 4 (1963): 541-53.

Watkins, Owen C. *The Puritan Experience: Studies in Spiritual Autobiography*. New York: Schocken Books, 1972.

Whitman, Walt. *Leaves of Grass: The Comprehensive Reader's Edition*. Deathbed Edition, edited by Harold W. Blodgett and Sculley Bradley. New York: W. W. Norton, 1965.

——. "November Boughs." *Prose Works*. Philadelphia: David McKay, n.d.

——. *Specimen Days*. Boston: David R. Godine, 1971.

Wiebe, Robert H. *The Search for Order, 1877-1920*. New York: Hill and Wang, 1967.

Wilner, Eleanor. *Gathering the Winds: Visionary Imagination and Radical Transformation of Self and Society*. Baltimore: Johns Hopkins University Press, 1975.

Wolf, William J. *Thoreau: Mystic, Prophet, Ecologist*. Philadelphia: United Church Press, 1974.

Woolman, John. *The Journal and Major Essays of John Woolman*, edited by
    Phillips P. Moulton. New York: Oxford University Press, 1971.
Wright, Frank Lloyd. *An Autobiography*. New York: Longmans, Green,
    1932.
———. *An Autobiography*. New York: Duell, Sloan, and Pearce, 1943.
———. *Genius and the Mobocracy*. 1949. Reprint. New York: Horizon Press,
    1971.
Wright, Luella M. *The Literary Life of the Early Friends, 1650-1725*. New
    York: Columbia University Press, 1932.
Ziff, Larzer. *Puritanism in America: New Culture in a New World*. New York:
    Viking Press, 1973.

INDEX

Library of Congress Cataloging in Publication Data
Couser, G. Thomas.
American autobiography
Bibliography: p.
Includes index.
1. Autobiography.   2. United States—Biography
3. Biography (as a literary form)
CT34.U6C68   920'.073   78-11835
ISBN 0-87023-263-0